Moses Mendelssohn

„Wir träumten von nichts als Aufklärung"

Moses Mendelssohn

„Wir träumten von nichts als Aufklärung"

Inka Bertz · Thomas Lackmann (Hg.)

Moses Mendelssohn
"We dreamed of nothing but enlightenment"

WIENAND

In dankbarer Erinnerung an Hans-Günter Klein (1939–2016), den langjährigen Leiter des Mendelssohn-Archivs der Staatsbibliothek zu Berlin, aus dessen Idee von einer Gesamtschau der Mendelssohn-Porträts diese Ausstellung entstanden ist.
In grateful memory of Hans-Günter Klein (1939–2016), the longtime director of the Mendelssohn Archive of the Staatsbibliothek zu Berlin, from whose idea of a complete show of Mendelssohn portraits this exhibition was born.

„Wir träumten von nichts als Aufklärung, und glaubten durch das Licht der Vernunft die Gegend so aufgehellt zu haben, daß die Schwärmerey sich gewiß nicht mehr zeigen werde. Allein wie wir sehen, steiget schon, von der andern Seite des Horizonts, die Nacht mit allen ihren Gespenstern wieder empor. Das Fürchterlichste dabey ist, daß das Uebel so thätig, so wirksam ist. Die Schwärmerey thut, und die Vernunft begnügt sich zu sprechen."

Moses Mendelssohn an Johann Georg Zimmermann, 1. September 1784

"We dreamt of nothing but Enlightenment and believed that the light of Reason would so illuminate the land that zealousness would never again show its face. But as we can see, from beyond the horizon night is ascending once again with all its ghosts. Most frightening of all is that evil is so active, so potent. Zealousness takes action, while Reason contents itself with speech."

Moses Mendelssohn to Johann Georg Zimmermann, September 1st 1784

Inhalt *Content*

Einführung *Introduction*
- 10 **Grußwort**
 Preface
- 12 **Namen, Bilder und Dialog-Werkstatt des „Juden von Berlin"**
 Names, Portrayals and Dialogue Workshop of "The Jew of Berlin"
- 34 **Mendelssohn im Porträt**
 Mendelssohn's Portraits

Bilderfabrik *Image Factory*
- 82 **Die Miniaturen**
 The Miniatures
- 86 **Das Porträt von Bernhard Rode**
 The Portrait by Bernhard Rode
- 88 **Das Porträt von Anton Graff**
 The Portrait by Anton Graff
- 96 **Die Porträts von Daniel Chodowiecki**
 The Portraits by Daniel Chodowiecki
- 104 **Mendelssohn in der Sammlung und den Schriften Lavaters**
 Mendelssohn in Lavater's Collection and Writings
- 108 **Das sogenannte Zingg-Porträt**
 The So-called Zingg Portrait
- 110 **Die Porträts von Johann Christoph Frisch**
 The Portraits by Johann Christoph Frisch
- 124 **Die Büste von Jean Pierre Antoine Tassaert**
 The Bust of Jean Pierre Antoine Tassaert
- 130 **Mendelssohns Nachleben im Bild**
 Posthumous Images of Mendelssohn

Objektverzeichnis *List of Objects*
- 150 **Von Dessau nach Berlin**
 From Dessau to Berlin
- 154 **Der „Jude von Berlin"**
 The "Jew of Berlin"
- 161 **Dialog & Netzwerk**
 Dialogue & Networks

166	**Aufklärung & Verdunkelung**	
	Enlightenment Versus the Shadows	
173	**Religion**	
	Religion	
178	**Übersetzung & Pädagogik**	
	Translation & Education	
183	**Menschenrechte**	
	Human Rights	
188	**Ästhetik & Freundschaft**	
	Aesthetics & Friendship	
193	**Bestimmung des Menschen**	
	Destiny of Man	
198	**Judenporzellan**	
	Jewish Porcelain	
201	**Was wird aus Moses Mendelssohn?**	
	What is Moses Mendelssohn's Legacy?	

Anhang *Appendix*

208	**Medienstationen**	
	Media Stations	
215	**Moses Mendelssohn (1729–1786)**	
	Biografische Daten und Zeitgeschichte	
	Moses Mendelssohn (1729–1786)	
	Biographical Data and Contemporary History	
218	**Räume & Themen**	
	Rooms & Topics	
220	**Literaturhinweise (Auswahl)**	
	Literature (Selection)	
222	**Wilde Mischung**	
	Wild Mixture	
234	**Personenregister**	
	Index of Names	
242	**Leihgeber der Ausstellung**	
	Lenders of the Exhibition	
243	**Abbildungsverzeichnis**	
	Table of Figures	
244	**Abkürzungsverzeichnis**	
	List of Abbreviations	
245	**Danksagung**	
	Acknowledgments	
248	**Impressum**	
	Credits	

Einführung

Introduction

Grußwort

Preface

Für die Geschichte der Juden in Deutschland und die der Berliner Aufklärung ist Moses Mendelssohn die Schlüsselfigur und Brückengestalt. Um zu verstehen, woher wir kommen, wohin wir als Gesellschaft gehen wollen, könnte uns gerade dieser kleinwüchsige große Talmudgelehrte und „Weltweise" die Augen öffnen. Mendelssohn wäre es sicher wichtig gewesen, dass dabei ebenso der Verstand und auch das Herz geöffnet werden.

Das Jüdische Museum Berlin und die Mendelssohn-Gesellschaft, der die biografische Erforschung der Mendelssohn-Familie ein Anliegen ist, haben gemeinsam eine Ausstellung realisiert, die solche Begegnungen ermöglichen soll. Der vorliegende Katalog dokumentiert unsere Unternehmung, damit deren wissenschaftlicher Ertrag weiterhin für viele nutzbar bleibt. Wir danken den Kuratoren und Herausgebern, dem engagierten Ausstellungsteam, allen privaten und institutionellen Leihgebern und den fördernden Organisationen für ihre großzügige Unterstützung. Es hat uns selbst begeistert festzustellen, wie dieser Herr Moses, der Emanzipationspionier aus dem fernen 18. Jahrhundert, zahlreiche Interessenten spontan begeistern kann – mit seinen Gedanken, seinen Themen und mit seiner aufrechten, glaubwürdigen Haltung.

Zum 200. Geburtstag Mendelssohns war 1929 in Berlin eine große Jubiläumsausstellung eröffnet worden, mit der – so stellt sich das heute dar, nach dem Bruch der NS-Zeit – eine Epoche des Judentums in Deutschland zu Ende ging. Wie in sieben Jahren, wenn Moses' 300. Geburtstag zu feiern wäre, die Zukunft der Juden und der Aufklärung in Deutschland reflektiert werden, ist aktuell schwer zu prophezeien. Eine inspirierende Stoffsammlung zur Reflexion solcher Fragen stellt dieser Katalog bereit.

Im April 2022
Hetty Berg, Direktorin des Jüdischen Museums Berlin
André Schmitz, Vorsitzender der Mendelssohn-Gesellschaft e. V.

For the history of the Jews in Germany and of the Berlin Enlightenment, Moses Mendelssohn is the key figure as a man bridging the epochs. In order to understand where we came from, and where we want to go as a society, it is none other than this Talmudic scholar, short of stature but great of intellect, a "worldly sage", who could open our eyes. Most likely, it would have been important to Mendelssohn that our minds and hearts be opened as well.

The Jewish Museum Berlin and the Mendelssohn-Gesellschaft, an association dedicated among other things to researching the biographical history of the Mendelssohn family, have joined forces to create an exhibition devoted to fostering this process of discovery. The present catalog documents our undertaking to ensure that its scholarly insights will continue to be useful to many. We wish to thank the curators and editors, the dedicated exhibition team, as well as all the various private and institutional lenders and sponsoring organizations for their generous support. We were thrilled to see how this Herr Moses, the pioneering champion of Jewish social emancipation from the distant 18th century, continues to inspire spontaneous interest in so many quarters—with his thoughts and arguments, with the topics he explored, with his rectitude and credibility.

In 1929, a comprehensive anniversary exhibition opened in Berlin to commemorate Mendelssohn's 200th birthday. Seen in hindsight, after the break with civilization that was the nazi era, this event essentially marked the close of what has been called the "German-Jewish epoch". Prophecies as to what the future of Jews in Germany and of the Enlightenment in Germany will look like seven years from now, when it would be time to celebrate Moses' 300th birthday, are difficult to make. This catalog provides inspiring materials to reflect on these and other questions.

April 2022
Hetty Berg, Director of the Jewish Museum Berlin
André Schmitz, Chairman of the Mendelssohn-Gesellschaft e.V.

Thomas Lackmann

Namen, Bilder und Dialog-Werkstatt des „Juden von Berlin"

Names, Portrayals and Dialogue Workshop of "The Jew of Berlin"

Nr. 266 Angelina Schüler
und Marie-Christin
Behrendt: Hommage
2015
Inkjet auf Leinwand
Privatbesitz, Berlin
(Foto: Anna Fischer)

„Was die Bestimmung meiner Landsleute seyn wird, fragen Sie? – Welcher Landsleute? Der Dessauer? Oder der Bürger zu Jerusalem?"[1]

MOSES MENDELSSOHN

Identity Card

Die spitze Reaktion des 34-jährigen Moses Mendelssohn auf einen Brief seines vertrauten Freundes Thomas Abbt im Sommer 1764 verweist auf das zwischen beiden Philosophen verhandelte Thema der „Bestimmung des Menschen" – und auf heutige Identitätsdebatten.

Mendelssohn, der tagtäglich eine Kippa trägt, mag es lebenslang gewohnt gewesen sein, auf den ersten Blick als Jude erkannt und manchmal deshalb schikaniert zu werden. Abbt ist Professor im westfälischen Rinteln. Mit seiner saloppen und etwas provinziellen Frage nach den „Landsleuten" sind „die Juden" gemeint. Das lässt Mendelssohn ihm so nicht durchgehen. Er selbst lebt nun immerhin schon über 20 Jahre in Berlin, als erfolgreicher Geschäftsmann, Familienvater, anerkannter Gelehrter. Seine Landsleute sind die Berliner.

Dennoch müsste die *Woher-kommst-du*-Frage, so übergriffig sie empfunden wird, nicht ganz abwegig sein – wann immer der Fragende sich für sein Gegenüber wirklich interessiert. Auch mit der noch viel intimeren *Wer-bist-du*-Frage hat die *Woher-kommst-du*-Frage durchaus etwas zu tun. Aber: Ob solche Erkundigungen übergriffig sind, entscheidet sich letztlich an der Qualität des Dialoges, in dem sie aufgehoben sind und korrigiert werden können.

"What the destiny of my compatriots will be, you ask?—Of which compatriots? The ones from Dessau? Or the citizens of Jerusalem?"[1]

Identity card

The tart response from the 34-year-old Moses Mendelssohn to a letter from his intimate friend Thomas Abbt in the summer of 1764 alludes to the ongoing discussion the two philosophers were having at the time on "the destiny of man—and also seems relevant to the debates about personal identity that preoccupy us today.

Mendelssohn, who wore a skullcap every day, was probably accustomed throughout his life to being immediately recognized as a Jew and to sometimes being harassed for it. Abbt, for his part, was a professor in Rinteln, Westphalia. With his casual and somewhat provincial question about "compatriots," he meant "the Jews". Mendelssohn refuses to let him get away with it. After all, he himself had been living in Berlin for over 20 years, a successful merchant, family man, and recognized scholar. His compatriots were the people of Berlin.

Nonetheless, the question "where do you come from?"—as intrusive as it can sometimes feel to the person being asked—need not be inappropriate in every case, provided the questioner is genuinely interested in his or her interlocutor. And this "where do you come from?"

Identität und Dialog: Wenn etwas dafür spricht, den Talmudgelehrten, Publizisten, Literaturkritiker, Ästhetiker, Seidenkaufmann und Emanzipationspionier Mendelssohn nicht als bezopfte Aufklärungsfigur in der Mottenkiste des Gutmenschentums verschwinden zu lassen, dann sind das diese beiden Lebensthemen (unter zahlreichen anderen).

Vom Begriff „Identität" oder gar von ihrer postmodern „multiplen" Version ist bei Moses zwar explizit nicht die Rede. Aber ob er nun als halachisch observanter Jude und zugleich moderner Aufklärer souverän oder hin- und hergerissen in sehr verschiedenen Welten verkehrt: Schon die Erfahrungen ideologischer Passagen von einer Debattenblase in die andere können so einem Passagier beibringen, Perspektiven der jeweils „anderen" mitzudenken.

Für eine klassische *Identity Card* sind die wichtigsten Elemente: der Name und das Konterfei. Von Mendelssohn existieren angesichts der kontrastreichen Darstellungen seiner Person und in Anbetracht seiner diversen Namen ausgesprochen unterschiedliche Personalausweise.

Die Ausstellung, für die dieser Katalog steht, zeigt viele changierende Konterfeis in einem Raum. Sie muss auch den Erwartungen

certainly relates to the even more personal question "who are you?" Still, whether or not such queries are actually transgressive will ultimately depend on the nature of the dialogue of which they form a part and in which, if need be, they can be corrected.

Identity and dialogue: if there were ever a reason for not relegating Mendelssohn the Talmudic scholar, publicist, literary critic, philosopher of aesthetics, silk merchant, and pioneer of Jewish emancipation to the mothballs of history as a bewigged Enlightenment figure with noble yet naïve ideals, then it is these two existential themes (among many others).

Admittedly, Moses never explicitly mentioned the term "identity", much less its more contemporary variant of "multiple identities". But regardless of whether he straddled two very different worlds as a Halachically observant Jew who was also a progressive Enlightenment thinker with ease or with a sense of inner conflict, the experience of such ideological transit passages from one bubble of intellectual debate to the other was surely enough to teach this passenger how to put himself into the mind of the respective "other".

o. Nr. **Johann Friedrich Fechhelm: Kurfürstenbrücke in Berlin**
um 1785
Öl auf Leinwand
Eigentum des Hauses Hohenzollern, SKH Georg Friedrich Prinz von Preußen, SPSG
(Foto: Jörg P. Anders)

Berliner unter Berlinern. Wo ist der „kleine Mausche aus Dessau"?
Berliner among Berliners. Where is the "little Moishe from Dessau"?

jener begegnen, die eine Ausschnittsidee von Mendelssohn als traditionsbewusstem Talmudgelehrten, jüdischem Reformer oder heutigem Toleranz-Prediger im Sinn haben, ohne auf die Figur der Widersprüche gefasst zu sein, und zugleich der Skepsis jener, die auf einen Mann von gestern eingestellt sind. Tatsächlich ist Mendelssohn auch eine Übergangsgestalt: Wo er zum Beispiel bei seiner Liebesheirat und partnerschaftlichen Ehe mit Fromet Gugenheim zwar modern scheint, aber bei der konventionellen (glücklosen) Verheiratung seiner Töchter rückwärtsgewandt. Das Kontrast-Tableau der Rezeptionskarte am Ende der Ausstellung passt zum Spektrum möglicher Erwartungen: Der multiple Moses ist Programm. Die Namensvielfalt spiegelt sich auf Ausstellungsebene in biografischen Phasen, Lebensthemen, Persönlichkeitsprofilen.

Die Namen

„Meines Vaters Vater hieß Mendel Dessau," scheibt der Kaufmann Abraham Mendelssohn Bartholdy 1829, im Jahr des hundertsten Moses-Geburtstags. „Als dessen Sohn, mein Vater, in die Welt getreten war, als er anfing genannt zu werden, als er den edlen, nie genug zu preisenden Entschluß faßte, sich selbst, und seine Mitbrüder, aus der tiefen Erniedrigung, in welche sie versunken waren, durch Verbreitung einer höheren Bildung zu reißen, fühlte er, daß es ihm zu schwer werden würde, als Moses Mendel Dessau in das nähere Verhältnis, welches ihm erforderlich war, zu denjenigen zu treten, die damals im Besitz dieser höheren Bildung waren: er nannte sich, ohne daß er fürchtete seinem Vater dadurch zu nahe zu treten, Mendelssohn. [...] Als Mendelssohn trennte er sich unwiderruflich von einer ganzen Classe, aus der er die besten zu sich hinaufzog, und an eine andre Gemeinschaft anschloß."[2]

Auf der Suche nach dem Mendelssohn von damals und für heute: ein Entwurf des Comic-Zeichners Typex für seine Graphic Novel „Moische" zur Begleitung der Ausstellung
In search of the Mendelssohn of yesteryear and for today: a design by comic artist Typex for his graphic novel "Moishe" to accompany the exhibition

The key elements of any identity card customarily are the subject's name and likeness. In Mendelssohn's case, any number of altogether different "identity cards" exist, given the various appellations and contrasting portrayals that have come down to us.

The exhibition that is the subject of this catalog presents many of these changing likenesses in a single space. Of necessity, it must also deal with the expectations of those who, unprepared to see Mendelssohn as a contradictory figure, have a clear-cut preconception in mind, e.g. as a Talmudic scholar steeped in tradition, Jewish reformer, or preacher of tolerance in the modern mold. At the same time, it will also have to face the skepticism of those who are determined to dismiss him as a man of the past.

In fact, Mendelssohn is a transitional figure: while he may seem modern in his respectful marriage partnership with Fromet Gugenheim, whom he married for love, he appears rather backward-looking when it comes to the conventionally arranged (and ultimately unhappy) marriages of his daughters. The map that closes out the exhibition illustrates how Mendelssohn was read by his contemporaries and posterity and presents a contrasting tableau that seems to run parallel with the range of potential visitor expectations. Moses the man of multiplicity is the way to tell his story. The many names under which he is known are reflected in this exhibition in the major phases of his life, the topics he grappled with, and profiles of personalities.

EINFÜHRUNG

Für Abraham Moses (wie bis zur Annahme des Taufnamens „Ernst" sein zweiter Name lautet) ist der bürgerliche Name seines Erzeugers vor allem ein Emanzipationskostüm. Ein so erfolgreiches, angeblich unabwaschbar jüdisches, dass er selbst nach seiner Taufe (vergeblich) versuchen wird, es loszuwerden: Ein christlicher Mendelssohn sei nun mal ebenso so unmöglich wie ein jüdischer Konfuzius, beschwört er seinen Komponisten-Sohn Felix.³

Noch anonym waren die ersten drei in deutscher Sprache gedruckten Bücher des Vaters Moses erschienen. Während seines Verlobungsjahres 1761/62 beginnt der 32-Jährige, gelegentlich an christliche Briefpartner mit dem selbst gebastelten Namen Nr. 2, „Moses Mendelssohn",⁴ zu zeichnen. Hebräische bzw. in Westjiddisch verfasste Briefe unterschreibt er dagegen weiter als *Ha-katan Mausche mi-Dessau*, der kleine Moses aus Dessau (Name Nr. 1) oder nur *Mausche Dessau*. In Berlin nennen sie ihn wiederum den Herrn Moses (Nr. 3).

Darüber hinaus zeugt auswärts der seit 1761 in Paris aufgekommene Ruhmestitel „juif à berlin"⁵ (Nr. 4), später auf der französischen Ausgabe seines Bestsellers „Phaedon" abgedruckt, von der Faszination der Nichtjuden. Den gelehrten Kollegen gilt dieser zivilisierte, brillante „Jude von Berlin" als Ausnahme seiner Spezies. In der Ehrung steckt mit der Wertschätzung des Geehrten die Abwertung jener „Anderen", zu denen er gehört.

Namen und Identität sind verbunden. Auch Ehrennamen können vereinnahmen. Die Kanonisierung — mit dem Propheten vom Sinai und der mittelalterlichen Autorität des Moses Maimonides — findet statt, wenn jüdische Verehrer folgender Generationen ihn nun in die rühmende Formel „Von Moses bis Moses war keiner wie Moses" einbeziehen (Nr. 5).⁶ Er wird auch als „Berliner Sokrates"⁷ (Nr. 6), als „Luther

The names

"My father's father was called Mendel Dessau," wrote the merchant Abraham Mendelssohn Bartholdy in 1829, the year marking the 100th anniversary of his father Moses. *"Once his son, my father, had entered the world, once he began to be called by name, once he had taken the noble decision, which can never be praised enough, to pull himself and his brethren out of the deep abasement into which they had sunk by exposing them to a higher level of education, he felt it in his heart that it would be too difficult for him, as Moses Mendel Dessau, to establish the closer relationship which he needed to have with those who, at time, were the stewards of this higher education: therefore, he called himself, without fearing to disrespect his father, 'Mendelssohn'. [...] As Mendelssohn, he irrevocably separated himself from an entire class of people, the best of whom he raised up to his level and joined to a different community."*²

For Abraham Moses (who later changed his middle name to "Ernst" following baptism), the civil name adopted by his progenitor was, above all, an emancipatory costume. One that was so successful and supposedly so ineffaceably Jewish that he would continue his attempts (in vain) to get rid of it, even after accepting baptism. A Christian Mendelssohn, he would later aver to his composer son Felix, was, after all, just as impossible as a Jewish Confucius.³

His father Moses had published his first three German-language books anonymously. Then, in the year of his engagement (1761/62), the 32-year-old budding author occasionally began to sign letters to Christian correspondents with his self-invented pen name "Moses Mendelssohn"⁴ (Name No. 2). When writing letters in Hebrew or Western Yiddish, however, he would continue to sign as Ha-katan Mausche mi-Dessau, "the little Moses from Dessau" (Name No. 1),

der Juden"⁸ (Nr. 7) gepriesen, als „echter Israelit, an dem kein Falsch ist"⁹ (Nr. 8, Zitat aus dem Johannes-Evangelium) und als „Moses der deutschen Juden"¹⁰ (Nr. 9). Für Karl Marx ist er ein typischer „Seichtbeutel"¹¹ (Nr. 10). Super-Moses oder Waschlappen? Mendelssohn entdecken heißt wohl auch: unter verschiedenen *Identity Cards* jene herausfinden, die zueinander im schärfsten Gegensatz stehen.

Ein Genießer und seine Gärten

Dass Moses, der verwachsene, kränkelnde Bücherwurm, nicht als sinnesstarker Naturbursche der Nachwelt vor Augen steht, ist verständlich. In jenen religiösen und intellektuellen Milieus, in denen sein Vermächtnis reflektiert wurde, hat man jeweils auszublenden gewusst, was dabei nebensächlich oder unpassend erschien. So wird auch der Ästhetiker und Kunstliebhaber Mendelssohn zumeist auf den Theoretiker reduziert, zumal er weder vom eigenen Klavierspiel noch von eigener Dichtkunst viel gehalten hat. Von seinen poetischen (Jugend-)Sünden in hebräischer Sprache ist uns nur ein Hymnus auf den Gartenempfang bei einem Freund in Hannover überliefert. Sein bestes deutsches Gedicht, die freie Bearbeitung

or simply as Mausche Dessau. In Berlin, on the other hand, he went by Herr Moses (No. 3).

Then there was the honorific soubriquet *le juif à berlin*⁵ (Name No. 4), which he acquired in Parisian literary circles in 1761 and which was later printed on the French edition of his bestseller "Phaedon". It testified to the fascination which he inspired in the Gentile community. To his learned fellow scholars, this cultured and brilliant "Jew of Berlin" was an exception to his kind. The esteem accorded to his person also implied a devaluing of the "others" in the community from which he sprang.

Names and identities are connected. Honorific names, too, can lock the bearer into a specific identity. Moses Mendelssohn is declared a person deserving veneration—on an equal footing with the Prophet of Sinai or the medieval authority Moses Maimonides—once subsequent generations of Jewish admirers begin to include him in the laudation "From Moses to Moses, there were none like Moses" (Name No. 5).⁶ He was praised as a "Berlin Socrates"⁷ (Name No. 6), as the "Luther of the Jews"⁸ (Name No. 7), as an "Israelite indeed in whom is no guile"⁹ (Name No. 8, which quotes from the Gospel of St. John) and as the "Moses of the German

Aufbruch, Befreiung, Natur. Illustration von 1756 für die von Moses übersetzte Rousseau-Abhandlung „Von dem Ursprunge der Ungleichheit unter den Menschen" sowie für die „Vermischten Abhandlungen und Urtheile über das Neueste aus der Gelehrsamkeit" mit seinen „Gedanken von der Wahrscheinlichkeit".
ULB Sachsen-Anhalt, Halle

Awakening, liberation, nature. Illustration from 1756 for the Moses-translated Rousseau treatise "Of the Origin of Inequality among Men" and for the "Miscellaneous Treatises and Judgments on the latest developments in scholarship" with his "Thoughts on Probability".
ULB Sachsen-Anhalt, Halle

von Versen des Breslauers Ephraim Kuh, ist ebenfalls eine Natur-Eloge („Ode zum Lobe Gottes. Nach einem Donnerwetter", 1771).

Aber Mendelssohns Lyrikübersetzungen, samt seinem deutschen Psalter, haben zahlreich überlebt; dazu zählt im Rahmen einer vergleichenden Literaturkritik folgende Übertragung von Horaz-Versen (Oden I 9), die der Übersetzer als „herrliches Gewächs" bezeichnet:

Jews"[10] (Name No. 9). For Karl Marx, he was a typical "shallow windbag"[11] (Name No. 10). Super-Moses or an ineffectual nebbish? Discovering Mendelssohn probably means to focus on those identity cards that stand out in sharpest contrast to one other.

„Siehe tiefen Schnee den glänzenden Soracte bedecken.
Belastete Wälder sinken unter ihrer Bürde, und vom scharfem Frost erstarren die Flüsse.
Zerlaß die Kälte, bedecke den Feuerheerd reichlich mit Brennholz,
und hole in Sabinischen Flaschen, o Thaliarchus!
Nicht sparsam, vierjährigen Wein.
Alles übrige stellet den Göttern anheim.
Sobald die aufbrausende Meere den Kampf der Winde gestillet,
schwanken Cypressen, schwanken bejahrte Buchen nicht mehr.
Forsche nicht heute, was morgen geschehen wird.
Welchen Tag das Glück dir schenkt, rechne zum Gewinnste.
Noch jung besuche die Chöre der Tänzer, so lange noch
kein mürrisches Grau das frische Haupthaar befleckt.
Des Mavors Kampfplatz geziemet dir jetzt, und der freye Markt,
und am Abend leises Flüstern zur abgeredeten Stunde."[12]

"See deep snow cover shining Mount Soracte,
Forests bend under their snowy loads, rivers congeal from the sharp frost.
Dispel the cold, pile firewood generously upon the hearth,
And fetch in Sabine bottles, oh Thaliarchus,
Unstintingly, the four-year-old wine.
All else commit to the gods.
Once the spuming seas have stilled the contending winds,
Cypresses and aged beeches will cease their swaying.
Seek not to know today what tomorrow will bring.
Whatever day fortune grants you, reckon it as profit.
While still young, visit the dancers' choruses, so long as
Sullen grey has not yet tarnished your fresh head of hair.
The arena of Mavors is proper for you now, and the free market,
And at eventide, quiet whispers at the appointed hour."[12]

Mendelssohn, aus kleinen Verhältnissen kommend, lebt auch als erfolgreicher Kaufmann bescheiden. Er weiß das gute Leben zu schätzen. Lustvoll und leibhaftig tritt er uns bei Gartenbesuchen und -passagen vor Augen. Die eigene Mietlaube (genannt „Moses Ruh"[13]) und die benachbarte des Freundes Nicolai, Gärten des Malers Frisch und des Akademiepräsidenten Sulzer, Sommerfrischen und Stadtrandvillen von verwandten Fabrikanten und Gemeindeältesten sowie den Lustgarten, den Tiergarten und Kurparks schätzt er nicht nur als Treffpunkte für Arbeitssitzungen, Business Lunchs und Gesundheitspflege.

Der durch mehrere Berufe eingespannte Stadtmensch genießt die Gärten; von floristischer Aktivität wissen wir nichts, aber er kultiviert seine Gärten im Kopf. Naturerlebnisse inspirieren die metaphysische Spekulation. Auch erscheinen hier, wie in weiteren Lebensbereichen, die Orientierungen des „jüdischen" Mendelssohn verschränkt mit den Ambitionen des säkularen „Weltweisen" – und sind keineswegs gegeneinander auszuspielen.

In seinem hebräischen Zeitschriften-Debüt äußert sich der Rousseau-Kritiker und -Übersetzer als Gegner antizivilisatorischer Naturverklärung. Den modischen Trend zu idealisierten Schäferidyllen und den Traum vom utopischen Arkadien spießt er in der Wochenschrift „Der Chamäleon" satirisch auf. Seine bodenständige Gartenlust, auf die in der Ausstellung mit *Open Air*-Elementen und Geräuschen angespielt wird, ist keine Fluchtbewegung, sondern Ausdruck seiner ganzheitlichen, biblisch fundierten Weltanschauung.

„Das Kommerz zwischen Seele und Körper"
Die schmerzvolle Erfahrung, dass unsere „beste aller Welten" sich jedoch so paradiesisch ganzheitlich wie gedacht oft nicht darstellt, hat

A lover of the good things in life— and of his garden
That Moses, the misshapen and sickly bookworm, is not known to posterity as a sensual outdoorsman is understandable. The various religious and intellectual circles preserving his legacy each found a way to bracket out what they considered tangential or out of place. Thus, Mendelssohn the aesthete and art-lover is usually reduced to a mere theoretician, all the more so as he himself thought little of his own piano playing or aptitude for poetry. Of his (youthful) dabblings in Hebrew poetry, the only work to survive destruction at his hands was a hymn inspired by a garden reception at the home of a friend in Hanover. His best German-language poem, a free reworking of verse by the Breslau poet Ephraim Kuh, is also an elegy to nature (Ode zum Lobe Gottes. Nach einem Donnerwetter, 1771—Ode in Praise of God. After a Thunderstorm).

Many of Mendelssohn's translations of lyric poetry have survived, however, along with his German psalter. Among them is this rendition of a famous poem by Horace (Odes I/9) which the translator, taking on the role of comparative literary critic, called a "splendid flowering".

Having come from humble circumstances, Mendelssohn continued to live frugally even after achieving commercial success as a merchant. He knew how to appreciate the good things in life, however. We see him depicted strolling jauntily and contentedly through various gardens and arcades. Among his favorite haunts were his rented garden house (called Moses Ruh or "Moses' Retreat"[13]) and the adjoining one of his friend Christoph Friedrich Nicolai, the gardens of the painter Johann Christoph Frisch and of the president of the Berlin Academy of Sciences Johann Georg Sulzer, the summer retreats and suburban villas owned by

für Mendelssohn und Zeitgenossen komplizierte Fragen aufgeworfen. Der Menschenkörper ist sterblich, die Seele soll unsterblich sein? Das fordert den Popular-Philosophen zu Publikationen heraus, die das Publikum als lesbar und hilfreich akzeptieren kann. Und wie funktioniert – in der psychosomatischen Interaktion – eine freie Willensentscheidung, was trägt die göttliche Vorbestimmung dazu bei?

Während sein „Phaedon oder über die Unsterblichkeit der Seele" (1767) vor allem nichtjüdische Leser erreicht, will der engagierte Aufklärer Moses das Thema mit weiterführenden Gedanken, unter Aussparung des platonischen Rahmens, auch Glaubensgenossen nahebringen. Gedruckt wird diese hebräische Schrift unter dem Titel „Abhandlung über das Kommerz zwischen Seele und Körper" erst ein Jahr nach seinem Tod. Darin heißt es, die Seele „perzipiert" alles (nimmt alles wahr), was dem Körper widerfährt: *„so dass sie sich freut, wenn sie seine Vollkommenheit und Gesundheit perzipiert – dies ist die sinnliche Lust (Voluptas sensualis) –, und dass sie sich betrübt, wenn sie seine Unvollkommenheit und Zerstörung perzipiert – dies ist die sinnliche Unlust (Dolor)."*[14]

Der Schmerz als Bedrohung, Phänomen und Herausforderung muss Moses zeitlebens beschäftigt haben. Das Tag und Nacht büffelnde, kränkelnde Kind in Fränkels Dessauer Talmud-Schule; der unbegleitet in die Fremde reisende Teenager; der hungernde Berliner Bettelstudent; der diskriminierte, bucklige Zuwanderer; der schüchterne, stotternde Gelehrte; der von Nervenkrankheit Deprimierte; von indiskreten Debattenpartnern öffentlich Vorgeführte; der Vater, dem vier von zehn Kindern sterben.

Auffällig ist, wie analytisch kühl der Betroffene vom Schmerz schreibt: *„Der Henker unsres Lebens, der sinnliche Schmertz hat keine*

relatives in the manufacturing sector and by community elders, not to mention the Lustgarten, Tiergarten, and the gardens of various health spas. Here he would meet people for working sessions and business lunches, or to stay fit.

As a busy urbanite engaged in multiple professions, he found great refreshment in the gardens. We know nothing of any actual flower-tending activities, but he cultivated his gardens in his mind. His experiences of nature inspired his metaphysical speculations. Here, as in other topical fields, the spheres of life and preoccupations of the "Jewish" Mendelssohn seem intertwined with the ambitions of the secular "worldly sage" in a way that does not admit of any evident contradiction.

Both a critic and translator of Jean-Jacques Rousseau, he took a firm stance, in his very first article published in a Hebrew periodical, against the idealization of nature as being superior to civilization. In the weekly journal Der Chamäleon, he satirically skewered the shepherds' idylls and dreamy visions of utopian arcadias that were the fashion of the day. His down-to-earth enjoyment of gardens—which the exhibition alludes to with open-air elements and sounds—was not a form of escapism, but rather an expression of his holistic, Bible-centered view of the world.

"The commerce between soul and body"
The painful experience that our "best of all possible worlds" is often not so paradisiacal as we would like raised complicated questions for Mendelssohn and his contemporaries. The human body is mortal, but the soul is supposed to live forever? It was a conundrum that challenged the popular philosopher to publish writings that the broad public could accept as readable and helpful. And how—in the interaction between

andere Schrecknisse als das gegenwärtige Bild einer Unvollkommenheit in dem Körper. Wenn nervigte Theile, die natürlicher Weise vereinigt seyn sollten, aus ihrer Verknüpfung gerissen werden; so erstrecken sich die traurigen Wirkungen davon auf das ganze organische Gebäude. Der Ton wird verändert, es äussert sich eine Mißstimmung in allen Sennadern; die Lebensbewegungen sind entweder träge oder in vollem Aufruhr. Die Nerven verkündigen diese Unordnung unverzüglich dem Gehirne. Was kann die Seele in dem Augenblick anders wahrnehmen, als das dunkele Gefühl einer Unvollkommenheit, die ihrem Körper drohet?"[15]

Doch neben solcher rationalen Bearbeitung seiner Lebensleiden findet Mendelssohn persönliche Wege zur Verwandlung des Negativen. In der Ausstellung wird dies durch ein Stegreif-Gedicht dokumentiert, dessen Abschrift sich bei den Nachkommen der Moses-Tochter Brendel/Dorothea und in einem gedruckten Zeitzeugenbericht erhalten hat.

mind and body—is our free will able to function? What role does divine predestination play?

With his treatise "Phaedon, or a Dialogue on the Immortality of the Soul" (1767), Moses was able to reach an audience of mainly non-Jewish readers. But as a committed Enlightenment philosopher, he also wanted to introduce the topic to his co-religionists, albeit after adding further ideas and leaving aside the Platonic framework. Written in Hebrew, the resulting "Treatise on the Commerce between Soul and Body" was not published until a year after his death. Here, we read that the soul becomes aware of everything that happens to the body, "so that it rejoices when it perceives its perfection and health—this being sensual pleasure (voluptas sensualis)—and grieves when it perceives its imperfection and destruction—this being sensual displeasure (dolor)."[14]

Pain—the threat, the phenomenon, the practical challenge—must have preoccupied Moses throughout his life: as a sickly child

NR. 193 JOHANN DAVID SCHLEUEN (1711–1771): PROSPECT DES GESUNDBRUNNENS BEI BERLIN. ANSICHT DER KURANLAGEN
Berlin, ca. 1770
Kupferstich, koloriert
JMB (Foto: Roman März)

Gartenlust und körperliche Zerbrechlichkeit: Während des Sommers 1779 verbringt der kränkelnde Mendelssohn Morgen- und Abendstunden in Gesundbrunnen.
Garden delight and physical fragility: during the summer of 1779, the ailing Mendelssohn spent morning and evening hours at Gesundbrunnen.

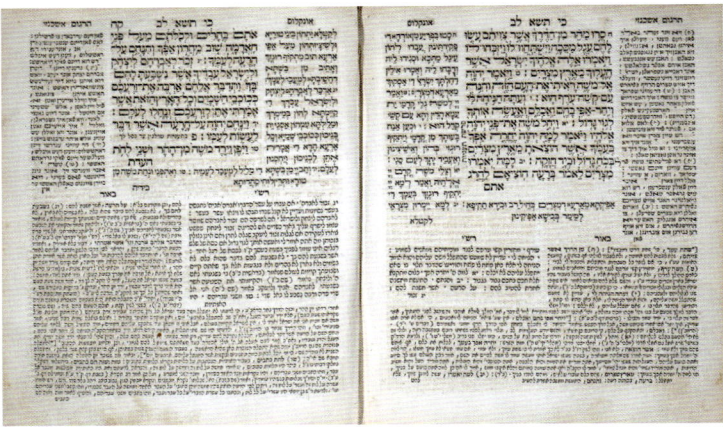

o. Nr. Moses Mendelssohn: Pentateuch-Übersetzung mit Biur, Exodus
Fürth, 1806
Privatbesitz
(Foto: Manfred Fuß)

Fundament und Opus magnum der Dialog-Werkstatt: das Interpreten-Konzert im Tora-Kommentar, dem Biur.
Foundation and magnum opus of Mendelsohn's dialogue workshop: the interpreter concert in the Torah commentary, the Biur.

Die Gelegenheitsverse entstanden Mitte der 1750er-Jahre im „Gelehrten Kaffeehaus", wo die Versammelten sich einmal gegenseitig aufforderten, Spontanreime über eigene Schwächen zu fabrizieren. Moses vergleicht sich in dieser Runde mit dem buckligen Dichter Aesop und dem stotternden Politiker Demosthenes, er schließt: „*Triumph! ich werd in Eurem Kreise/ Gedoppelt gros und weise seyn, Der glücklich ich in mir verein/Was man getrennt im Demosthen, und im Aesop gehöret und gesehen.*"[16]

Mit Witz und Charme *Handicaps* in Pluspunkte verwandeln: die Überlebenstechnik. Aus der Verarbeitung von Nachteilen, Beschränkungen, Schwächen wird ein „Triumph" der Persönlichkeit. Niederlagen konnte der vom Schicksal wenig Verwöhnte in Erfolge verwandeln. Das Desaster des Lavater-Streites ist ein Beispiel: seine aufgrund von Stress samt Krankheitsfolgen erzwungene langjährige Abstinenz von spekulativer Metaphysik und die so beförderte Hinwendung zu seinem innerjüdisch wirkmächtigsten Lebenswerk, der Tora-Übersetzung.

Mendelssohn hinterlässt kein philosophisches System, weshalb Philosophie-Geschichten ihn oft unter „ferner liefen" führen. Sein

cramming day and night at David Fränkel's Talmudic school in Dessau; as an unaccompanied teenager traveling far from home; as an indigent, practically starving student in Berlin; as the butt of prejudice due to his hunched back and immigrant background; as a shy, stuttering scholar; as a sufferer of debilitating nervous illness; as a debater exposed to public opprobrium by indiscreet opponents; as a father who had to watch four of his ten children die prematurely.

It is striking how coolly and analytically he was able to write about the pain afflicting him: "That executioner of our life, sensual pain, has no other horrors in store than the present image of an imperfection in the body. When the nerve-containing parts that by nature should be conjoined are torn from their connection, then the resulting unhappy effects extend across the whole organic structure. The tone is altered, a discord is apparent in all the brain's channels; the vital movements are either sluggish or in full turmoil. The nerves immediately announce this disorder to the brain. What else can the soul perceive at that moment but the dark feeling of an imperfection threatening its body?"[15]

But besides processing his existential suffering through reason, Mendelssohn also found

schriftliches, politisches, emanzipatorisches, ästhetisches und religiöses Werk wird aber von der Nachwelt als Gesamtkunstwerk wahrgenommen: in Kombination mit der Überwindungskraft seiner starken, charismatischen, vermittelnden Persönlichkeit. Als Faszination des Trotzdem. Gerade das macht ihn zum „Moses der deutschen Juden". Hier fallen Parallelen zur nachhaltigen Ausstrahlung des als hässlich verrufenen Sokrates auf (von dem ebenfalls außer dem glaubwürdigen Lebenszeugnis keine Schrift und kein System erhalten ist).

Schöne Seele, kaputter Körper: Dieses Paradox, die Überwindungsenergie des Moses, ließ schon seine Zeitgenossen staunen. Sein Arzt Johann Georg Zimmermann vermerkte dazu 1764, der „Urheber der Natur" habe wohl „*in den elendesten und unter uns Thoren verachtetsten Leib eine göttliche Seele gradezu seiner Schöpfung zur Zierde*" gelegt. Er vergleicht den Patienten mit zwei Philosophen, zwei Dichtern, einem Naturwissenschaftler: „*Eine ganz Esopische Gestalt hat der Jude, Schriftsteller und Kaufmann Moses Mendelssohn in Berlin, der so tief als Leibniz sieht, so groß als Plato denkt, so wizig als Pope redt, so schön als Addison schreibt, und so fromm als Boerhave lebt.*"

Dialog-Werkstatt
Dass Moses, der widerständige Überwinder, als starker Typ angesehen wird, ist aus seiner Rezeptionsgeschichte weniger bekannt. Menschenfreundlichkeit, Vermittlerqualitäten und sein Einsatz für Toleranz wurden ihm eher als Nachgiebigkeit und Schwäche ausgelegt. Zum Verständnis für seine echte Stärke führt jedoch die Rehabilitierung seiner Idee von Tugend. Aufklärer verstehen unter Tugend keine moralinsaure Lustfeindlichkeit, kein verzopftes Artigsein. Ihr Begriff davon ist kämpferisch, von antiken und mittelhochdeutschen Wortfeldern

personal ways to make the best of adversity. This is documented in the exhibition by an impromptu poem, a copy of which was preserved by the descendants of Moses' daughter Brendel/Dorothea, as well as in the printed account of a contemporary witness. The lines were casually composed in the mid-1750s at the "Gelehrtes Kaffeehaus" (Learned Coffee House), when the members of the club had challenged one another to concoct spontaneous rhymes about their own faults. In this group, Moses compares himself to the hunchbacked poet Aesop and the stuttering politician Demosthenes, concluding with the lines: "Triumph is mine! In your circle I will be reckoned/Twice-over great and wise, who happily unite in one/ That seen and heard in Demosthenes and Aesop both."[16]

Using wit and charm to turn physical handicaps into assets: a survival technique. Working through disadvantages, limitation, and weaknesses turns into a personal "triumph". This enabled the man who had hardly been spoiled by fate to turn setbacks into successes. The disaster of the Lavater controversy is just one example. The resulting stress—coupled with ill health—forced him to abstain from speculative metaphysics, which allowed him to devote himself to his German translation of the Torah, the work which ultimately had the greatest impact within the Jewish community.

Mendelssohn did not leave any philosophical system behind, which is why histories of philosophy often classify him among the also-rans. Yet his writings on politics, emancipation, aesthetics, and religion are perceived by posterity as a total work of art, seen in combination with the strong, charismatic, and diplomatic personality that made its author so indomitable. As the fascination of the "contrary". This is what makes him the "Moses of German

geprägt, auf denen es um Tüchtigkeit, Kraft und Gestaltungsfertigkeit geht. Praktizierte soziale Tugenden des Individuums tragen bei zu seiner gottbestimmten Vervollkommnung, welche sich wiederum auf die partielle Vervollkommnung der Welt auswirkt. So klingt dann die – sehr verhaltene – Fortschrittsvision Mendelssohns: „Gesetzt, wir fahren fort, unsere Künste so zu verbessern, daß der Arbeiter weder Kopf noch Routine braucht, sein Werk hervorzubringen; wir reinigten unsere Religionsbegriffe von allen Vorurtheilen; wir trieben es in der Handlung so weit, daß die Produkte aller Länder in allen Ländern zu allen Zeiten vorräthig seyen; wir befreieten die Regierungen von Tyranneyen, die Gerichtshöfe von Chicanen; die Zollbude von Plackereyen, und die Recensionen von allen Neckereyen. Was sollen nun unsere Kinder? Immer vorwärts eilen? – Der Weg gehet freylich ins Unendliche. Allein sie kommen so zur Welt, wie wir gekommen sind. […] Wie sollen sie ihre Verstandeskräfte üben, wenn alle ihre Bedürfnisse ohne Anstrengung befriediget werden können? ihre Liebe zur Freyheit, wenn keine Tyranney drücket? zur Wahrheit, wenn sie ihnen vorgekauet wird? – Es ist offenbar, daß das menschliche Geschlecht hier und da zurük muß, wenn die Individua fortkommen sollen."*[17]

Mit Stärke und Widerstandskraft hat Mendelssohn persönliche Widersprüche bewältigt, Konflikte zwischen Tradition und Reformbedarf, zwischen Zaudern und Entschlossenheit, Schüchternheit und Selbstbewusstsein. Stärke, Widerstandskraft, Beharrlichkeit benötigt man, unter anderem, für sein zeitloses Projekt der Dialogwerkstatt: jenen lebenslangen Lernprozess der Meinungsbildung und des Austausches, samt Wahrheitsfindung und Positionierung, der Demokratie so mühsam macht (und manchen an ihr verzweifeln lässt).

Jews". Particularly evident, too, are the similarities of his enduring aura to that of Socrates, who was defamed for being physically ugly (and who likewise left no formal system of philosophy behind apart from what we can glean from credible eye-witness accounts of his life).

A beautiful soul in a broken body. This paradox, and the resilient energy applied to overcoming it, made Moses a source of amazement to his contemporaries. His physician Johann Georg Zimmermann speculated in 1764 that the "Author of Nature" must have implanted "a divine soul, as if intending to ornament his creation, into the most miserable body of the sort that we, being fools, are most wont to despise." He went on to compare his patient to no less than two philosophers, two poets, and one natural scientist: "Entirely Aesop-like is the figure of the Jew, the writer, and the merchant Moses Mendelssohn of Berlin, who sees as deeply as Leibniz, thinks as widely as Plato, converses as wittily as Pope, writes as beautifully as Addison, and lives as piously as Boerhave."

The dialogue workshop
That Moses, the robust overcomer of odds, was regarded as a tough guy by posterity is rather less evident from the reader responses throughout reception history. Indeed, his love of people, diplomatic skills, and commitment to tolerance were more often interpreted as weakness and a propensity to accommodate. However, his true strength can be understood based on a rediscovery and appreciation of his conception of virtue. The Enlightenment thinkers did not understand virtue as a hyper-moral condemnation of pleasure, as an outdated duty to be proper and well-behaved. No, their concept of virtue was quite pugnacious, laced with a vocabulary drawn from classical and middle-high German literature relating to competence, energy, and

Für Mausche Dessau hat diese Sozialisation in der Talmudschule begonnen, mit der Entdeckung des mittelalterlichen Vernunftpatrons Maimonides und der traditionell unterstützten Vielfalt von Interpretationen im jüdischen Synagogenbetrieb. Dialogisch geprägt durch Einbeziehung der jeweils „anderen" Argumente sind dann auch viele seiner säkularen Bücher, verfasst im Gesprächs- oder Brief(wechsel)format. Er überwindet Hemmungen, sich offen zu äußern, artikuliert sich in Gelehrtenclubs, bei Caféhaustreffen, Gartendisputen: als Protagonist einer neuen Öffentlichkeit. Er zeigt publizistisch Flagge im Zeitschriftenmarkt, als Rezensent und Feuilletonist. Das Panorama dieser Korrespondenzen, Kontakte und Sparringpartnerschaften wird im „Netzwerk"-Raum der Ausstellung skizziert.

Mit Rabbinern, die ihn kritisch sehen, setzt er das freundschaftliche Gespräch ebenso fort wie mit christlichen Gelehrten, die eine Judenemanzipation ablehnen. Zur Geschichte seiner Dialog-Werkstatt gehört vor allem auch sein monumentales Werk der Pentateuch-Übersetzung mit Kommentar, das die Interpreten-

the skill to create. By practicing such virtue, the individual was realizing the process of perfection intended by God, thereby making a contribution to perfecting the world. Which leads to the (very restrained) vision of progress developed by Mendelssohn:

"Suppose that we continue to improve our arts and skills such that the worker needs to use neither his head nor some routine to produce his work; suppose that we purify our religious concepts from all prejudices; that we push commerce so far that the products of all countries become available in all countries at all times; that we free the governments from tyrannies, the courts from chicanery; the customs house from drudgery, and the critics' reviews from all derision. What should our children do then? Constantly hurry forward? Obviously, that path leads towards infinity. Yet they come into the world just as we have come. [...] How are they to exercise their powers of reason when all their needs can be satisfied without effort? Their love of freedom when no tyranny oppresses? Of truth, when it is pre-masticated for them to swallow? It is obvious that the human race must take a

O. NR. DISMAR DEGEN
(CA. 1690–1753): HÄUSERBAU
IN DER FRIEDRICHSTRASSE
um 1735
Öl auf Leinwand
SPSG

Fortschrittsvisionen: „Der Weg gehet freylich ins Unendliche."
Visions of progress: "The path, however, goes to infinity".

EINFÜHRUNG

O. NR. SAMUEL HIRSCHENBERG:
DER EXKOMMUNIZIERTE
SPINOZA
1907
Öl auf Leinwand
Kursker Gemäldegalerie
„A. A. Dejneka"

Plädoyer für Gewissensfreiheit
und die Dissidenten von gestern
und heute.
*Plea for freedom of conscience
and the dissidents of yesterday
and today.*

Paraden der Jahrhunderte mit wissenschaftlichen und eigenen Einsichten der Gegenwart kombiniert. Gegen die dogmatische Engführung religiöser Diskussionen durch Glaubenswächter und Kirchenzucht setzt er wiederum sein Plädoyer für Gewissensfreiheit in „Jerusalem oder über religiöse Macht und Judentum". Dissidenten von gestern, wie Spinoza, und seiner Tage, wie der polnische Querkopf Abba Glosk, motivieren ihn dazu.

Er wird in seinem Wohnhaus Spandauer Straße 68 zum Gastgeber und Moderator für Debattierer verschiedener Standpunkte, Religionen und Milieus. Getragen von seiner Dialogkunst, die sich mit den engsten Diskursfreunden herausbildet, lässt sich während der Jahrzehnte vor der Französischen Revolution ein Kairos ausmachen, ein Hoffnungsfenster öffnet sich: für ein utopisches Momentum der milieuübergreifenden Verständigung. Weitere Kollegen der Haskala und der christlichen Berliner Aufklärung sind in solche Erfahrungen einbezogen. Das stärkste Dokument dieser Kommunikations-Highlights, aus dem schon früh er-

step back from time to time if individual human beings are to progress."[17]

It was strength and resilience that allowed Mendelssohn to overcome his own personal contradictions, along with the conflict between upholding traditions and the need for reform, between hesitation and determination, shyness and self-confidence. This same strength, resilience, and perseverance remain essential prerequisites if we are to carry forward his timeless project of a dialogue workshop: that lifelong process of learning, of forming opinions, of exchanging ideas—while also seeking the truth and adopting a position of one's own—which makes democracy so arduous (and which makes some people give up on it).

For Mausche Dessau, this socialization began in the Talmudic school, where he discovered Maimonides, the medieval champion of reason, and where he took part in the freewheeling interpretation of scripture traditionally enabled in Jewish synagogue activities. Many of his secular books, written in a conversational or epistolary format, became a sort of dialogue in which the

sichtlich wird, wie so etwas geht und welchen Einsatz es für so etwas braucht, ist Nicolais, Mendelssohns und Lessings Brief- und Disputserie „Briefwechsel über das Trauerspiel".

Darin zeigt sich, was für solch eine Werkstatt wichtig wäre und gelernt werden muss: Höflichkeit, Offenheit, Herzlichkeit, Witz und Ironie, Interesse und Neugierde, scharfe Kritik. Formulieren der Argumente des Anderen besser als dieser selbst. Engagement, Lust am spielerischen Gefecht, Sachlichkeit, Gründlichkeit, Leidenschaft. Zuhören, Hinterfragen, Einfordern der Meinungen, Kritikfähigkeit, Suche nach Übereinstimmung. Einsatz fürs eigene Argument, Suche nach Konsens, Mut zur Differenz, Zwischenresümees von beidem. Freundschaft trotz der Differenzen. – *Yes, we can.* Dialog ist schön, macht aber viel Arbeit.

Die Ausstellung

Aus Identitätszweifeln, Menschenbildern und Dialogproblemen der Zeit Mendelssohns sind Fragen des Jahres 2022 herauszuhören. Zugleich erscheinen er und sein Aufklärungsjahrhundert fremd und fern. Eine Erzählung, die hier Zugänge ermöglicht, muss sich annähern, ohne Erkenntnisoptionen der Fremdheit auszublenden. Zur Provokation der fremden Figur gehört im 21. Jahrhundert der Glaubenskrisen und des Fundamentalismus der fromme, das mosaische Gesetz observierende Mendelssohn: die Religion und Vernunft verbindende Spiritualität seiner Aufklärung.

Nach den Biografen, Interpreten und Werkeditoren Mendelssohns haben seinerzeit die Ausstellungsmacher begonnen, solche Brücken der Vermittlung zu entwickeln. Die bisher größten Präsentationen in Berlin 1929 (Jüdische Gemeinde zu Berlin und Preußische Staatsbibliothek) und Wolfenbüttel 1986 (Herzog August Bibliothek) nahmen Jahrestage

arguments of the respective "other" were duly included. Overcoming his inhibitions to express himself openly, he began articulating himself in scholars' clubs, at get-togethers in coffee houses, in garden disputations, playing to a new public. He published his opinions in the magazine market as a reviewer and feature writer. A panoramic overview of his relationships with postal correspondents, personal contacts, and intellectual sparring partners is presented in the "Network" space of the exhibition.

Moses kept up the amicable dialogue even with those rabbis who viewed him critically, as well as with those Christian scholars who rejected the very idea of Jewish emancipation. One of the most notable achievements of his dialogue workshop was his monumental translation of the Pentateuch with commentary, which brought together interpretations from centuries past with scholarly opinions from his own day as well as his own personal insights. Opposed to allowing religious debate to be constrained by self-appointed "guardians of the faith" or by religious dogma, he made an impassioned plea for freedom of conscience in the treatise "Jerusalem, or on Religious Power and Judaism". Here he drew inspiration from famous dissidents of the past, like Spinoza, as well as of his own day, like the Polish free-thinker Abba Glosk.

In his Berlin home at Spandauer Straße 68, he became a host for the exponents of different viewpoints, religious traditions, and social groups, moderating their intellectual discourse. His artful debating skills, which he honed with the help of his closest friends and partners in discussion, can be regarded as part of a kairo— a window of hope and opportunity, a utopian moment of cultural understanding transcending societal strata—occurring in the decades leading up to the French Revolution. It was an experience that also included other colleagues from

zum Anlass: den 100. Geburtstag und den 200. Todestag. Damals wurden Bestände versammelt und katalogisiert, ohne deren Dokumentation diese Ausstellung im 21. Jahrhundert kaum hätte zustande kommen können.

In den über 50 Jahren zwischen einerseits 1929 – als zum letzten Mal der Pionier des deutschen Judentums ungebrochen gefeiert wurde – und andererseits 1986 lag die katastrophale Zäsur des „Dritten Reiches". Forscherwissen, Objekte und Dokumente waren mit der Vertreibung und Vernichtung der europäischen Juden und ihrer Kultur verloren gegangen. War nicht das optimistische, zivilisatorische Lebenswerk Mendelssohns selbst durch diesen Bruch *ad absurdum* geführt worden?

Manche Quellen und Standorte waren während der Jahre des Kalten Krieges nicht mehr auffindbar oder zugänglich. Insofern konnte die Ausstellung von Wolfenbüttel immerhin vieles feststellen, was überhaupt noch recherchierbar, anfragbar, ausleihbar war. Zwei sehr unterschiedliche Biografen, der Rabbiner und Herausgeber der „Gesammelten Schriften" Alexander Altmann und der Feuilletonist Heinz Knobloch („Herr Moses in Berlin") hatten diese Bestandserkundung auf Wissenschafts- und Publikumslevel mit angebahnt.

Ein knappes Jahrhundert später haben sich die Koordinaten der Rezeption und der Darstellung weiter gedreht. Auf Forschungsebene ist die Neu- und Wiederentdeckung des jüdischen, des hebräischen Mendelssohn wichtiger geworden. Die 1938 durch Beschlagnahmung durch die Gestapo gestoppte Edition der kritischen Werkausgabe („JubA") kommt, nach ihrer Wiederaufnahme durch den Stuttgarter Verleger Holzboog, im laufenden bzw. kommenden Jahr mit den letzten beiden von 40 Bänden zum Abschluss. Gerade wurden „1700 Jahre jüdisches Leben in Deutschland" gefeiert; einen

the Haskala movement as well as Christian exponents of the Enlightenment in Berlin. Perhaps the clearest record of these communicative fireworks—which readily demonstrates how such a process works and the level of commitment it requires—is the series of philosophical letters exchanged among Nicolai, Mendelssohn, and Gotthold Ephraim Lessing on the "nature of tragedy".

In it, we witness the finer touches that are so important and that must be learned for such a dialogue workshop to function smoothly: politeness, openness, heartfelt kindness, wit and irony, interest and curiosity, incisive critical thinking. Being able to formulate the arguments of the other side even better than they can. Remaining engaged, delighting in playful combat, being objective, thorough, and passionate. Listening, questioning, and soliciting opinions while accepting criticism and trying to reach common ground. Defending one's own arguments while aiming for consensus. Daring to disagree while encouraging both sides to take honest stock of the progress made. Staying friends in spite of all differences in a "yes, we can" spirit. Dialogue can be beautiful, but it takes a lot of work.

The exhibition
The identity conflicts, divergent understandings of human existence, and impediments to dialogue that prevailed in Mendelssohn's time still seem pertinent to the controversies that bedevil us today in 2022. Yet both he and the century of Enlightenment in which he lived can appear foreign and distant to us as well. Thus, any exhibition narrative that aims to make Moses and his times more approachable must refrain from robbing visitors of the ability to gain insights based on what they regard as alien. Still, as an observant Jew who sought to reconcile religion and reason within a spiritual understanding of

unmittelbaren Mendelssohn-Jahrestag gibt es gerade nicht, aber der 300. Geburtstag des „Juden von Berlin" naht.

Diese kulturhistorische Ausstellung ermöglicht Besichtigungen, die so bisher nicht möglich waren. Porträts und Dokumente, die vor kurzem verschollen oder noch unbekannt waren, können gezeigt werden: Glücksfunde auf dem Kunstmarkt, aus Privatbesitz, aus Institutionen Tschechiens, Polens und Israels. Dazu gehören die Funde verschiedener Fassungen der frühesten Miniatur von 1767 und die Präsentation der ältesten Handschrift des 14-jährigen Moses aus dem Jüdischen Museum in Prag. Verschollen bleibt seit den 1930er-Jahren die Miniatur der Fromet Mendelssohn, geb. Gugenheim.

Zeit, Themen und Biografie Mendelssohns sind in Wechselwirkungen zu entdecken. Der zur Ausstellung erscheinende Comic des holländischen Zeichners Typex zeigt uns Anekdoten aus Mendelssohns Biografie mit den Augen eines Künstlers des 21. Jahrhunderts. Eingangssätze am Treppenaufgang sollen den Bogen

enlightened progress, Mendelssohn remains a provocative figure for this 21st century of ours, in which loss of faith collides with religious fundamentalism.

Following the lead of Mendelssohn's biographers, interpreters, and editors, exhibition organizers, too, began to foster the sort of bridge-building he had pioneered. The largest shows dedicated to him until now were those mounted in Berlin in 1929 (by the Jewish Community of Berlin and Prussian State Library on the 200th anniversary of his birth) and in Wolfenbüttel in 1986 (by the Herzog August Library on the 200th anniversary of his death). Without the records and exhibits that were compiled and catalogued for these events, this exhibition in the 21st century would scarcely have been possible.

The catastrophic caesura of the so-called "Third Reich" was to overshadow the more than fifty years between 1929—the last time this pioneer of German Jewry could be celebrated unreservedly—and 1986. Knowledge, objects, and documents were irretrievably lost with the expulsion and annihilation of Europe's Jews and

O. NR. TYPEX: MOISCHE. SECHS ANEKDOTEN AUS DEM LEBEN DES MOSES MENDELSSOHN
Amsterdam, 2022

Comic-Held für das 21. Jahrhundert: Der 14-jährige Zuwanderer Moische am Halleschen Tor.
Comic hero for the 21st century: 14-year-old immigrant Moische at Hallesches Tor.

schlagen von Fragen der Gegenwart zu den Raumthemen, wo sie aufgenommen werden. An den biografischen Dessau / Berlin-Raum grenzt das Balkonzimmer, in dem es um Erfahrungen von Öffentlichkeit und Dialog im „Netzwerk" geht. Im Saal der Auf- und Gegenaufklärung, der Religionsdiskussion sowie der Übersetzungs- und Schulprojekte stoßen wissenschaftliche, theologische und sprituelle Aspekte des epochalen Aufbruchs zur Mündigkeit aneinander.

In drei getrennten Räumen kreisen die Erzählungen zum einen um Politik und Menschenrechte, um die Theorie eines multireligiösen Staats, die Forderung nach Gleichberechtigung des Judentums ohne Aufgabe seiner Besonderheit; zum anderen um ästhetische Wahrnehmung mit der Spannung zwischen Kopf und Bauch sowie um Menschenbilder und Un-Sterblichkeit. Im letzten großen Saal korrespondiert die „Bilderfabrik" der erstmals versammelten Moses-Porträts zu Lebzeiten mit der Installation des New Yorker Künstlers Izhar Patkin zur Moses-Erzählung vom „Judenporzellan", gefolgt vom Ausblick in das Nachleben – auf Denkmalprojekte, Souvenirproduktion und Rezeptionsdissonanzen.

Für das Ausstellungsteam war die intensive Begegnung mit der Persönlichkeit und dem Vermächtnis Mendelssohns ein Erlebnis. Was bei uns im Jahr 2022 von seiner Stärke, seiner Gesprächsfähigkeit ankommt, hat viel mit seinem bedrängten, letztlich unbeirrten Festhalten an der Wahrheitssuche zu tun. Jeder könne durch Gottes Allgüte die Wahrheit finden, der sie „mit offenen Augen sucht, und sich nicht selbst das Licht verstellen will", erklärte Mendelssohn in seiner Vermächtnisschrift „An die Freunde Lessings" (1785).[18]

Sein Appell gegen die Resignation an einen Aufklärungsmitstreiter hatte wenige Wo-

their culture. Was not Mendelssohn's optimistic and civilizing life's work itself reduced to absurdity by this rupture?

Many sources and locations could no longer be found or accessed during the Cold War. Fortunately, the Wolfenbüttel exhibition at least succeeded in creating an inventory of what could still be researched, requested, or borrowed. Two very different biographers of Moses, the rabbi and editor of the collected works Alexander Altmann and the feature writer Heinz Knobloch (Herr Moses in Berlin), were instrumental in getting this stock-taking process off the ground for both an academic and a general audience.

Almost a century later, the key reference points for Moses' legacy and public image have continued to evolve. For researchers, uncovering and/or re-discovering the Jewish or the Hebrew, respectively, Mendelssohn has become increasingly important. Publication of the critical edition of Mendelssohn's collected works (the Jubliäumsausgabe or "JubA"), which was blocked by the Gestapo confiscation in 1938 but later resumed by Holzboog in Stuttgart, is set to be completed in the current or coming year, when the last of its 40 volumes will appear. Just last year, "1700 Years of Jewish Life in Germany" were celebrated; while there is no Mendelssohn anniversary on the calendar just now, the 300th birthday of the "Jew of Berlin" is not far off.

The present exhibition offers visitors cultural and historical insights that were not available before. Portraits and documents considered lost or unknown until only recently can now be shown, having been discovered fortuitously on the art market, in private collections, or among the holdings of institutions in the Czech Republic, Poland, and Israel. They include the findings of various versions of the earliest miniature portrait dating from 1767. Also on view is

chen zuvor so geklungen: „*Es ist nicht alles verloren, und auch die geringste Bemühung, die man anwendet, die Wahrheit aufrecht zu halten, oder wieder aufzurichten, ist nicht verloren. Die Schreier führen das große Wort, und machen einen Lerm, als wenn sich alle Stimmen schon für sie erklärt hätten. Es ist aber nicht an dem.*"[19] Ob von dieser Ermutigung etwas weitergegeben werden kann, soll sich auch in den Auge-in Auge-Begegnungen mit Mendelssohn-Porträts erweisen, zu denen die „Bilderfabrik" der Ausstellung einlädt.

a holograph from the Jewish Museum of Prague which Moses made as a fourteen-year-old, making it the oldest one extant. The miniature portrait of Fromet Mendelssohn, née Gugenheim, which went missing in the 1930s, remains untraceable, however.

Mendelssohn's life and times, the topics shaping them both, and the interlinking of all three are waiting to be discovered. The comic strip by Dutch illustrator Typex, published to accompany the exhibition, shows us anecdotes from Mendelssohn's biography through the eyes of a 21st century artist. The introductory phrases greeting visitors at the entrance stairway are meant to bridge the gap between current issues and the themes highlighted in the various exhibition spaces. Adjacent to the biographical Dessau / Berlin room is the balcony room, where

„Es ist nicht alles verloren, und auch die geringste Bemühung, die man anwendet, die Wahrheit aufrecht zu halten, oder wieder aufzurichten, ist nicht verloren. Die Schreier führen das große Wort, und machen einen Lerm, als wenn sich alle Stimmen schon für sie erklärt hätten. Es ist aber nicht an dem."

Moses Mendelssohn

we learn about the public relations activities and dialogue that characterized Mendelssohn's network. The room highlighting the Enlightenment and Counter-Enlightenment, which focuses on Moses' religious debates, translation work, and school projects, presents the often colliding scientific, theological, and spiritual aspects of the epochal shift towards autonomy.

Three separate rooms present narratives revolving, on the one hand, around politics and human rights, around the theory of a multi-religious state, the demand for equal rights for Judaism without giving up its specificity: on the other hand aesthetic perception, and the tension between intellect and intuition, as well as philosophical conceptions of human existence and (im)mortality. In the final large room, the "image factory" of portraits of Moses made during his lifetime, assembled here for the first time, ties in with an installation by New York artist Izhar Patkin on the "Jewish porcelain" story associated with Mendelssohn. This is followed by an examination of his posthumous impact, as exemplified by various memorial projects, commemorative souvenirs, and varying interpretations of his legacy.

For the exhibition team, the intensive encounters with Mendelssohn's personality and legacy were quite an experience. That his strength and eloquence continue to resonate with us today in 2022 has much to do with his ultimately unswerving determination to search for truth despite the hurdles placed in his way. As Mendelssohn himself declared in his final publication "To the Friends of Lessing" (1785), which he completed only a few days before his death, anyone can find the truth through God's all-embracing benevolence so long as he "seeks it with open eyes and does not willfully block the light from his eyes."[18]

Just a few weeks earlier, he had written to a fellow champion of the Enlightenment, urging him not to despair: "It is not all that is lost, and the least effort which one expends to uphold the truth, or to raise it up again, does not go to waste. The shouters are holding forth and making a big noise, as if all votes had already been cast in their favor. But that is not the case."[19] Whether some of this encouragement can be conveyed to visitors will become apparent as they stand eye-to-eye with the Mendelssohn portraits in the exhibition's "image factory".

O. NR. VIGNETTE MOSES SAMUEL LÖWES FÜR EIN PORTRÄT FRIEDRICH NICOLAIS, DES MITSTREITERS VON MOSES MENDELSSOHN (NR. 76):
Vor der aufgehenden Sonne der Aufklärung kämpfen die Pioniere der Vernunft gegen den vielköpfigen Drachen des Aberglaubens, der *Fake News* und der Verschwörungstheorien. Stiftung Stadtmuseum Berlin. *Against the rising sun of the Enlightenment, the pioneers of reason battle the many-headed dragon of superstition, fake news and conspiracy theories.*

Quellenverzeichnis

[1] Brief vom 20. Juli 1764, in: Mendelssohn, Moses: Gesammelte Schriften. Jubiläumsausgabe (JubA). Stuttgart, Bad Cannstatt 1976, Bd. 12,1, Nr. 249, S. 52; abgekürzt: JubA

[2] Brief an Felix Mendelssohn Bartholdy vom 8. Juli 1829. In: Oxford, Bodleian Library, Grüne Bücher, Bd. 1, Nr. 71

[3] Ebd.

[4] So am Ende des Briefes vom 5. Januar 1762 an Johann Friedrich Loewen: „Ew. Hochedelgebohrenen gehorsamster Diener Moses Mendelssohn". In JubA 11, 1974, Nr. 170, S. 284

[5] Nicolas-Charles-Joseph Trublet an Jean Henri Samuel Formey am 27./28. Juli 1761: "Wer ist der Moses genannte Jude aus Berlin, der auf deutsch eine Abhandlung über die Empfindungen verfaßt hat [...]?", zitiert nach JubA 22, 1995, "Anfragen aus Paris", S. 16

[6] Der Erste, der sagte, von Moses Maimonides bis Moses Mendelssohn habe es keinen Juden wie Mendelssohn gegeben, war allerdings 1761 der Ansbacher Pfarrer und Übersetzer rabbinischer Literatur Johann Jacob Rabe.
However, the first to say that from Moses Maimonides to Moses Mendelssohn there had been no Jew like Mendelssohn was the Ansbach priest and translator of rabbinical literature Johann Jacob Rabe in 1761.
So Friedrich Niewöhner S. 119 in: Mendelssohn als Philosoph – Aufklärer – Jude. Oder: Aufklärung mit dem Talmud. Zeitschrift für Religions- und Geistesgeschichte, 1989, Bd. 41, Heft 2, S. 119–133.

[7] "Ein Weiser wie Sokrates, Unsterblichkeit lehrend und unsterblich wie er", formulierte Karl Wilhelm Ramler für die Widmung am Postament der Mendelssohn-Büste von Tassaert.

[8] So David Jenisch in: Skizze von dem Leben und Charakter Mendelssohns, in: Moses Mendelssohns philosophische Schriften, Berlin 1789, zitiert nach JubA 23, 1998, S. 266

[9] Daniel Berger: Moses Mendelssohn, 1786, Kupferstich, in: JubA 24, 1997, S. 84. Unter dem Stich steht der griechische Urtext Joh. 1,47.

[10] Livius Fürst: Dem Moses der deutschen Juden. In: Lessing-Mendelssohn-Gedenkbuch. Zur hundertfünfzigsten Geburtsfeier von Gotthold Ephraim Lessing und Moses Mendelssohn, sowie zur Säcularfeier von Lessing's „Nathan". Leipzig 1879, S. 135

[11] Am 27. Juni 1870 schrieb Karl Marx an seinen damaligen Freund Ludwig Kugelmann (Werke, Bd. 32, p. 686): „In vieler Hinsicht erinnert er [der Philosoph Friedrich Albert Lange] mich an Moses Mendelssohn. Dieser Urtyp eines Seichtbeutels schrieb nämlich an Lessing, wie es ihm einfallen könne, „den toten Hund Spinoza" au sérieux zu nehmen." Für die Verifizierung des Zitats danke ich Thomas Kuczynski.
On June 27th, 1870, Karl Marx wrote to Ludwig Kugelmann, who was still his friend at the time (Works, vol. 32, p. 686): "In many a regard, he [the philosopher Friedrich Albert Lange] reminds me of Moses Mendelssohn. After all, that archetype of a shallow windbag wrote to Lessing, inquiring where he could ever have gotten the idea of taking 'the dead dog Spinoza' seriously." We would like to thank Thomas Kuczynski for verifying this quote.

[12] Aus einem Brief Mendelssohns an Thomas Abbt, Ende August 1764, in: JubA 12,1, 1976, Nr. 252, S. 57. Mavors (Mars) Kampfplatz spielt an auf ein Gedicht der Anna Louisa Karsch.
The arena of Mavors (Mars) is a literary reference to a poem by Anna Louisa Karsch.

[13] So Mendelssohn in einem hebräischen Brief an seinen Schwiegersohn Mendel Meyer vom 20. Juni 1784, deutsche Übersetzung in: JubA 20,2, 1994, Nr. 276, S. 447

[14] In: JubA 3,1, 1932, Berlin, „Die Seele", S. 228

[15] Briefe über die Empfindungen, 10. Brief, in: JubA 1, Berlin 1929, S. 84

[16] Zitiert nach dem Autograf in Privatbesitz, Sammlung Dopfer, Depositum bei der Mendelssohn-Gesellschaft

[17] An August Hennings, 25. Juni 1782, in: JubA 13, 1977, Nr. 571, S. 65

[18] JubA 3,2, 1974, S. 218

[19] An Johann Albert Reimarus, 1. September 1785, in: JubA 13, 1977, Nr. 703, S. 298

Inka Bertz

Mendelssohn im Porträt
Notizen aus der Bilderfabrik

Mendelssohn's Portraits
Notes from the Image Factory

o. Nr. David Joseph Curländer (1761–1852): Porträt Moses Mendelssohn

aus dem „Taschenbuch von dem Jahre 1845"
1844/45
Tinte, Bleistift, Aquarell
JMB

Moses Mendelssohn war ein Medienereignis. Vor allem aber: das erste moderne Bild-Medienereignis der jüdischen Geschichte. Ob er die anderen Medienstars seiner Zeit – Voltaire, Rousseau, seinen Freund Lessing oder Jahrzehnte später Goethe – darin überflügelte, das sei zunächst dahingestellt. Tatsache ist, dass zwischen dem Erscheinen des „Phädon" 1767 und Mendelssohns 200. Geburtstag 1929 eine kaum übersehbare Zahl von Porträts, Büsten, Denkmälern, Erinnerungsobjekten und historischen Genreszenen entstand.

Das Bild Moses Mendelssohns begleitete mithin die gesamte „Epoche des deutschen Judentums", wie Dan Diner den Zeitraum vom Beginn bis zum gewaltsamen Ende von Emanzipation und Teilhabe genannt hat. Aber auch darüber hinaus und bis in die jüngste Gegenwart regte Mendelssohn zur künstlerischen Auseinandersetzung an.

Die Bilderflut um Mendelssohn wurde schon früh ein Gegenstand des Interesses: Sein Sohn Joseph Mendelssohn widmet ihr 1843 einen Abschnitt seiner die „Gesammelten Schriften" einleitenden Lebensbeschreibung. 1886, zu Mendelssohns 100. Todestag, veröffentlichte der Mainzer Rabbiner Siegmund Salfeld einen Beitrag über „Bilder und Büsten Mendelssohns" in Brülls Monatsschrift. Ludwig Geiger folgte 1890 in der „Zeitschrift für die Geschichte der Juden in Deutschland". Einen ersten Katalog mit Maßangaben und Inschriften veröffentlichte der Sammler Albert Wolf 1900 im „Gedenkbuch für David Kaufmann". Die Ausstellungen zum 200. Geburtstag in Dessau und Berlin stellten Originalmaterial vor und regten weitere Forschungen an, etwa von Moritz Stern, dem Bibliothekar der Berliner jüdischen Gemeinde.[1]

Moses Mendelssohn was nothing short of a media personality. More than that, he was the first personage in Jewish history to enjoy the sort of image recognition that we associate with modern celebrities. Whether he outstripped the other media stars of his time—Voltaire, Rousseau, his friend Lessing or, decades later, Goethe—is a question we can put aside for the moment. For between the publication of his treatise "Phaedon" in 1767 and the bicentennial of his birth in 1929, his image was reproduced in an almost incalculable number of portraits, busts, monuments, historical genre scenes, and other reverently commemorative artwork.

Thus, the image of Moses Mendelssohn was present throughout the "epoch of German Jewry", as Dan Diner calls the period of Jewish emancipation and social inclusion from its earliest beginnings to its cataclysmic end. Yet even today, the great man's likeness retains its power to stimulate artistic interest and debate.

The veritable flood of Mendelssohn images attracted attention early on. In 1843, Joseph Mendelssohn discussed it in his biographical introduction to the edition of his father's collected works. In 1886, on the centenary of Moses' death, Rabbi Siegmund Salfeld of Mainz published an article on "Images and Busts of Mendelssohn" in the monthly journal Brülls Monatsschrift. Ludwig Geiger followed suit in 1890 in the "Zeitschrift für die Geschichte der Juden in Deutschland" (Periodical for the History of the Jews in Germany). The very first catalog of such images, including dimensions and inscriptions, was published in 1900 by the collector Albert Wolf in the Gedenkbuch für David Kaufmann (Memorial Book for David Kaufmann). Much of this material was presented in original form at the exhibitions held in Dessau and Berlin in honor of Moses' 200th birthday. These in

EINFÜHRUNG

Hermann Meyer, der Sammler und Bibliophile, bildet mit seinem Wissen über die Bildkultur um Mendelssohn eine der wenigen Brücken zwischen dem Wissen der Zeit vor und nach der Katastrophe. Der Abschnitt „Mendelssohn im Bilde" in seiner Bibliografie von 1965 ist immer noch ein unentbehrliches Referenzwerk. Der von Gisbert Porstmann betreute 24. Band der Jubiläumsausgabe bot den ersten illustrierten systematischen Überblick über das Material.[2] Einen erweiterten Überblick gab Richard Cohen.[3] Zu einzelnen Objekten und Themen publizierten Hermann Simon, Bernd G. Ulbrich und Holger Jacob-Friesen,[4] während Leah Hochman die Mendelssohn-Porträts im Kontext der zeitgenössischen ästhetischen Diskurse behandelte.[5]

Seit dem letzten systematischen Überblick sind 25 Jahre vergangen, in denen zahlreiche neue Stücke auftauchten, was einen erneuten Blick auf einzelne Aspekte des Materials lohnend erscheinen lässt.[6] Dabei möchte ich mich auf drei Fragen konzentrieren: die nach dem frühesten Porträt Mendelssohns und seinem jüdischen Kontext, die nach seiner Darstellung in den Jahren unmittelbar vor und nach seinem Tod und dem Verhältnis zwischen dem Bild Mendelssohns in antikem und in modernem Gewand sowie die nach der jüdischen Porträtkultur in Berlin und Mendelssohns Rolle darin.

Überblick über die Porträts

Zur Orientierung sei die Abfolge der Mendelssohn-Porträts kurz rekapituliert: Das früheste Porträt Mendelssohns ist die 1767 entstandene Miniatur, zusammen mit dem seine Ehefrau Fromet darstellenden Pendant. Von beiden wird noch ausführlich die Rede sein.

Auf die Miniaturen folgte 1768 das von Johann Wilhelm Ludwig Gleim „wegen seines

turn stimulated further research by scholars such as Moritz Stern, the librarian of Berlin's Jewish Community.[1]

Hermann Meyer, a collector and bibliophile with expertise in the iconography of Mendelssohn, is one of the few who bridge the gap between the state of knowledge before and after the Holocaust. His 1965 bibliography is still an indispensable reference work, particularly the chapter "Mendelssohn im Bilde" (Mendelssohn in Pictures). The first illustrated, systematic summary of the material was provided in volume 24 of the Jubilee Edition (Jubiläumsausgabe) of the Collected Works supervised by Gisbert Porstmann.[2] A more extended overview was provided by Richard Cohen.[3] Individual objects and topics were also covered in publications by Hermann Simon, Bernd G. Ulbrich and Holger Jacob-Friesen,[4] while Lea Hochman has examined Mendelssohn's portraits in the context of the aesthetic debates of his time.[5]

In the twenty-five years since the last systematic survey of this subject was published, many new works have come to light, making it worthwhile to take another look at individual aspects of the material.[6] In so doing, I would like to focus on three key topics: When was the earliest portrait of Mendelssohn made and in which Jewish cultural context? How was Moses portrayed in the years right before and after his death and what is the relationship between the images showing him in ancient dress to those in which he wears clothes of his time? How did portraiture figure in Jewish culture in the Berlin of Mendelssohn's day and what role did he play in this context?

Overview of the portraits

By way of providing orientation, it makes sense to look at the key Mendelssohn portraits in their chronological order. The earliest known image of

O. NR. DOSE MIT MINIATUR-
PORTRÄT MOSES MENDELS-
SOHN
nach 1767 (Miniatur)/
nach 1788 (Dose)
Gouache auf Elfenbein, Leder
The Jewish Museum, New York

Phaedon" bei dem Berliner Maler Christian Bernhard Rode in Auftrag gegebene Porträt für seinen Halberstädter „Freundschaftstempel".[7] Doch bedurfte es keiner engen persönlichen Freundschaft, um hier aufgenommen zu werden. Wie bei den Gelehrtengalerien von Bibliotheken waren auch die Verdienste der Dargestellten ein wichtiges Kriterium. Über den Stich von Krüger hinaus, der 1768 als Frontispiz der „Berlinischen Monatsschrift" erschien, erfuhr das Gemälde keine weitere Verbreitung.

Noch im selben Jahr bestellte der Königsberger Buchhändler Kanter, Hauswirt Immanuel Kants, ein Porträt Mendelssohns. Dies jedenfalls berichtet Johann Georg Hamann an Johann Gottfried Herder am 28. August 1768 und gibt uns dabei auch einen Einblick in die Praxis der Zeit: „*Kanter wird diese Woche seinen Laden beziehen und er hat es sich was kosten laßen um dem Publico zu gefallen. Die Einrichtung verdient meines Erachtens Beyfall. Er hat über ein Dutzend alte Busten hier schnitzeln laßen ein treffl. Porträt des Königes von Berlin gebracht, das zwischen Pindar Caesar Tacitus Plutarch - - - stehen soll. In die Schreibstube des Ladens werden gemahlte Köpfe kommen, wovon er Moses und Ramler gleichfalls von Berlin mitgebracht, und hier Schäffner, Willamof, Hippel, Lindner p. sammelt; auch Kant sitzt bereits, und*

Mendelssohn is a miniature painted in 1767, along with a matching counterpart depicting his wife Fromet. Both will be discussed in detail below.

These miniatures were followed by a portrait created in 1768 by the Berlin painter Christian Bernhard Rode under a commission from Johann Wilhelm Ludwig Gleim in Halberstadt, who wished to include Moses in his personal portrait gallery of cultural luminaries "on account of his Phaedon".[7] However, the induction into this "Temple of friendship" did not require any of those depicted to be close personal friends of Gleim's. As is the case for the galleries of writers and scholars found in libraries, the subjects' achievements were the key qualifying aspect for their inclusion. This painting was not reproduced further, except in an engraving by Krüger which served as the frontispiece of the journal "Berlinische Monatsschrift" in 1768.

That same year, the Königsberg bookseller Kanter, Immanuel Kant's landlord, ordered his own portrait of Mendelssohn. A letter written by Johann Georg Hamann to Johann Gottfried Herder on August 28th, 1768, reports on this and provides further insights into the practice of the time: "*Kanter will be moving into his store this week, and has gone to some expense to please the public. The furnishings deserve applause, in*

EINFÜHRUNG

NR. 52 DER „FREUND-
SCHAFTSTEMPEL" IN
GLEIMS GEBURTSHAUSE
ZU HALBERSTADT
(NACH CARL JORDAN)

1862
Stahlstich
Gleimhaus Halberstadt –
Museum der deutschen
Aufklärung

Sie werden doch auch wohl Lust haben nächstes Jahr Ihre Lares und Penates zu sehen."[8] Ob es sich bei diesem Porträt um eine Kopie desjenigen von Rode handelte oder ein gänzlich neues, wissen wir nicht.[9]

Ganz anders das nächste Porträt, das der Leipziger Buchhändler Philipp Erasmus Reich bei Anton Graff in Auftrag gab. Der Inhaber der Weidemann'schen Buchhandlung hatte den Dresdner Hofmaler bei seinem Besuch in Leipzig kennengelernt. Seit 1769 entstand bei Reich – sicher in Kenntnis der Sammlung von Gleim – die Idee zu einer Freundschaftsgalerie. Im Januar 1771 reiste der Maler mit seinem Auftraggeber nach Berlin, um Sulzer, Ramler, Mendelssohn und Spalding zu porträtieren.[10] Mendelssohns Porträt gehörte damit zu den frühesten in Reichs Sammlung, die bis 1779 auf mindestens 40 Gemälde anwuchs.

Inwieweit die publizistische Auseinandersetzung Mendelssohns mit Reichs Verlagsautor Lavater für die Wahl des Porträtierten eine

my opinion. He has had over a dozen old portrait busts carved here, including an excellent likeness of the King of Berlin which is to stand between Pindar, Caesar, Tacitus and Plutarch - - -. The store's office will feature more heads—painted ones. He has already brought along those of Moses and Ramler, also from Berlin, and is hereabouts collecting ones of Schäffner, Willamof, Hippel, Lindner, etc. Kant, too, is already sitting in place, and you will probably also be keen to see your own Lares and Penates here next year."[8] Whether the portrait mentioned here was a copy of the one by Rode or a completely new one is not known.[9]

The next portrait, by the Dresden court painter Anton Graff, is altogether different. It was commissioned by Philipp Erasmus Reich, owner of Weidemann's bookshop in Leipzig, who had met Graff when the latter visited the city. Almost certainly aware of Gleim's collection, Reich began working to assemble his own gallery of friends from 1769 onwards. In January

Rolle spielte, muss offenbleiben. Auch über den Minister Fritsch gab es eine Verbindung zwischen Reich und Mendelssohn. Doch gleichwie: Mendelssohn war damals einer der bekanntesten unter den Berliner Aufklärern.[11]

Über den Entstehungsprozess berichtet Christian Garve am 6. Februar 1771 aus Leipzig an Katharina Garve: „*Unser Herr Reich hatt mit Herrn Grafen, dem Portrait-Mahler (…) eine Reise nach Berlin gethan, lediglich in der Absicht, die 4 Köpfe Spaldings, Sulzers, Moses und Ramlers abzumalen. In 8 Tagen ist die Sache Geschehen. Herr Graf ist wieder hier, und ich habe die Köpfe gesehen. Ich kenne nur Moses unter diesen 4. Aber der ist auch so frappant ähnlich, daß es mir schien, ich sähe ihn wieder vor mir. […] Die halbe Stadt ist gegangen diese Köpfe zu besehen. Morgen nimmt sie Graf nach Dresden mit, dort wird er sie vollends ausmahlen und dann wird sie Bause nacheinander stechen.*"[12]

Graff arbeitete nicht nur direkt für seine Auftraggeber, sondern auch für den entstehenden Kunstmarkt. Er ließ das Mendelssohn-Porträt, wie auch die gemeinsam mit ihm entstandenen, von Johann Friedrich Bause stechen und verbreitete damit nicht zuletzt seinen Namen als Porträtist. Daneben fertigte er mehrere eigenhändige Repliken, sowohl auf Bestellung – was damals eine übliche Praxis war – als auch auf eigenes unternehmerisches Risiko. Die Verbreitung des Mendelssohn-Porträts verdankt sich also ebenso sehr den Arbeitsweisen Anton Graffs und Johann Friedrich Bause, wie diese auf einen aufnahmebereiten Markt reagierten. Im Gegensatz zu den drei anderen Porträts stach Bause das Mendelssohns bereits im darauffolgenden Jahr.[13]

Durch die Übernahme einer Kopie als Wandmalerei in der Bibliothek des Gotischen Hauses im Garten von Wörlitz um 1780 wurde Mendelssohns Porträt ein weiteres Mal in eine

1771, he had Graff accompany him to Berlin so that the painter could create portraits of Sulzer, Ramler, Mendelssohn, and Spalding.[10] Mendelssohn's portrait was thus one of the earliest in Reich's collection, which grew to at least 40 paintings by 1779.

Did the decision to include Mendelssohn in the bookseller's gallery have something to do with his famous religious disputation by letter with the theologian Lavater, who also happened to write for Reich's publishing house? We do not know. Reich and Mendelssohn may also have become acquainted through their mutual friend Thomas von Fritsch, Foreign Minister of the Kingdom of Saxony. Either way, Mendelssohn was certainly among the best known of Berlin's Enlightenment thinkers at the time.[11]

The creation of Graff's work is described in a letter dated February 6th, 1771, from the Leipzig philosopher Christian Garve to his mother Katharina: "*Our Mr. Reich took a trip to Berlin with Mr. Graff, the portrait painter [...], exclusively with the aim of painting the four heads of Spalding, Sulzer, Moses, and Ramler. It was all done in a matter of 8 days. Mr. Graff is back here now and I have seen the heads. Of these four, I only know Moses in person. But the likeness is so strikingly lifelike that I thought I saw him before me again. [...] Half the city has gone to inspect these heads for themselves. Tomorrow, Graff will take them to Dresden, there to fully flesh them out in paint; Bause will then engrave them one after the other.*"[12]

Graff worked directly for his clients—but he also worked for the public art market that was beginning to emerge. He had the Mendelssohn portrait, as well as the others he had created along with it, engraved by Johann Friedrich Bause, not least for the purpose of enhancing his fame as a portraitist. He would go on to produce several additional replicas by his own

EINFÜHRUNG

Gelehrtengalerie eingereiht. Und dann erneut in dreidimensionaler Form: auf dem um 1790 entstandenen Tête-à-tête Service der Porzellanmanufaktur Fürstenberg, das Mendelssohn im Kreise Lessings, Sulzers, Spaldings, Ramlers und anderer zeigt.[14]

Graffs Darstellung wurde das „offizielle" Porträt und findet sich in institutionellen Zusammenhängen[15] wie der Hochschule für die Wissenschaft des Judentums, der Hochdeutschen Israelitengemeinde in Altona sowie bei der Gesellschaft der Freunde.[16]

Zwei oder drei Jahre nach Graffs Porträt entstanden die Zeichnungen Daniel Chodowieckis. Anders als Graff zeichnete Chodowiecki zunächst nicht im Auftrag, sondern hielt Porträts als visuelle Notiz fest, um für verschiedene Zwecke darauf zurückkommen zu können. So entstand aus einer fast karikierenden Federskizze ein idealisiertes, strenges Porträt im Medaillon als Rötelzeichnung. Es sind davon mehrere, in Abklatschtechnik vervielfältigte Exemplare bekannt. Sie wurden vom Künstler selbst, vom Dargestellten oder auch von dritter Hand weitergegeben.[17]

Die ausgearbeitete Rötelzeichnung bildete die Grundlage für den Kupferstich von Peter Haass, der 1774 im Illustrationsband zu Basedows „Elementarwerk" erschien. Im selben Jahr prägten Jakob Abraham und Abraham Abramson, ebenfalls auf der Grundlage der Zeichnung Chodowieckis, eine Porträtmedaille als Teil ihrer Serie von Gelehrten. Wiederum erschien Mendelssohn als Teil der *république des lettres*.[18] Die Rückseite nahm mit einer Darstellung von Totenschädel und Schmetterling Bezug auf den „Phädon". Wie das Buch, so wurde auch die Medaille ein Bestseller und übertraf mit mehr als 500 verkauften Exemplaren die anderen der Serie um das Zehnfache.[19]

hand—not just on commission, as was normal for the time, but also at his own entrepreneurial risk. This means that the wide dissemination of the Mendelssohn image is the result both of the working methods applied by Graff and Bause and of their response to market demand. Bause engraved Graff's depiction of Mendelssohn just one year after its creation, while putting aside the other three portraits for a later time.[13]

Around 1780, this Mendelssohn portrait was once again included in a gallery of scholars, this time as a mural adorning the library of the "Gothic House" in the ducal gardens of Wörlitz. It was then translated into three-dimensional form in a "tête à tête" service for two made by the Fürstenberg Porcelain Manufactory around 1790. Here, the figure of Mendelssohn could be seen in the company of Lessing, Sulzer, Spalding, Ramler, and others.[14]

Graff's rendering of Mendelssohn eventually became the "official" portrait and was displayed on the premises of many prominent organizations,[15] such as the Higher Institute for Jewish Studies in Berlin, the High-German Israelite Congregation in Altona, Hamburg, and at the Society of Friends, a Berlin-based Jewish cultural association.[16]

Two or three years after the creation of Graff's portrait, Mendelssohn was drawn by the artist Daniel Chodowiecki. Unlike Graff, Chodowiecki did not start his drawing as a commission, but sketched out his portraits as visual records to which he could later refer for various purposes. In this process, he elaborated what essentially began as a caricature of Moses in pen and ink into an idealized and austere portrait in red chalk that was set into a medallion. Several specimens are known to exist, having been reproduced through the technique of impression. They were likely brought into circulation by the artist, by Mendelssohn himself, or by a third party.[17]

O. NR. JOHANN FISCHER:
PORTRÄT MOSES
MENDELSSOHN IN DER
SCHLOSSBIBLIOTHEK IM
GOTISCHEN HAUS
Wörlitz, um 1780
Wandmalerei auf Putz
Kulturstiftung Dessau-Wörlitz
(Foto: Peter Dafinger)

Als dritte Veröffentlichung dieses Jahres erscheint das von Otto Christian Sahler gezeichnete und von Daniel Berger gestochene Frontispiz zur Sammlung der Briefe zwischen Lavater, Mendelssohn und Kölbele. Ob es wirklich „nach dem Leben" gezeichnet wurde, scheint angesichts der großen Ähnlichkeit zu Chodowieckis Bildfindung fraglich. Gleiches gilt für die Silhouette von Johann Ulrich Schellenberg, die 1775 in Lavaters „Physiognomischen Fragmenten" erschien.

Schon im August des Jahres 1776 entstand auf einer Reise nach Dresden, die Mendelssohn gemeinsam mit August Hennings unternahm, ein weiteres Porträt. Hennings berichtet an Elise Reimarus, dass der Dresdner Maler Adrian Zingg das Bild des Philosophen „im Profil sehr sauber gezeichnet hätte".[20] 1937 gelangte bei der Auflösung des Lessing-Museums in der Brüderstraße ein Pastellporträt Mendelssohns an die Kunstsammlung der Jüdischen Gemeinde.[21] Der Gemeindebibliothekar Moritz Stern identifizierte es mit dem in Hennings Brief erwähnten Porträt.[22] Seine

The detailed drawing in red chalk subsequently served as a model for the copperplate engraving by Peter Haass, which appeared in 1774 in Basedow's Elementarwerk (Elementary Book), a popular illustrated textbook for children. That same year, Jakob Abraham and Abraham Abramson minted a Mendelssohn portrait medallion as part of their series of famous scholars, likewise using Chodowiecki's drawing as a basis. Once again, Mendelssohn was featured as a prominent member of that abstract intellectual arena known as the "Republic of Letters".[18] The medal's obverse side made reference to Moses' "Phaedon" with a depiction of a skull and butterfly. Just like the book, it became a bestseller. Indeed, with more than 500 copies sold, it proved ten times as popular as any of the other medals in the series.[19]

The third image of Moses to be published during this same year was drawn by Otto Christian Sahler and engraved by Daniel Berger as a frontispiece for a published collection of correspondence between Lavater, Mendelssohn, and Kölbele. Whether it was really drawn "from life"

41

EINFÜHRUNG

NR. 250 RING DER STIFTUNG
1791 MIT PORTRÄT MOSES
MENDELSSOHN
1791
Rotgold, Perlmutt,
Glasüberfang
Privatbesitz

stärksten Argumente waren die Provenienz aus der Familie Hennings, aus der es durch Zwischenhand ins Lessing-Museum gekommen war, sowie die rückseitige Beschriftung: „Frauenhand in moderner Schrift ‚Moses Mendelssohn, den Großvater Hennings in Berlin hat malen lassen.'" Doch seine Zuschreibung enthält auch spekulative Elemente: Die Formulierung „in Berlin" könnte sich auf den Entstehungsort des Porträts, aber auch auf den Aufenthaltsort ihres Großvaters beziehen. Dann ist die Rede vom „Profil", während das Pastell ein Halbprofil zeigt. Auch würde ein Pastell eher „gemalt" als „gezeichnet" werden. Überdies ist von Zingg nur ein Porträt, das von Daniel Chodowiecki, bekannt. Sein späterer Ruhm als Landschaftsmaler und „Wegbereiter der Romantik" überstrahlt heute die Hochachtung der Zeitgenossen für den Illustrator, Raumkünstler und Porträtisten.[23] Vor allem aber stellt sich hier, wie auch bei anderen Porträts, die Frage der Haartracht. Denn Reimarus schreibt an Hennings: „Sie wissen, lieber Hennings, was Lessing von Mendelssohn hält. Es befremdete ihn, daß er jetzt in Dresden sei, befremdete ihn, daß er sein eigenes Haar trägt, nur Ihre Freude, ihn bei sich

seems questionable, given its close resemblance to Chodowiecki's rendition. The same applies to a silhouette created by Johann Ulrich Schellenberg which appeared in Lavater's "Physiognomische Fragmente" (Physiognomic Fragments) in 1775.

Shortly thereafter, in August 1776, yet another portrait resulted from a trip to Dresden that Mendelssohn undertook with August Hennings. As Hennings reported to Elise Reimarus, the Dresden painter Adrian Zingg "drew the philosopher's likeness very neatly in profile."[20] In 1937, a pastel portrait of Mendelssohn passed into the art collection of Berlin's Jewish Community following the dissolution of the Lessing Museum on Brüderstraße.[21] The Community's librarian, Moritz Stern, identified it as the portrait mentioned in Henning's letter.[22] He based this conclusion on the fact that the portrait he had at hand could be traced back to the Henning family, whence it had passed into the Lessing Museum via various intermediaries. And he relied on the inscription on the verso side of the work, noting it was "in modern script in a woman's hand: 'Moses Mendelssohn, whom Grandfather Hennings had painted in Berlin'".

zu sehen, befremdete ihn nicht."[24] Auch durch Joseph ist überliefert, dass Mendelssohn der Mode, eine Stutzperücke zu tragen, seit seinem 30. Lebensjahr und bis etwa 10 Jahre vor seinem Tod folgte.[25] Doch wird sich dieser Wandel vermutlich nicht plötzlich, sondern allmählich vollzogen haben, sodass er für die Jahre um 1775/76 kein eindeutiges Kriterium bildet. Daher spricht trotz aller Gegenargumente auch viel für Sterns Zuschreibung.

Wieder vergingen nur wenige Jahre bis zum nächsten Porträt. Erneut erfahren wir davon aus einem Brief, diesmal von Mendelssohn an Nicolai, dem er am 3. September 1778 berichtet: *„Morgen Vormittags bin ich bei dem Maler Frisch, allwo ich in cameo gemalt werde."* Diese Bemerkung wurde häufig auf das spätere farbige Porträt von Frisch bezogen,[26] bis Gisbert Postmann die Verbindung zu dem Stück herstellte, das Meyer nur aus einem Auktionskatalog bekannt war: einem in Grisaillemalerei ausgeführten ovalen Porträt in Anlehnung an eine antike Gemme.[27] In den Jubiläumsausstellungen von 1929 wurde es nicht gezeigt, nach einer Auktion im Dezember 1932 verliert sich erneut seine Spur.

Nach 1778 entsteht eine bemerkenswerte Pause. Sie war vielleicht Mendelssohns Krankheit und seinem allgemeinen Rückzug aus der publizistischen Öffentlichkeit geschuldet. Nach fünf Jahren, 1783, lässt er sich erneut von Johann Christoph Frisch porträtieren. Diesmal in farbiger Ölmalerei und zeitgenössischer Kleidung. Doch trägt das Bildnis auch einen sehr viel weniger repräsentativen Charakter als die vorangegangenen. So mag man einen privaten Zusammenhang vermuten, fand doch in diesem Jahr die erste Hochzeit in der Familie statt, zwischen der ältesten Tochter Brendel und dem Bankier Simon Veit.

But Stern's attribution of provenance was also partly speculative, since the phrase "in Berlin" could refer either to the portrait's place of origin or to the grandfather's place of abode at the time. Another problem is that Henning's letter spoke of a "profile" (the pastel image is in half-profile) which had been "drawn" ("painted" would be more appropriate for a pastel). Finally, the only portrait by Zingg known to us is the one he made of the artist Daniel Chodowiecki. Today, the fame he eventually acquired as a landscape painter and "pioneer of Romanticism" outshines the esteem in which he was held by his contemporaries as an illustrator, decorator, and portraitist.[23]

But the biggest issue, as in the case of other portraits, is the sitter's hairstyle. The pastel portrait shows Mendelssohn wearing a bob wig, but this contradicts what Reimarus wrote to Hennings in a letter contemporary with the portrait: "You know, my dear Hennings, what Lessing thinks of Mendelssohn. It bothered him that he is now in Dresden; it bothered him that he wears his own hair; the only thing that did not bother him was your joy at having him with you."[24] *We are also told by Joseph Mendelssohn that his father began wearing his bob wig at the age of 30 and did not stop doing so until roughly 10 years before his death.*[25] *On the other hand, it could also be that this change in appearance occurred gradually rather than all at once, and should thus not be taken as a strict criterion for precluding a dating to 1775/76. So, despite all evidence against it there is much to be said for Stern's attribution.*

Only a few years passed until the next portrait was created. We know this from another letter, this time from Mendelssohn to Nicolai on September 3rd, 1778: "Tomorrow morning I shall be with the painter Frisch, where I am to be painted in cameo." This remark was usually taken

So berühmt es ist, so unsicher war lange die Datierung des Gemäldes. Einziger Anhaltspunkt dafür war die Bemerkung Josephs, das Porträt sei entstanden, als sein Vater „zwischen vierzig und fünfzig Jahre alt war". Nicht nur durch die Verwechselung mit dem Porträt „in cameo" existierten unterschiedliche Angaben zu diesem Porträt sowie seinen Repliken und Kopien. Bekannt war die große Fassung, die sich im Besitz von Cécile Lowenthal-Hensel befand, die aus dem Besitz von Albrecht Mendelssohn Bartholdy stammende, stark verkleinerte Fassung sowie das verschollene Gemälde, das sich einst im Besitz von David Friedländer befand und danach an die Jüdische Gemeinde und das Jüdische Museum gelangte. Von ihnen war einzig die verkleinerte Fassung signiert und aufgrund einer älteren Notiz auf 1786 datiert.[28] Der „große Frisch" ist weder datiert noch signiert. Über das verschollene Gemälde besitzen wir keine Angaben. 2009 konnte das Jüdische Museum, dank der Vermittlung von Thomas Lackmann, eine weitere Fassung erwerben, die etwas größer als die bisher bekannte große Fassung sowie signiert und auf 1783 datiert ist.[29]

Das Bild von Frisch sollte zum beliebtesten aller Mendelssohn-Porträts werden, doch wurde es dies nicht auf Anhieb. Nach dem Stich von Müller, von dem noch zu sprechen sein wird, dauerte es einige Jahrzehnte, bis Friedrich Wilhelm Bollinger es 1819 als Punktierstich veröffentlichte. 1843 erschien es auf dem Frontispiz der „Gesammelten Schriften" und dann immer wieder, bis zu August Beckers für das Jubiläum 1929 geschaffenen Holzschnitt. Noch populärer (von der Auflagenhöhe her betrachtet) wurde es jedoch in der Variante, die der in Dresden tätige Kupferstecher Moritz Steinla (1791–1858) im Jahr 1821 schuf und die auf das alte „Finger im Buch"-Motiv rekurrierte. Noch

to refer to a later, colored portrait made by Frisch,[26] until Gisbert Porstmann successfully linked it to a piece which the expert Hermann Meyer had come across in an auction catalog: an oval portrait executed in grisaille in the style of an antique gem cameo.[27] This had not been shown in the Jubilee Exhibition of 1929 and, after being offered at auction in December 1932, it vanished without trace.

There is a noticeable break in the output of Mendelssohn images after 1778. Perhaps this was due to the philosopher's illness and his general withdrawal from the publishing world. Five years later, in 1783, he had himself portrayed once more by Johann Christoph Frisch, this time in colorful oils and contemporary clothing. This later image is much less formal and stately than the previous ones. We can assume that it was created in a more private context, given that this was the year in which the Mendelssohn family celebrated its first wedding, namely between the eldest daughter Brendel and the banker Simon Veit.

As famous as the Frisch painting is, its date long remained uncertain. The only clue was Joseph's remark that the portrait was painted when his father "was between forty and fifty years old." All other information available about the portrait, along with its replicas and copies, is contradictory, not least because of the aforementioned confusion with the "in cameo" portrait. The large version owned by Cécile Lowenthal-Hensel is known, as are a much scaled-down version stemming from the estate of Albrecht Mendelssohn Bartholdy and a now-lost painting originally owned by David Friedländer and later by the Berlin Jewish Community and the pre-war Jewish Museum. Of these, only the reduced version is signed, and can be dated to 1786 based on an older written notation.[28] But the version known as the "great Frisch" is nei-

O. NR. DEUTSCHE BUNDESPOST
BERLIN: SONDERBRIEFMARKE
ZUM 250. GEBURTSTAG MOSES
MENDELSSOHNS
1979
Papier, gummiert
JMB (Foto: Jens Ziehe)

1979 wählte es die Deutsche Bundespost als Vorlage für ihre Mendelssohn-Briefmarke.

Während also das farbige Porträt Frischs seine öffentliche Breitenwirkung erst im Laufe des 19. Jahrhunderts entfaltete, erfuhr die von Antoine Tassaert 1785 geschaffene Büste unmittelbar nach ihrer Entstehung eine breite Rezeption. Dies lag freilich auch an den Umständen ihrer Entstehung:

Nach dem Abschluss der Tora-Übersetzung und dem Erscheinen von „Jerusalem" reflektiert sie diese Jahre intensiver Produktivität und öffentlicher Wirksamkeit. Und ihre Entstehung war selbst ein öffentliches Projekt: 1774 fanden sich 20 Freunde Mendelssohns zusammen und stifteten das Geld für den Auftrag an den Hofbildhauer. Jede und jeder erhielt einen Gipsabguss, während das Marmor-Original für die Jüdische Freischule bestimmt war, die 1781 ihren Unterricht aufgenommen hatte.[30]

Leider kennen wir nicht die Namen der Subskribenten. Elise Raimarus und Friedrich Nicolai sollen Gipsabgüsse der Büste besessen haben.[31] In der Stiftung Preußische Schlösser und Gärten und der Alten Nationalgalerie haben sich Exemplare erhalten, weitere sind in der älteren Literatur erwähnt,[32] deren Verbleib unbekannt ist. Das Original befindet sich heute in der Jüdischen Gemeinde zu Berlin in der Fasanenstraße und die 1930 von Arnold Zadikow

ther dated nor signed. We also have no information about the lost painting. In 2009, thanks to the mediation of Thomas Lackmann, the Jewish Museum managed to acquire yet another version, which is somewhat bigger than the previously known large version and which is also signed and dated to 1783.[29]

Frisch's picture eventually became the best-loved of all the Mendelssohn portraits, but it took time to achieve this status. Following its initial engraving by Müller, which will be discussed later, it would not be reproduced again until several decades later, this time as a stipple engraving (by F. W. Bollinger in 1819). It would appear again in 1843 as the frontispiece for the "Collected Works" and with increasing regularity thereafter. August Becker would also create a woodcut version for the 1929 Jubilee. But perhaps the most popular version of the Frisch image (in terms of circulation) was the one made in 1821 by Moritz Steinla (1791 – 1858), an engraver working in Dresden, which resorted to the old "finger in the book" motif. In 1979, when the German Federal Post Office was designing its Mendelssohn stamp, this was the model it chose.

While Frisch's colorful portrait acquired its broad popularity only gradually over the course of the 19th century, the bust sculpted by Antoine Tassaert in 1785 received wide acclaim right from the start. For one, this was thanks at least in part to the circumstances of its creation. It

für das Jüdische Museum in der Oranienburger Straße angefertigte Kopie in der Stiftung Neue Synagoge – Centrum Judaicum. Gleichfalls erhalten haben sich der originale Sockel und seine Kopie.

Bereits um 1800 fügte die Manufaktur Fürstenberg Mendelssohn in dieser Gestalt in ihre Serie von Gelehrtenbüsten *en miniature*.[33] Im Laufe des 19. Jahrhunderts entstehen bei Fürstenberg und bei der Berliner Königlichen Porzellan-Manufaktur weitere verkleinerte Fassungen, bis die Bronzegießerei Noack im Rahmen der Jahrhundertausstellung 1906 eine originalgroße Bronzekopie anfertigt.

Die Büste wurde oft für die erste vollplastische Porträtbüste gehalten, die einen Juden darstellt. Doch gilt dies nur, wenn man das Maskulin spezifisch versteht: Denn schon 1783 wurde Henriette Herz von Tassaerts Schüler Johann Gottfried Schadow als Büste porträtiert.[34]

Die Miniaturen
Zu den wichtigsten Ergebnissen der Recherchen für das Ausstellungsprojekt zählt das Auftauchen der verloren geglaubten Miniatur von 1767. Sie war bislang nur aus einer Abbildung bekannt. Ihre Datierung beruhte auf der ihres Pendants, des Porträts von Fromet Mendelssohn. Während diese Miniatur trotz umfangreicher Recherchen weiterhin verloren ist,[35] kennen wir vom Porträt des Moses mittlerweile sieben Fassungen, zwei davon lediglich aus der Literatur, fünf als Objekte.

Nach einem Vergleich der verschiedenen Fassungen des Moses-Porträts mit dem Fromets im Hinblick auf die Ausführung des Gesichts, die Anlage des Bildraums, den Faltenwurf des Vorhangs und seine Ausgestaltung mit oder ohne Fransen und Quasten handelt es sich bei dem heute im Familienbesitz befindlichen Exemplar mit großer Wahrscheinlichkeit

was made just as Mendelssohn's productivity and public profile were at their apex—he had just completed his Torah translation and published "Jerusalem". For another, the bust's genesis was a very public affair: in 1774, twenty of Mendelssohn's friends got together and donated the money needed to commission the Prussian court sculptor. Each sponsor received a plaster cast, while the marble original was destined for Berlin's Jewish Free School, which had begun holding classes in 1781.[30]

The names of the sponsors have not come down to us, unfortunately, but Elise Reimarus and Friedrich Nicolai are said to have owned plaster casts of the bust.[31] Further specimens have also been preserved by the Prussian Palaces and Gardens Foundation and in Berlin's Alte Nationalgalerie. Additional ones are mentioned in some of the older scholarly literature, but their whereabouts are unknown.[32] The original marble is now located in the offices of the Jewish Community of Berlin on Fasanenstraße, while the copy made in 1930 by Arnold Zadikow for the Jewish Museum on Oranienburger Straße is now at the New Synagogue Foundation—Centrum Judaicum, also on Oranienburger Straße. The original pedestal and its copy have been preserved as well.

As early as around 1800, the Fürstenberg Porcelain Manufactory added Mendelssohn, in the form of this bust, to its series of miniature-busts of scholars.[33] The Fürstenberg Manufactory and the Berlin Royal Porcelain Manufactory would both produce further, scaled-down versions over the course of the 19th century. An original-sized bronze copy was created for the Centennial Exhibition in 1906 by the bronze foundry Noack.

This sculpture is often thought to be the first full-scale portrait bust of a Jewish person. But this view is colored by male-dominant dis-

um das Original und das ursprüngliche Pendant zum Porträt Fromets. Bei den anderen Exemplaren ist vor allem der Vorhang weniger detailreich gezeichnet, der Faltenwurf unnatürlicher und das Gesicht gröber ausgeführt; der Bildausschnitt sowie die Anordnung der Bücher und Accessoires des Gelehrten variieren.

Die Originalminiatur zeigt Mendelssohn als Brustbild vor einem Regal, in dem neben Büchern zwei Globen und ein Totenschädel erkennbar sind. Aus einer der Bücherreihen hängt ein Zettel mit der Signatur „Dr. P.S. fecit / A. 1767". Vor dem Dargestellten liegen drei Bücher. Auf dem untersten, hell gebundenen ist die Aufschrift „M M / Phaedon" erkennbar. Das mittlere zeigt einen repräsentativen Ledereinband mit Goldprägung, während der Dargestellte im obersten Buch mit dem Zeigefinger seiner linken Hand eine Seite markiert.

Die Darstellung Fromets ist einzig, denn außer einer Silhouette kennen wir kein weiteres Porträt von ihr. Überdies könnte es sich sogar

course: the honor rightfully belongs to the famous salon hostess Henriette Herz, who was immortalized in bust form in 1783 by Johann Gottfried Schadow, a student of Antoine Tassaert.[34]

The miniatures

One of the most important findings of the research carried out for our exhibition project is the discovery of a miniature portrait of Moses from 1767 which was previously known only from an illustration and believed to be lost. Its dating was based on that of its matching counterpart, the portrait of Fromet Mendelssohn. While the whereabouts of the miniature showing Fromet remain unknown despite extensive research,[35] *we now know of seven versions of the miniature portrait of Moses, two of them only from the literature and five as tangible objects.*

After comparing the various versions of Moses' miniature portrait with the surviving reproduction of Fromet's miniature in terms of the

NR. 262 KÖNIGLICHE PORZELLAN-MANUFAKTUR: BÜSTE MOSES MENDELSSOHN (NACH ANTOINE TASSAERT)
Berlin, ca. 1800
Biskuitporzellan, teilweise glasiert
JMB (Foto: Roman März)

o. Nr. Miniaturporträt
Moses Mendelssohn
(nach Dr. P. S.; vermutlich
Elimelech Pilta ben
Schimschon Rofe)
nach 1767
ehemals Besitz der
Jüdischen Gemeinde zu
Berlin, verschollen
Abb. in: Gemeindeblatt der
Jüdischen Gemeinde zu Berlin,
19. Jg. 1929, Nr. 9, S. 433

um das früheste Porträt einer jüdischen Frau im deutschsprachigen Raum handeln.[36] Bis dahin kennen wir Damenporträts nur aus der sephardischen Oberschicht Amsterdams.[37]

Moses' Darstellung hingegen knüpft an eine bereits bestehende jüdische Porträtkultur an. Auch sie begann im 17. Jahrhundert in Italien, Amsterdam und London.[38] Doch gab es in den ersten Jahrzehnten des 18. Jahrhunderts auch im deutschsprachigen Raum die ersten Porträts, vor allem in Wien mit den Hoffaktoren Samson Wertheimer und Samuel Oppenheimer, und in Frankfurt mit Süßkind Stern. Noch vor den 1730er-Jahren und der antijüdischen Bilderflut um Süß Oppenheimers Prozess und Hinrichtung 1737/38 ließ sich 1733 bis 1737 der Mannheimer Hoffaktor Elias Hayyum als junger Mann porträtieren, und später ein weiteres Mal als Erwachsener.[39] In Hamburg entwickelte sich nicht zuletzt durch den Austausch mit London und Amsterdam schon früh eine jüdische Porträtkultur. Erhalten ist das Porträt von Issachar Bär Cohen (Berend Cohen), dem Gründer der ältesten Hamburger Klaus, des Synagogen-

execution of the face, the layout of the pictorial space, and the fall of the drapery (with or without fringes and tassels), we can conclude that the specimen in question, which is currently in private hands, is most probably the original counterpart to Fromet's miniature portrait. In the other copies, the curtain especially is less detailed and looks less natural while Moses' face is more coarsely rendered. The picture layout and the arrangement of the scholar's books and accessories vary as well.

The original miniature shows Mendelssohn from the chest up before a shelf on which two globes and a skull are discernible alongside various books. From one of the rows of books hangs a note with the signature "Dr. P.S. fecit / A. 1767" (Dr. P.S. made this in the year of the Lord 1767). Three of the books lie in front of the sitter. On the lowest one, which has a brightly colored binding, the inscription "M M / Phaedon" can be made out. The middle book features an elaborate leather binding with gold embossing, while the sitter marks a page in the uppermost book with the index finger of his left hand.

Lehrhauses von 1680, der 1728 starb. Auch in der Geschichte des Rabbinerporträts gehörte Hamburg für den deutschsprachigen Raum zu den Vorreitern. Zu den frühesten Beispielen zählt das Porträt des Jonathan Eybeschütz.[40]

Für die Identifizierung des Malers der beiden Miniaturen bietet es den Schlüssel. Das Monogramm „P.S." mit dem vorangestellten „Dr." konnte bislang nicht gedeutet werden. Unter den bekannten Fassungen des Eybeschütz-Porträts[41] ist hier jenes von Interesse, das noch zu seinen Lebzeiten entstand, wie die Bemerkung „ad vivum" bezeugt, also vor 1764. Die Signatur zeigt ein ähnliches „D", mit einem über den Punkt gestellten „r" und einem geschwungenen, nach rechts geneigten „S".[42] Die hebräische Adresse des Stiches identifiziert den Künstler als Arzt („rofe") „Elimelech Pulta/Pilta". In einer 1775 datierten Variante seines Stiches fügte der Künstler seinem Namen den Zusatz „Sohn des Simson" hinzu.[43] Aus letzterem erklärt sich das „S" in seiner Signatur, das sich mit „Pilta" zu dem Monogramm „Dr. P.S." verbindet, der Signatur der nur wenige Jahre nach dem Porträt Jonathan Eybeschütz' entstanden Miniaturen des Ehepaars Mendelssohn.

Das erste Porträt Moses Mendelssohns wäre damit von einem jüdischen Künstler geschaffen worden, der seinen Beruf als Laie oder zumindest im Nebenberuf ausübte. Bemerkenswert ist dabei, dass der Künstler seinen Arztberuf angibt, denn ganz offensichtlich ist er es, aus dem er seinen Status und sein Selbstbewusstsein bezieht, und nicht aus seinem Künstlertum. Doch über keinen seiner drei Namensbestandteile ist er bislang nachweisbar. Sein Status als Arzt in Hamburg muss daher ebenso unklar bleiben wie alles Weitere zu seiner Biografie.[44]

Viele der frühen Rabbinerporträts im deutschsprachigen Raum zeigen einen ähn-

The miniature depiction of Fromet is one-of-a-kind, for we know of no other picture of her, apart from a silhouette. In fact, it may even be the earliest portrait of a Jewish woman in the German-speaking world.[36] The only portraits of women that are known to us from before that time were commissioned by the Sephardic upper class of Amsterdam.[37]

Moses' portrayal, on the other hand, ties in with an already existing Jewish culture of portraiture that also originated in 17th century Italy, Amsterdam, and London.[3] In the first decades of the 18th century, such portraits began to be made in German-speaking countries as well, particularly in Vienna, where the sitters included the court factors Samson Wertheimer and Samuel Oppenheimer, and in Frankfurt with the merchant Süsskind Stern. Before the flood of anti-semitic images that would accompany the trial and execution in 1737/38 of Süss Oppenheimer, the Mannheim court factor Elias Hayyum had himself painted as a young man circa 1733 – 1737 and later as an adult.[39] Hamburg nurtured a culture of Jewish portraiture relatively early on, not least due to the city's trading links with London and Amsterdam. One example that has come down to us is the portrait of Issachar Bär Cohen (Berend Cohen), who founded Hamburg's oldest Klause, or synagogue school, in 1680, and who died in 1728. Hamburg was also one of the cities in which the evolution of rabbinical portraiture in the German-speaking world began. Among the earliest portraits of this type is that of Rabbi Jonathan Eybeschütz.[40]

And it is this particular portrait that provides the key to identifying the painter of the two miniatures discussed earlier. Thus far, it had not been possible to determine the person behind the monogram "P.S." and the prefixed title "Dr." Among the several known versions of the Eybeschütz portrait,[41] the one of interest is that

lichen Aufbau wie seine Darstellung von Eybeschütz. Ob Elimelech Pilta ben Schimschon dabei Amsterdamer oder Londoner Rabbinerporträts oder die Hamburger christlichen Gelehrtenporträts der 1740er- und 1750er-Jahre, etwa von Christian Friedrich Fritzsch, zum Vorbild nahm, sei hier dahingestellt.[45]

Jedenfalls aber folgte der Künstler seinem eigenen Porträt Jonathan Eybeschütz' für das Miniaturporträt Mendelssohns. Ähnlich wie dort, aber deutlich anders als in den auf Repräsentation von Status und Amtswürde angelegten Gelehrtenporträts von Fritzsch, zeigt er den Rabbiner dicht an den Bildrand gerückt. Im Hintergrund sehen wir ein ähnlich über Eck gestelltes Bücherregal, die Dargestellten halten ein Buch in einer Hand, während die andere mit dem Arm unter dem Bildrand verschwindet. Doch ist Mendelssohns Porträt bewegter. Er lehnt sich gleichsam aus dem Bild heraus und seinem Gegenüber mit leicht geneigtem Kopf entgegen. Dabei zeigt er eine gewisse Lässigkeit der Haltung. Sie mag freilich auch dem vergleichsweise jugendlichen Alter des damals 38-Jährigen geschuldet sein.

Moses Mendelssohns erstes Porträt entstand vermutlich in Hamburg, der Heimatstadt Fromets, die hier durch die Kontakte ihres Vaters nach Wien in puncto Luxus und Lebensstil einen differenzierteren Geschmack entwickeln konnte. Hier existierte bereits eine jüdische Porträtkultur und neben den christlichen zumindest ein jüdischer Künstler, die diesen Bedarf bedienten. Und wiewohl wir nichts über die genauen Umstände des Auftrags wissen, können wir doch vermuten, dass die Initiative nicht von einem Verehrer des Gelehrten ausging, denn dazu hätte es des Gegenstücks von Fromets Porträt nicht bedurft.[46] Dies und die Entstehung in Hamburg sprechen für die Beteiligung von ihr oder ihrer Familie. Doch muss

made while he was still alive, i.e. before 1764, as evidenced by the notation "ad vivum". The signature found on the work features a letter "D" similar to that on the miniature, along with an "r" placed above the period and a curvy "S" that inclines towards the right.[42] The Hebrew dedication on the engraving identifies the artist as the physician ("rofe") "Elimelech Pulta/Pilta". In a version of the engraving dated 1775, the artist added "son of Simson" after his name.[43] This explains the "S" in his signature, which combines with the name "Pilta" to form the "Dr. P.S." monogram on the miniatures of Moses and Fromet Mendelssohn, which were created just a few years after the portrait of Jonathan Eybeschütz.

This would mean that the very first portrait of Moses Mendelssohn was created by a Jewish artist who worked as an amateur or at least as a side pursuit. It bears noting that the artist describes himself as a "physician". This, rather than his artistry, is evidently what he regards as the main source of his social status and selfesteem. However, by none of his three name components he can be traced so far. His status as a physician in Hamburg and everything else about his life must remain in the dark.[44]

Many of the early portraits of rabbis made in the German-speaking regions of Europe exhibit a basic layout similar to the one Elimelech Pilta ben Schimschon used for his rendering of Eybeschütz. Whether he modeled it on portraits of rabbis from Amsterdam or London or on the portraits of Christian scholars from Hamburg made in the 1740s and '50s by Christian Friedrich Fritzsch and others is a question that must remain open for now.[45]

In any case, the artist used his own portrait of Jonathan Eybeschütz as a template for the miniature portrait of Mendelssohn. In both cases, the sitter is positioned close to the picture frame, thereby creating a very different effect

O. NR. DR. S.
(VERMUTLICH ELIMELECH
PILTA BEN SCHIMSCHON
ROFE): PORTRÄT
JONATHAN EYBESCHÜTZ
vor 1764
Kupferstich
Universitätsbibliothek
Hamburg

auch Moses am Entstehungsprozess und der Ausarbeitung des ikonografischen Programms beteiligt gewesen sein, denn es reflektiert subtil auf seine Position in der jüdischen Gelehrtenwelt seiner Zeit und führt einen Dialog mit dem in seinem Umfeld sicher bekannten Porträt von Eybeschütz.

Mit dem großen Oberrabbiner verband Mendelssohn eine heikle Beziehung: 1761, im Jahr vor seiner Hochzeit, hatte er ihn in Hamburg aufgesucht und gehofft, von ihm die Erlaubnis zu erhalten, sich fortan als Rabbiner bezeichnen zu können. In dem auf das Treffen folgenden Brief zeigt sich Eybeschütz zwar voll des Lobes für den jungen Gelehrten, vergleicht ihn gar mit dem biblischen Moses,[47] doch eine rabbinische Approbation erteilt er ihm nicht. Der Titel „chawer", Gefährte, sei zu gering für ihn, doch den Titel „morenu" könne er ihm als Unverheiratetem nicht verleihen. Der Ehestand sei eine unerlässliche Vorbedingung. Damit folgt Eybeschütz dem Statusdenken der traditionellen rabbinischen Elite.[48]

Sechs Jahre später ist Mendelssohn ein geachtetes Mitglied der Berliner Gelehrten-

from Fritzsch's portraits of scholars, which tend to reflect their subjects as dignitaries of academia. The background of both works features a similar bookshelf placed diagonally across a corner. Both sitters hold a book in one hand while the other is obscured by the bottom of the frame. Mendelssohn's portrait is livelier, however. He seems to be almost leaning out of the picture towards the viewer, his head slightly bowed. His bearing exhibits a certain casualness, due perhaps to his relatively youthful age of 38.

This first portrait of Moses Mendelssohn was presumably made in Hamburg, the hometown of his wife Fromet, who was exposed to a more sophisticated lifestyle and sense for luxury thanks to her father's contacts to Vienna. Hamburg was a city where Jewish portraiture was already flourishing and where at least one if not more Jewish artists served the market alongside their Christian counterparts. Although we do not know the specific circumstances of the miniature's commission, we can assume that it did not come from anyone who admired Moses as a scholar, since they would hardly have needed a matching portrait of Fromet.[46]

gesellschaft und ein erfolgreicher Autor. Noch im Jahr des Erscheinens seines „Phaedon" verfasst er eine bildliche Antwort auf das vermutlich als kränkend und kleinlich empfundene Schreiben, in dem er sich vom Porträtisten des inzwischen verstorbenen Rabbiners als selbstbewusster Philosoph malen lässt.

Sein offen fallendes Obergewand zeigt zwar noch die für Rabbinermäntel übliche Fülle, entspricht jedoch ohne deren breiten Kragen eher den auf Gelehrtenporträts üblichen Hausmänteln. Auch gegen seine Haar- und Barttracht hätten die Rabbiner einige Jahrzehnte zuvor noch heftigen Widerstand erhoben: Er trägt eine Perücke und hat den Bart bis auf einen schmalen Streifen über Wangen und Kinn rasiert.[49]

Eine viel schwerwiegendere Übertretung der religiösen Gebote wäre hingegen der Totenschädel, der im Regal im Hintergrund dargestellt ist. Doch enthält das Bild durch die Aufschrift „M M / Phaedon" auf dem Rücken des untersten Buches den Verweis auf Mendelssohns Schrift. Ob die bildliche Darstellung eine Übertretung darstellt, dazu gab es unter den Zeitgenossen sicher unterschiedliche Auslegungen. Die beiden Globen und das Bücherregal zeigen die beiden Wissenswelten des jungen Gelehrten: die religiöse Tradition und die modernen Naturwissenschaften, Empirie und Philosophie. Mit dem Porträt seiner Gattin zeigt Mendelssohn, dass die damaligen Gründe, ihm die Approbation zu verweigern, jetzt nichtig sind. Und auch sie ist als zugleich traditionell und modern inszeniert: Nach den traditionellen Regeln der Sittsamkeit gekleidet, ist ihr ein Spiegel als Symbol der Weisheit auf den Tisch gestellt, eine Standhaftigkeit und Stärke bezeugende Säule im Hintergrund beigegeben, während das Fenster sich zu einer Landschaft mit Bäumen hin öffnet.

This and the work's presumed origin in Hamburg suggest that Fromet and/or her family were involved. Yet Moses, too, must have had a say in the work's creation and in its iconographic design since it delivers a subtle commentary on his position among the Jewish scholars of the time and enters into a dialogue with the Eybeschütz portrait, which was surely familiar to Moses and those in his social circle.

As it happened, Mendelssohn had had a fraught relationship with the well-known Chief Rabbi. In 1761, the year before his wedding, Moses had called on Eybeschütz in Hamburg in the hopes of gaining his permission to call himself "rabbi". In a letter written to Moses after the meeting, Eybeschütz heaps generous praise on the young scholar, even comparing him to a prophet of the Bible,[47] but withholds his rabbinical approbation. While the title chaver ("companion") may be too modest, the rabbi explains, he simply cannot accord Moses the title morenu ("our teacher") since he does not fulfill the indispensable precondition of being married. In this, Eybeschütz was following the status-conscious thinking of the traditional rabbinical elite.[48]

Fast-forward six years to 1767: Mendelssohn had become a respected member of the Berlin world of scholars as well as a successful author. Having just published his "Phaedon", he is now ready to create a pictorial response to the letter, which he must have found hurtful and petty, and has himself painted in the pose of a self-assured philosopher by the very same artist who had portrayed the rabbi, who had since passed away.

The portrait shows Moses wearing an upper garment that falls open with a fullness reminiscent of a rabbi's coat, but without the typical broad collar. The effect is more like that of the housecoat usually seen in portraits of scholars.

Nr. 29 Dr. P. S.
(vermutlich Elimelech
Pilta ben Schimschon
Rofe): Porträt Fromet
Mendelssohn geb.
Gugenheim (1737–1812)
verschollen
Abb. in: Moses Mendelssohn:
Brautbriefe, Berlin 1936
JMB

Das erste Porträt, das wir von Mendelssohn kennen, ist ein Zeugnis bewusster Bildpolitik. Es ist von einem jüdischen Künstler mit Verbindungen in die traditionelle Rabbinische Elite geschaffen und an diese Elite gerichtet. Unschwer werden die zeitgenössischen Betrachter das Vorbild des bekannten Rabbinerporträts erkannt haben, ebenso die markanten Abweichungen davon. Damit markiert das Miniaturporträt Mendelssohns Abschied von der Sphäre der rabbinischen Gelehrten und den Beginn seiner Entwicklung „zum herausragenden Repräsentanten einer nichtrabbinischen jüdischen Elite" (Feiner).

Es gehört zu den Paradoxien der visuellen Rezeptionsgeschichte Mendelssohns, dass im Verlag von Wolf Pascheles in Prag 1835 ein Porträt entstand, das die Komposition dieses Porträts aufnimmt und – unter Anleihen bei Frischs Porträt für die Physiognomie – Mendelssohn als traditionellen rabbinischen Gelehrten zeigt. Die Bücher im Regal hinter ihm haben nun erkennbare Titel erhalten: auf dem unteren Brett die fünf Bücher der Tora, der Prediger und das Hohe Lied; auf dem Regal darüber die Vertreter

Then there is Moses' hairstyle and beard couture, which surely would have caused offence to rabbis of the older generation: he wears a wig and has trimmed his beard down to a narrow strip running over his cheeks and chin.[49]

A potentially far more serious breach of Jewish religious tradition is visible as well: the skull sitting on the shelf in the background. On the other hand, the inscription "M M / Phaedon" on the binding of the bottom book clearly alludes to Mendelssohn's treatise on the immortality of the soul. The ambiguity of this symbolism probably led Moses' contemporaries to take differing views on whether it constituted a transgression or not. The two globes and the bookshelf, meanwhile, represent the two spheres of knowledge in which the young scholar moved: religious tradition and the natural sciences, philosophy and empiricism. With the portrait of his wife, Mendelssohn shows that the reasons given at the time for denying him his approbation are no longer valid. She, too, is depicted in a manner that is both traditional and modern at the same time. Her attire fits the traditional rules of propriety, a mirror symbolizing wisdom lies on the

der andalusischen Tradition,⁵⁰ unter ihnen Maimonides, Nachmanides, Jehuda Halevi, Isaak Karo und Josef Albo. Der Text nennt seine Lebensdaten und Hauptwerke und endet mit einem Lobgedicht, das seine Treue zur Tradition lobt und dabei sein Buch „Jerusalem" besonders hervorhebt.

Nicht nur initiiert hier mit Pascheles nach Reich und Kanter der dritte Buchhändler und Verleger ein Mendelssohn-Porträt. Erneut sehen wir ihn im Kreis anderer Gelehrter. Nun jedoch sind es die Vertreter einer traditionell bis neoorthodox ausgerichteten rabbinischen Elite: Der Verlag Pascheles publizierte die Porträts des Prager Rabbiners Samuel Kauder, von Abraham Tiktin und Samson Raphael Hirsch sowie nicht zuletzt eine Biografie von Jonathan Eybeschütz.⁵¹

In derselben Darstellungsform, mit der Mendelssohn sich einst von der rabbinischen Elite verabschiedete, findet er sich nun in diese eingereiht.

table before her, the pillar in the background stands for constancy and strength, while the window opens out onto a tree-lined landscape.

This very first portrait of Mendelssohn to come down to us bears witness to his deliberate image politics. It was fashioned by a Jewish artist with ties to the traditional rabbinical elite and was intended to be seen by this same elite. Contemporary viewers will have easily recognized its similarities to the well-known portrait of the Hamburg rabbi, as well as the marked deviations from it. Thus, the miniature portrait of Mendelssohn marks his departure from the sphere of rabbinical scholars and the start of his evolution "to become an outstanding exponent of a non-rabbinical Jewish elite" (Feiner).

The visual reception history of Mendelssohn portraits is full of paradoxical elements, one of them being that the portrait released in 1835 by Wolf Pascheles' publishing house in Prague follows the miniature's compositional layout while depicting Mendelssohn as a tradi-

Nr. 108 Johann August Krüger (vermutlich): Porträt Hirschel Loebel (1721–1800)
ca. 1787/99
Öl auf Leinwand
Jewish Museum London/ United Synagogue

Der antike und der moderne Mendelssohn

Mendelssohns erstes Porträt war eng mit dem sozialen und kulturellen Kontext der Hamburger jüdischen Gemeinde verbunden. Die darauffolgenden Porträts hingegen wurden von Künstlern geschaffen, die eine Kunstakademie besucht hatten, in den Netzwerken und kunstkritischen Diskursen verankert waren und dies in ihrer Formensprache zur Anwendung brachten. Dies galt für Rode, für Graff und Chodowiecki.

Doch im Folgenden möchten wir uns den Darstellungen zuwenden, die in den Jahren vor und nach Mendelssohns Tod besonders verbreitet waren. Der Stich von Krüger nach Rode aus dem Jahr 1768 mochte dem Zeitgeschmack der 1780er-Jahre kaum noch entsprochen haben. Das antikisierende „Cameo"-Porträt hingegen verlieh erstmals der Rede vom „Sokrates von Berlin" einen prägnanten bildlichen Ausdruck.

Der erste Nachstich erschien sowohl separat als auch 1784 auf dem Titelblatt von Zöllners Kritik an Mendelssohns „Jerusalem". Vier Jahre später hingegen schmückte er das Titelblatt von Isaak Euchels Mendelssohn-Biografie. Mendelssohn-Kritik und Mendelssohn-Eulogie bedienten sich also derselben bildlichen Darstellung. Dies wirft die Frage auf, ob Text und Bild unabhängig voneinander oder nur im Zusammenhang funktionierten.

Sie stellt sich auch bei dem nächsten Stich nach Frischs Gemälde, den Daniel Berger schuf und der zuerst 1787 als Titelkupfer zum neunten Jahrgang der „Berlinischen Monatsschrift" erschien. Das Zitat aus dem Johannesevangelium – „Siehe ein rechter Israelit, in welchem kein Falsch ist." (Joh. 1, 47) – könnte für heutige Ohren ambivalent klingen, denn es entstammt der Erzählung von der Bekehrung Nathanaels. Doch könnte das Zitat auch in durchaus positivem Sinne den Streit mit Lavater tional rabbinical scholar (and borrowing a few facial details from Frisch's portrait). The books on the shelves behind the sitter have now been given legible titles. On the lower shelf lie the five books of the Torah, the Book of Ecclesiastes, and the Song of Songs; on the shelf above, works by representatives of the Andalusian tradition,[50] including Maimonides, Nachmanides, Jehuda Halevi, Isaac Karo, and Joseph Albo. The text below shows the key dates of the sitter's life and his main works, ending with a poetic eulogy that praises his loyalty to tradition and particularly his book "Jerusalem".

This makes Pascheles the third bookseller and publisher after Reich and Kanter to have commissioned a Mendelssohn portrait. Once again, Moses is placed in the company of other learned men. But this time, they happen to be exponents of a rabbinical elite with decidedly traditional to neo-orthodox convictions: Pascheles published portraits of the Prague rabbi Samuel Kauder, as well as Abraham Tiktin, and Samson Raphael Hirsch, not to mention a biography of Jonathan Eybeschütz.[51]

Using the same symbolism Mendelssohn once used to separate himself from the rabbinical elite, he is depicted here as its member.

The classical and the modern Mendelssohn

Mendelssohn's first portrait was closely associated with the social and cultural milieu of Hamburg's Jewish community. The portraits that followed, by contrast, were created by artists who had attended art academies, who were at home in the artistic networks and currents of their times, and who brought this to bear in their visual language. This certainly held true for Rode, Graff, and Chodowiecki.

The following section will deal with those depictions of Mendelssohn that were widely disseminated in the years shortly before and after

55

EINFÜHRUNG

reflektieren, den Nicolai, der Herausgeber der „Monatsschrift", einst mit seinem Machtwort zum Schweigen gebracht brachte: *„Sie wünschen, dass er ferner kein Jude bliebe, er hat aber nichts dawider einzuwenden, dass Sie ein Christ bleiben."*[52]

Hingegen irritiert das falsche Todesdatum 1785. Warum Moses' Freund Nicolai diesen Fehler nicht korrigieren ließ, bleibt rätselhaft. Vielleicht war dieser Fehler der Grund, aus dem die Platte noch im selben Jahr in Hamburg auftauchte, nunmehr mit der Signatur „I.C.G. Fritzsch cs", und der Schrift von Friedrich Wilhelm von Schütz über Mendelssohns „Leben und Meinungen" vorgebunden wurde. Insofern hinterlassen beide zu seinem Gedächtnis gedachten Veröffentlichungen einen zwiespältigen Eindruck.

Zur Perspektive Fromets und ihrem Umgang mit den Porträts ihres verstorbenen Mannes his death in 1786. By that time, the engraving made by Krüger in 1768 from the Rode portrait was probably well out of fashion. Not so the classicist "cameo-style" portrait, which became the first work to give cogent visual expression to Moses' honorific title of "Socrates of Berlin".

An engraving of this cameo portrait was first issued both separately and, in 1784, on the title page of Zöllner's critique of Mendelssohn's "Jerusalem". Four years later, it adorned the title page of Isaac Euchel's biography of Mendelssohn. Thus, a work criticizing Mendelssohn and another eulogizing him were using one and the same image. This gives rise to the question of whether text and image are truly independent of one another or whether they work only in tandem.

This question also seems pertinent to the next engraving to be made on the basis of Frisch's painting: a copper plate made by Daniel Berger that first appeared in 1787 as the title page of

O. NR. JOHANN CHRISTIAN GOTTFRIED FRITZSCH (CA. 1720–1802/03): PORTRÄT MOSES MENDELSSOHN
1785/86
Kupferstich
Rijksmuseum, Amsterdam

nes gibt es nur eine Quelle, die der Mendelssohn-Biograf Meyer Kayserling 1891 veröffentlichte.⁵³ Es ist ein Brief, den sie am 2. Nissan 1786, wenige Monate nach Moses' Tod, an einen Hamburger Verwandten schrieb. Sie dankt ihm für sein Kondolenzschreiben und fährt fort: „Ich habe auch den überschickten Kupferstich bekommen, er gefällt mir sehr gut und danke ich Ihnen sehr dafür. Sie würden mir eine Gefälligkeit erzeigen, wenn Sie mir in Kurzem neun Stück hievon einschicken könnten. Ich bitte mir den Preis anzuzeigen."

Aus dem Umstand, dass der Stich aus Hamburg geschickt wurde, schloss Kayserling, dass er dort erschienen ist, und vermutete daher, dass es sich um das Frontispiz der in Hamburg bei Müller verlegten Schrift von Schütz handeln müsse. Der Sammler Albert Wolf widerspricht dem, nicht zuletzt, weil das Buch noch nicht erschienen war, als Fromet den Brief verfasste.⁵⁴ Doch sie hätte kaum – abgesehen vom christlichen Zitat – einen Stich mit falschem Todesdatum verschickt. Handelte es sich also bei der Bestellung um den Stich von Henne? Oder um den sehr verehrungsvollen Stich von Löwe, der schon 1784 im „HaMeassef" gedruckt worden war?⁵⁵ Vermutlich fand aber Fromet eher Gefallen an der Wiedergabe eines lebensnäheren Porträts, wie dem von Graff durch den Hamburger Kupferstecher Fritzsch.⁵⁶

Im Gegensatz zur späteren Bilderflut dominierte um 1786 noch das Bild von Mendelssohn im antiken Gewand. Auch der Stiftungsring von 1791 geht auf das Gemälde der Gemme zurück. Prägnanter und eindrucksvoller als dieses Gemmenporträt war jedoch die Büste Tassaerts. Vom letzteren unterschied diese sich insbesondere durch ihren öffentlichen Charakter, den die Gattung bereits nahelegt, den sie dann aber durch die Aufstellung in der Freischule offensichtlich erhielt.

Annual Volume 9 of the journal "Berlinische Monatsschrift". It features a quote from the Gospel of St. John—"Behold, a righteous Israelite in whom is no falsehood" (John 1:47), which may sound ambivalent to modern ears, since it belongs to the story of the conversion of Nathanael. Yet it could also be read as a friendly allusion to the theological dispute with Lavater, who had been finally silenced by a withering riposte from Nicolai, the journal's publisher: "You wish him not to remain a Jew, but he has no objection to you remaining a Christian."⁵²

By contrast, the erroneous date of death of 1785 found on the plate is strange. It remains a puzzle why Moses' friend Nicolai did not have this mistake corrected. Maybe this error was the reason why the copper plate re-surfaced in Hamburg that same year, but this time bearing the signature "I. C. G. Fritzsch cs" and why it was then used for the cover of Friedrich Wilhelm von Schütz's text on Mendelssohn's "Life and Opinions". Consequently, these two publications, which were both intended to honor Moses' memory, leave behind a conflicting impression.

The only historical source for Fromet's perspective on the portraits of her late husband is a letter published by the Mendelssohn biographer Meyer Kayserling in 1891.⁵³ Fromet wrote it on 2nd Nissan 1786, just a few months after Moses' passing, to thank a relative in Hamburg for his written condolences: "I have also received the copper engraving you sent. I like it a great deal and I thank you very much for it. You would do me a favor if you could send me nine copies in the near future. Please let me know the price."

Given that the engraving had been sent from Hamburg, Kayserling concluded that it must have been published there, and thus surmised that it had to have been the frontispiece of the book by Schütz published by Müller in Hamburg. The collector Albert Wolf disputes

Auch die Spannung zwischen antikem Gewand und Gegenwärtigkeit des Ausdrucks, der sowohl als Lächeln als auch als zum Sprechen geöffneter Mund gedeutet wurde, wurde Gegenstand kunstkritischer Erörterungen. So verwundert es nicht, dass es vor allem Künstler waren, die sich von dieser Büste faszinieren ließen und sie in bildliche Darstellungen übersetzten.

Schon wenige Monate nach Mendelssohns Tod berichtet Daniel Chodowiecki seiner Vertrauten, der Gräfin von Solms-Laubach, über den kurz zuvor in Berlin eingetroffenen Künstler Joseph Friedrich August Darbes: „Er zeichnet sehr schön mit Silberstift. In Oehl hat er hier noch nichts Gemacht als die Büste von M. Mendelson (!) [von] tassaert hat er in Oehl beynah im Profil gemahlt mit sehr guter Wirkung."[57]

Das Gemälde existiert noch und ist Teil der Kunstsammlung des Leo Baeck Instituts in New York und als Leihgabe auch in der Dauerausstellung des Jüdischen Museums zu sehen. Julius Held, der Kunsthistoriker, eminenter Kenner der niederländischen Malerei und Sammler von Mendelssohn-Porträts,[58] schenkte das Gemälde 1981 dem Leo Baeck Institut in Erinnerung an seine nach Israel ausgewanderte Schwester Ida Bloch. Er hatte es im New Yorker Kunsthandel erworben. Mitte des 19. Jahrhunderts befand es sich in der Sammlung des Prinzen zu Hohenzollern-Hechingen im Schlesischen Löwenberg, die 1890 aufgelöst und versteigert wurde. Dieser Hinweis führt uns geradewegs zu den außergewöhnlichen Frauen, die sich Mitte der 1780er-Jahre in Mendelssohns Umkreis und in den Berliner Salons bewegten: die Salonière Dorothea von Kurland und ihre Halbschwester, die Schriftstellerin Elisa von der Recke. Sie verehrten den Philosophen und korrespondierten mit ihm, Dorothea lud ihn in ihr Schloss Friedrichsfelde ein. Von ihr führt

this, however, not least because this book had not yet appeared at the time Fromet wrote her letter.[54] Yet she would hardly have sent out an engraving bearing an erroneous date of death—leaving aside the matter of a Christian quotation. So could it have been the engraving by Henne that she was requesting? Or the highly reverential engraving by Moses Samuel Löwe, which had already been printed in the journal "HaMeassef" back in 1784?[55] Perhaps it is more likely that Fromet would have preferred a more life-like portrait, such as one which the Hamburg engraver Fritzsch had made from the painting by Graff.[56]

Unlike in the later proliferation of images, most of the Mendelssohn portraits created around the year 1786 show him wearing classical garb, as in the cameo-style painting that also served as the model for the commemorative membership ring (Stiftungsring) created in 1791. Even more eloquent and impressive than this cameo portrait, however, was the bust fashioned by Tassaert. By its nature, the free-standing piece of sculpture was intended to be admired by a broad public, and was prominently displayed at the Free Jewish School (Freischule) in Berlin.

The contrast between the classical vestments worn by Moses and the informal immediacy of his expression—is he smiling or opening his mouth as if about to speak?—was a feature of the bust that intrigued art critics. Small surprise then, that it was artists above all who were inspired by this sculpture and who transposed it into their own visualizations.

Just a few months after Mendelssohn's death, Daniel Chodowiecki reported to his confidante, the Countess of Solms-Laubach, that a new artist had recently arrived in Berlin, Joseph Friedrich August Darbes: "He draws very beautifully in silverpoint. He has not yet done any-

Nr. 180 Antoine Tassaert (1727–1788): Büste Moses Mendelssohn
1785
Gips
SPSG

dann die Spur nach Löwenberg: Denn Dorothea von Kurlands Tochter heiratete Friedrich von Hohenzollern-Hechingen, deren Sohn Konstantin dann die berühmten Sammlungen der Herzöge von Kurland aus Sagan nach Löwenberg überführte. Johann Friedrich August Darbes wiederum hatte lange in Kurland und Russland gelebt, bevor er 1785 nach Berlin kam und hier Akademiemitglied und 1786 Professor für Porträtmalerei wurde. Auf der Akademieausstellung dieses Jahres zeigte er ein Gemälde „Einer Marmorbüste neben einem Todtenkopf". Ob es sich dabei um eine frühe Fassung des hier besprochenen Gemäldes handelt, der als Verweis auf den „Phaedon" ein Totenkopf beigegeben war?

Auch wissen wir nicht, ob Dorothea von Kurland nur die Käuferin oder sogar die Auftraggeberin des Gemäldes war. Von ihrer Halbschwester Elisa von der Recke wird hingegen berichtet, dass sie auch einen Gipsabguss der Büste besaß, also für die Marmorfassung gespendet hatte.

thing in oil here yet, except for the bust of M. Mendelson (!) [by] Tassaert, which he has painted nearly in profile to excellent effect."[57]

The painting in question still exists and forms part of the art collection of the Leo Baeck Institute in New York. It is currently on display in the permanent exhibition of the Jewish Museum, to which it has been loaned. Julius Held, art historian, eminent expert in Dutch painting and collector of Mendelssohn portraits,[58] donated it to the Leo Baeck Institute in 1981 in memory of his sister Ida Bloch, an émigré to Israel. He had acquired the painting on the New York art dealers' market. During the 19th century, it was known to have been in the collection of the Prince of Hohenzollern-Hechingen in Löwenberg, Silesia. The collection was dissolved in 1890 and then auctioned off.

This piece of information takes us directly to the extraordinary women who, in the mid-1780s, figured prominently in the literary salons of Berlin and in Mendelssohn's social circle: the salon hostess Dorothea, Duchess of Courland, and her half-sister, the writer Elisa von der

EINFÜHRUNG

O. NR. JOHANN CHRISTOPH
FRISCH (1738–1815): PORTRÄT
MOSES MENDELSSOHN
1783/86
Öl auf Leinwand
ehemals Besitz der
Jüdischen Gemeinde zu
Berlin, verschollen
Abb. in: Kat. Moses-
Mendelssohn-Ausstellung,
Berlin 1929, S. 9

Doch bei dieser einen Version des Wettstreits zwischen Malerei und Skulptur blieb es nicht: Tassaerts Sohn fertigte – unabhängig von Darbes Gemälde – einen Stich der Büste, der sogar in verschiedenen Varianten erschien.[59] Tassaerts Schüler Johann Gottfried Schadow schließlich platzierte die Büste vor einer Monumentalarchitektur in ein Arrangement der Schriften Mendelssohns, „Jerusalem", „Phaedon" und „Psalmen", einer Harfe mit dem Kopf König Davids, dazu Lorbeerkranz, Öllampe, Tintenfass und Feder. Der Detailreichtum zeigt uns, was dem in jüdischen Dingen vertrauten, vorurteilslosen Schadow und seinem Publikum wichtig schien.

Das Motiv der bildlichen Darstellungen einer Büste kennt man als Wandmalerei, meist in Grisaille, aus antikisierenden Gelehrtengalerien, wie der Bibliothek im Gotischen Haus in Schloss Wörlitz. Doch ein seltenes Phänomen ist die Verarbeitung in einem eigenständigen Gemälde oder einem grafischen Blatt. Man könnte darin auch – ähnlich wie Schadow es etwa zehn Jahre später mit der Prinzessinnengruppe tat – eine Art kunsttheoretisches „Diskursstück" sehen.

Recke. Both of them venerated the philosopher and corresponded with him; Dorothea even invited him to her palace Friedrichsfelde. From here, the trail leads to Löwenberg: Duchess Dorothea's daughter married Friedrich von Hohenzollern-Hechingen and it was their son Konstantin who relocated the famous art collection of the Dukes of Courland from Sagan to Löwenberg. Johann Friedrich August Darbes, for his part, had spent many years in Courland and Russia before arriving in Berlin in 1785 and joining the Prussian Academy of Arts the following year as a professor of portrait painting. At an exhibition held by the Academy in 1786, he exhibited a painting entitled "Marble Bust Beside a Skull". Was this an early version of the painting discussed here, which also featured a skull as an allusion to the "Phaedon"?

We also do not know whether Dorothea of Courland was merely the buyer of the painting by Darbes or whether she also commissioned it. It is reported that her half-sister Elisa von der Recke owned a plaster cast of the bust featured in the painting, which implies that she had donated money for the sculpting of the marble version.

Jedenfalls steht dabei, im Gegensatz zu Chodowieckis Profilporträts, nicht mehr die Physiognomie im Zentrum des Interesses. Neben der Idealisierung des Verstorbenen sehen wir hier auch eine Reflexion über die Frage der Vorbildhaftigkeit der Antike, das Problem von antiker Idealität und gegenwärtigem Abbild. Solche kunsttheoretischen Debatten wurden unter den Berliner Künstlern im Kontext der Akademiereform Mitte der 1780er-Jahre intensiv geführt.

Die Akademiereform konfigurierte jedoch auch das Verhältnis von Politik und Ästhetik neu. Nun fanden nicht nur halbprivate Besichtigungen in Künstlerateliers oder in Häusern der Auftraggeber statt, sondern öffentliche Kunstausstellungen. Kunst wurde zum Gegenstand von öffentlicher Debatte und Vergnügung. Und sie ermächtigte das Publikum, nun seinerseits Kunst für eigene politische Interessen einzusetzen.

Ein solches Beispiel ist das von Johann Gotthard von Müller in Stuttgart für die Jüdische Freischule gestochene Porträt Mendelssohns. Die Vermutung liegt nahe, dass hierfür das Gemälde aus dem Besitz von David Friedländer, eines ihrer Mitgründer, als Vorlage diente.

Folgt man der Biografie, die Moses' Sohn Joseph 1843 als „Lebensgeschichte" der Ausgabe der Gesammelten Werke voranstellte, stellt man fest, dass dieser nur die Porträts von Graff und das zweite von Frisch gelten ließ: „*alle anderen Bilder von Mendelssohn, die wir gesehen haben, gezeichnet, gemalt in Kupfer gestochen, in Stein geschnitten oder in Glas abgedrückt, sind mehr oder weniger Zerrbilder, die von den Zügen des Originals nichts wiedergeben.*"[60]

Es war wohl nicht so sehr der Tod Mendelssohns, der den entscheidenden Anlass für diesen Stich bildete, als die Thronbesteigung

But this "competition" between painting and sculpture would go further still. Tassaert's son fashioned his own engraving of the bust, quite independently of Darbes' painting. This was issued in several variants.[59] *Tassaert's student Johann Gottfried Schadow, meanwhile, depicted Mendelssohn's bust against a monumental architectural backdrop, ringed by his books "Jerusalem", "Phaedon", and his translation of the "Psalms", along with a harp adorned with the head of King David, a laurel wreath, an oil lamp, an inkwell and a pen. The wealth of detail provided by Schadow, who was free of prejudice and conversant with Jewish culture, tells us which aspects the artist and his public deemed to be most important.*

The painted image of a bust is a motif familiar from mural painting, usually executed in grisaille, to be found in scholars' galleries echoing classical antiquity, such as the one in the Gothic House in the Wörlitz Garden Realm. But it is comparatively rare to see such a motif integrated into a standalone picture or a folio of graphic art. This could be regarded as a sort of "contribution to the debate" of theoretical artistic analysis—much like the one Schadow would create roughly ten years later on the basis of his sculptural "Princesses Group" (Prinzessinnengruppe).

In any case, these images of busts no longer focus on the sitter's face as the main point of interest, in contrast to Chodowiecki's portraits in profile. Besides idealizing the departed personage, they also reflect on the questions of whether or not classical antiquity can serve as a model and how to deal with the idealization typical for the classical period and the exigencies of creating the sitter's likeness. This was just the sort of theoretical discourse that was playing out among Berlin's artists during the move to reform the Prussian Academy of Arts in the mid-1780s.

Friedrich Wilhelms II. Ihm, dem neuen König, ist er „unterthänigst gewidmet / von der Jüdischen Freyschule zu Berlin 1787". Im Lichte der Erwartungen auf eine Reform der Judengesetzgebung, die mit seinem Regierungsantritt verbunden wurden, ist dieses Blatt vielleicht gar nicht so „untertänig" gemeint, sondern vielmehr ein Stück aktiver jüdischer Interessenpolitik, unterstützt durch das Medium des Bildes.

In diesem Zusammenhang erklärt sich möglicherweise, warum dafür nicht das Bild des „antiken" Mendelssohn gewählt wurde. Nur mit dem Bild des „modernen" Juden, der sich in seiner äußeren Erscheinung von seinen christlichen Zeitgenossen nicht unterschied, konnte die Forderung nach Gleichberechtigung untermauert werden. Mendelssohn wurde hier, wie bereits im Kontext der Emanzipationsdebatte am Beginn der 1780er-Jahre, zum Beweis für das Recht der Juden auf Gleichheit.

Vielleicht ist vor diesem Hintergrund verständlich, warum der „antike" Mendelssohn schon so bald in Vergessenheit geriet. So wie

The Academy's reform not only reconfigured the prevailing aesthetics, but also the way they related to politics. The semi-private viewings held in artists' studios or in the homes of patrons were now supplemented for the first time by public art exhibitions. Art was becoming an object of discussion and enjoyment for society at large. And this in turn empowered the audience to co-opt art in order to advance their own political interests.

One example is the Mendelssohn portrait engraved by Johann Gotthard von Müller in Stuttgart for the Jewish Free School. There is reason to believe that the model he used for this purpose was the painting owned by David Friedländer, one of the school's co-founders.

According to the biographical "Story of His Life" (Lebensgeschichte) which Joseph Mendelssohn added as a preamble to his father's "Collected Works" in 1843, only the portraits by Graff and the second portrait by Frisch passed muster: "All the other pictures of Mendelssohn that we have seen, whether drawn, painted, engraved

O. NR. JACOB PLESSNER (1871–1936): BÜSTE MOSES MENDELSSOHN
Entwurf 1909/19, Guss 1928
Bronze, patiniert
JMB (Foto: Jens Ziehe)

bei der in den folgenden Jahren viel diskutierten Frage, welche Kleidung die in öffentlichen Denkmälern Geehrten tragen sollen, obsiegte schließlich auch für Mendelssohn das zeitgenössische Kostüm.

Und diese „querelle des anciens et des modernes" um Mendelssohn wiederholte sich im frühen 20. Jahrhundert – mit umgekehrtem Ausgang. Als die Berliner Jüdische Gemeinde 1909 wieder ein Mendelssohn-Denkmal vor der Knabenschule in der Großen Hamburger Straße sehen wollte, denn das Original befand sich mittlerweile im Sitzungssaal des Vorstands der Jüdischen Gemeinde, veranstaltete sie einen Wettbewerb.

Zwei der Einsendungen kennen wir: von Jacob Pleßner und von Rudolf Marcuse.[61] Jacob Pleßner zeigte den „gegenwärtigen" Mendelssohn, indem er den 1821 von Steinla geprägten Bildtypus weiterentwickelte, der Mendelssohn mit einem Buch im Arm und erhobener Hand zeigte.[62] Doch der seinerzeit gegenwärtige war nun nicht mehr der moderne. Er

on copper, sculpted in stone, or printed on glass, are essentially distortions which do not replicate any of the features of the real person."[60]

This particular engraving seems to have been occasioned less by the death of Mendelssohn and instead by the enthronement of Friedrich Wilhelm II. It is to him, the new Prussian King, that the engraving is "dedicated, in the most humble obedience,/by the Jewish Free School of Berlin 1787." In light of the fact that Prussia's Jews were expecting the new monarch to promote progressive legislative reforms in their favor, the gift was perhaps not so much a token of "subservience" than an active lobbying effort using the visual medium.

This state of affairs perhaps also helps to explain why the image of the "classical" Mendelssohn was not the one selected for this purpose. The only way to effectively support the demand for equal rights, so the thinking may have gone, was to resort to the image of a "modern" Jew who was outwardly indistinguishable from his Christian contemporaries. As during

o. Nr. Rudolf Marcuse:
Denkmal mit Büste Moses Mendelssohn
1909
ehemals Berlin, Große Hamburger Straße, zerstört
Abb. in: Das Jüdische Magazin, 1. Jg. 1929, Heft 3, S. 20

verfehlte den Geschmack der Juroren. Den Wettbewerb gewann Rudolf Marcuse, ein technisch brillanter, versierter Bildhauer des späten Jugendstils, der sich an die Büste Tassaerts anlehnte und uns eine Wiederkehr des „jüdischen Sokrates" zeigt.

Als damals, zu Beginn des 20. Jahrhunderts, die Zeit um 1800 wiederentdeckt wurde, war es der „antike" Mendelssohn, in dem sich die Epoche der jüdischen Emanzipation mit derjenigen der deutschen Klassik zu einem Bild vom „*Judentum jenseits des Judentums*" (George L. Mosse) verschmelzen konnte.

Mendelssohn und die Porträts der Haskala
Betrachtet man die Porträts, die zu Mendelssohns Lebzeiten entstanden im Kontext der jüdischen Porträtkultur, stellt sich die Frage, wo sie in deren Entwicklung zu verorten sind. Beginnt auch auf diesem Feld mit Mendelssohn etwas radikal Neues oder werden Entwicklungen fortgesetzt?

Die tiefgreifenden kulturellen Veränderungen, die jüdische Gemeinden im 18. Jahrhundert durchliefen, begannen nicht in Berlin, das weder in wirtschaftlicher noch in kultureller Hinsicht ein für die jüdische Welt besonders bedeutender Ort war. Das waren Frankfurt am Main, Hamburg und Altona, Amsterdam, Prag und Wien.[63]

In den ersten Jahrzehnten des 18. Jahrhunderts hören wir Nachrichten über das jüdische Luxusleben vor allem aus Altona und Mannheim, aus Wien und Fürth.[64] Zu dieser Zeit war die Berliner Gemeinde noch zu klein und noch nicht vermögend genug. Sie erlebte ihren Aufschwung erst nach dem Ende des Siebenjährigen Krieges 1763.[65]

Erst danach, mit dem Aufstieg der von der merkantilistischen Wirtschaftspolitik geförderten Münz- und Manufakturunternehmer,

the emancipation debate of the early 1780s, Mendelssohn was thus adduced as a paragon to prove that the Jews were worthy of emancipation.

Against this backdrop, it might be understandable why the "classical" Mendelssohn was relegated to oblivion soon after. The question of which attire was most proper for personages honored by public monuments would continue to be hotly debated in the years to come. But in practically all cases—and also in Mendelssohn's —contemporary costume was ultimately preferred.

This "querelle des anciens et des modernes" (quarrel between the ancients and the moderns) centering on the person of Mendelssohn would repeat itself in the early 20th century – but this time with the opposite outcome.

In 1909, Berlin's Jewish Community invited artists to tender designs for a new Mendelssohn bust. This was to be placed in front of the Jewish Boys' School (Knabenschule) on Große Hamburger Straße, since the original had been moved to the executive conference room of the Jewish Community.

We know two of the designs that were submitted: those of Jacob Plessner and Rudolf Marcuse.[61] Jacob Plessner proposed to portray the "contemporary" Mendelssohn by elaborating on the visual type developed by Steinla in 1821: Mendelssohn with a book under one arm, raising his other hand.[62] But what had been deemed up-to-date by Steinla was no longer modern enough for the jurors' taste. So the award went to Rudolf Marcuse, a technically brilliant sculptor steeped in the late art nouveau style. He went on to use Tassaert's bust as a starting point to bring the "Jewish Socrates" to the fore once again.

This being the early 20th century, a period of renewed appreciation for the neo-classicism prevailing around 1800, it was the "classical"

O. NR. GEORG FRIEDRICH
SCHMIDT (1712–1775):
PORTRÄT HIRSCH MICHEL
1762
Radierung
JMB (Foto: Jens Ziehe)

entwickelte sich eine kleine wirtschaftliche Elite. Die wohlhabendsten unter ihnen teilten den Lebensstil des Adels, mit Stadtpalais und Sommerhäusern, Kunstsammlungen und Gärten. Für die jungen Gelehrten, die nach Berlin strebten und sich hier zur jüdischen Aufklärungsbewegung formierten, bildeten sie die wirtschaftliche Basis. Mendelssohns Stellung als Hauslehrer bei Bernhard Isaak ist ein Beispiel dafür.

Ein Versuch, diese Entwicklung mit den Porträts der Berliner Juden zu verbinden, steht freilich noch auf unsicherem Grund, denn nur von wenigen besitzen wir eine gesicherte Datierung oder Identifikation der dargestellten Person. Aus der Zeit vor 1760 kennen wir kaum Beispiele. Als das früheste Bildnis galt lange das 1702 von Anthoni Schoonjans gemalte Porträt, dessen Identifikation mit dem Hoffaktor Jost Liebmann heute als fraglich gilt. Ein um 1720 entstandener Kupferstich zeigt den Besuch der Königsfamilie in der Synagoge. 1762 radiert Georg Friedrich Schmidt das Porträt des Potsdamer Rabbiners Hirsch Michel. Doch vermischt er hier das reale mit einem literarisch inspirierten „Typenporträt".⁶⁶ Es verdankte sich

Mendelssohn who was deemed to best embody a visual merging of Jewish emancipation with German classicism that would give expression to a "Jewishness beyond Judaism" (George L. Mosse).

Mendelssohn and the portraits of the Haskala
Looking at the Mendelssohn portraits created during his lifetime, within the context of Jewish portrait culture, the question of their role in the evolution of that culture comes to mind. Did the visual image of Mendelssohn touch off radically new trends in this area as well, or was it merely a continuation of existing trends in Jewish portraiture?

The deep-seated cultural changes that Jewish communities underwent during the 18th century did not originate in Berlin, which was not a place of great importance to the Jewish world, either culturally or economically. Frankfurt am Main, Hamburg (including Altona), Amsterdam, Prague, and Vienna were far more significant.⁶³

In accounts from the early decades of the 18th century, we read reports of affluent Jews living a life of luxury, especially in places like Altona and Mannheim, Vienna and Fürth.⁶⁴ Ber-

EINFÜHRUNG

O. NR. ANNA DOROTHEA
THERBUSCH, (1721–1782):
PORTRÄT HENRIETTE HERZ
(1764–1847)
1778
Öl auf Leinwand
SMB PK, Alte Nationalgalerie

dem Einfluss Rembrandts, vor allem seiner als Judendarstellungen gedeuteten anonymen Porträts, ebenso wie dem Umgang mit Juden im Potsdamer und Berliner Alltagsleben.

Beschränkt man sich auf die gesicherten Porträts, außerhalb von jenen Mendelssohns, beginnt die Reihe mit den Porträts von Isaak Daniel Itzig, 1777 von Johann Christoph Frisch, Henriette Herz, 1778 von Anna Dorothea Therbusch, Marcus Herz, 1779 ebenfalls von Frisch, Moses Wessely, 1779 von Chodowiecki nach Tischbein, und vermutlich Marcus Elieser Bloch, ebenfalls in diesen Jahren und ebenfalls von Frisch.[67] Ein weiteres frühes Indiz für die Berliner Juden als Auftraggeber an bildende Künstler ist das Exlibris, das David Friedländer 1774 bei Daniel Chodowiecki bestellte.

Die Mendelssohn-Porträts von Rode, Graff und Chodowiecki stünden somit am Beginn dieser kulturhistorisch erstaunlichen Entwicklung. Die meisten der so zahlreichen Porträts Berliner Juden und Jüdinnen entstanden hingegen erst nach Mendelssohns Tod, vor allem in den 1790er-Jahren.

lin's Jewish community was still not large or rich enough to claim such status; its boom times would not begin until after the end of the Seven Years' War in 1763.[65]

Only after peace came, and with the introduction of the mercantilist economic policies which encouraged the proliferation of coin-minting enterprises and manufacturing workshops of various kinds, did a small Jewish elite establish itself in the Prussian capital. The most prosperous among them enjoyed lifestyles comparable to those of the nobility, with palatial town houses and summer retreats, art collections and gardens. It was these entrepreneurs who provided an economic basis for the young Jewish scholars who gravitated to Berlin to join the ranks of the Jewish Enlightenment. Mendelssohn's position as a private tutor at the home of the silk manufacturer Bernhard Isaak bears witness to this movement.

Any attempt to tie in these trends with the portraits painted of Berlin's Jews must currently remain tentative since in only a few cases can the works' dates of creation and the identity of the people depicted be determined with cer-

Dabei hatten die Künstler der Mendelssohnschen Porträts zu Juden recht unterschiedliche Beziehungen. Von Rode, der vor allem als Historienmaler tätig war, ist kein weiterer Kontakt zu Juden überliefert. Gleiches gilt für Tassaert. Von Chodowiecki hingegen, dem fleißigen Brief- und Tagebuchschreiber, sind wir am besten unterrichtet: über seine Zusammenarbeit mit Abramson an verschiedenen Medaillen, über seine jüdischen Schüler und Schülerinnen und auch über seine Ressentiments. In Mendelssohns Debatte mit Lavater bezog er für letzteren Position und teilte dessen Unverständnis darüber, dass ein aufgeklärter Jude Jude bleibt. Mit jüdischen Lebensweisen war er soweit vertraut, dass er seiner Freundin, der Gräfin Solms-Laubach, berichten konnte:

„Es scheint, dass in Ihren Gegenden die Juden noch orthodox sind, hier sind die, die nicht zu dem Pöbel gehören, es keineswegs; sie Kaufen und verkaufen am Sonnabend, Essen alle verbothenen Speisen, halten keine Festtage u. s. w."[68]

tainty. Also, hardly any examples from before 1760 are known. The earliest such image was long considered to have been painted in 1702 by Anton Schoonjans. The identification of its sitter as the court factor Jost Liebmann is now doubtful. There is an engraving from around 1720 which shows the Prussian royal family visiting a synagogue. In 1762 Georg Friedrich Schmidt etched a portrait of Hirsch Michel, Rabbi of Potsdam. However, this was as much a likeness from life as a stylized "type portrait" inspired by literary sources.[66] It was certainly influenced by Rembrandt, particularly by his portraits of (what are thought to be) unnamed Jewish people, as well as by random encounters with Jews living in Berlin and Potsdam.

If we limit ourselves to those portraits that can be dated and identified with certainty (other than those of Mendelssohn), we come up with the following series: a portrait of Isaac Daniel Itzig painted in 1777 by Johann Christoph Frisch; one of Henriette Herz, made in 1778 by Anna Dorothea Therbusch; of Marcus Herz from 1779,

O. NR. JOHANN CHRISTOPH FRISCH (1738–1815):
MARCUS UND RAHEL LEVIN (SPÄTER VARNHAGEN VON ENSE)
ca. 1783
Öl auf Leinwand
SBB PK, Abt. Handschriften und Historische Drucke
(Foto: Susanne Welther)

EINFÜHRUNG

Diejenigen Juden, die in seinen Stichen als solche erkennbar sind, hätte er vermutlich dem „Pöbel" zugerechnet. Die anderen, wie etwa den Vater Rahel Levins, Marcus Levin, oder Moses Wessely oder eben Mendelssohn, zeigt er – zumindest in den ausgearbeiteten Fassungen – so, wie er sie vermutlich auch erlebte, nämlich ohne, dass sie durch ihre Kleidung als Juden erkennbar wären. Seine Ressentiments gegen Juden sind in erster Linie sozial und religiös grundiert. Seine Kritik an Affektiertheit, Heuchelei und anderen Lastern geht noch nicht, wie das nach seinem Tod seit den 1810er-Jahren zunahm, mit proto-rassistischen visuellen Stereotypen einher. Die Konstruktion einer speziell „jüdischen" Physis ist dem Freund des Physiognomikers Lavater noch fremd, ebenso das Phantasma des „maskierten" Juden. Doch als solche markiert werden Juden durchaus, wo er sie in seiner Korrespondenz erwähnt. Er beobachtet ihre Teilnahme am kulturellen Leben mit dem Bewusstsein, dass sich hier etwas grundlegend Neues vollzieht, das auch die

again by Frisch; of Moses Wessely, made in 1779 by Chodowiecki after a work by Tischbein; and (presumably) of Marcus Elieser Bloch, also painted by Frisch during these years.[67] *Another early example of how Berlin's Jews were busily commissioning visual art is the ex libris which David Friedländer ordered from Daniel Chodowiecki in 1774.*

Thus, the Mendelssohn portraits created by Rode, Graff, and Chodowiecki would have come at the very inception of this amazing cultural and historical development. This said, the majority of the numerous portraits of Berlin's Jewish men and women would not be created until after Mendelssohn's death, particularly during the 1790s.

The relations that the artists behind the Mendelssohn portraits maintained with the Jewish community differed significantly from one another. Rode, who worked primarily as a historical painter, did not have any wide-ranging contacts with Jewish people according to historical records. The same holds true for Tassaert.

O. NR. JOHANN FRIEDRICH AUGUST DARBES (1747–1810): PORTRÄT MIRJAM ITZIG (1727–1788)
ca. 1787
Öl auf Leinwand
JMB (Foto: Roman März)

O. NR. KÖNIGLICHE
PORZELLAN-MANUFAKTUR
TASSE MIT UNTERSCHALE,
MIT PORTRÄT ISAAK DANIEL
ITZIG (1750–1806)
(NACH ANTON GRAFF) UND
DARSTELLUNG SEINES
SCHÖNEBERGER FREIGUTES
Berlin, ca. 1795
Porzellan
JMB (Foto: Roman März)

sozialen Verhältnisse innerhalb der Künstlerschaft nicht unberührt lässt: „*Herr Frisch ist der Mahler der Juden, hatt auch mehrerentheils nur umgang mit ihnen*"[69], berichtet er seiner Vertrauten.

Dass Frisch „der Maler der Juden" sei, erstaunt nicht mehr angesichts der Vielzahl von Porträts Berliner Juden und Jüdinnen, die wir von ihm kennen. Neben den oben erwähnten schuf er in den 1780ern das Kinderbild von Rahel Levin mit ihrem Bruder, das Porträt des Kantors Aaron Beer und, unser Thema streifend, die Folge von Szenen aus „Nathan dem Weisen". Freilich gab es zu dieser Zeit wenig Alternativen. „*Jetzt ist Berlin von guten Porträtmalern sehr entblößt*", schrieb Chodowiecki 1784 an Anton Graff, der inzwischen nach Dresden übergesiedelt war. „*Es ist niemand mehr als Frisch, der etwas Erträgliches malt und er malt sehr langsam.*"[70]

Interessant ist Chodowieckis Hinweis auf den geselligen Austausch zwischen Frisch und seinen jüdischen Auftraggebern. Was bei Mendelssohns Freundschaften mit Lessing, Nicolai und Abbt in den 1750er- und 1760er-Jahren noch ein Novum war, hatte nun offenbar breitere Kreise erfasst. Doch war es noch nicht so selbstverständlich, dass es keiner Erwähnung mehr bedurfte.

But not for Chodowiecki: thanks to his many surviving letters and diary entries, we know all about his collaboration with Abramson on various medals, about his male and female Jewish students, and also about his pet prejudices. During Mendelssohn's theological debate with Lavater, for example, he expressed sympathy for the latter's inability to understand why an enlightened Jew would choose to remain a Jew. But he was certainly well acquainted with the Jewish way of life, as evidenced by this report to his friend the Countess Solms-Laubach:

"It seems that the Jews living in your parts are still orthodox. The ones here—at least those who are not part of the rabble—are anything but: they buy and sell on Saturdays, eat all the forbidden foods, do not observe holidays, etc."[68]

So Chodowiecki would probably have assigned those Jews in his engravings who were outwardly identifiable as such to the "rabble". The others, such as March Levin, father of Rahel Levin, or Moses Wessely or particularly Mendelssohn, are portrayed in his works—at least in the finished versions—just as he encountered them in person, i.e. without being recognizable as Jews through their clothing. His anti-Jewish biases were evidently based primarily on religious intolerance and class consciousness. Although his illustrations often critizised pretentiousness,

Als Porträtist war Anton Graff freilich renommierter als Frisch und auch er erhielt Ende der 1780er-Jahre etliche Porträtaufträge, vor allem aus den Familien Itzig und Friedländer, die er als Silberstiftzeichnungen ausführte. Erst nach 1790 entstanden die Gemäldeporträts von Marcus Elieser Bloch, Dorothea Veit-Schlegel und Henriette Herz. So viele Aufträge müssen es gewesen sein, dass er diese Kundschaft an den gerade wieder nach Berlin zurückgekehrten Kollegen Joseph Friedrich August Darbes weiterreichte:

„Die Überbringer," schreibt Graff am 4. Juli 1786 in einem Empfehlungsschreiben an Darbes, „sind Herr und Madame Levi [die Salonière und Bach-Wiederentdeckerin Sara Levy, I. B.]; die Frau ist eine Tochter der Hrn. Itzig: dieses ist genug, um zu wissen, daß sie ehrlige Leute sind [...]. Ich habe den Mann gemahlt, sollte die Frau auch mahlen; aber das neulich angefangene Portrait meiner Herzogin [von Kurland] u. andere welche eiligst geendigt werden müßen, rauben mich die*

hypocrisy or other vices, they did so without resorting to the proto-racist stereotypes that would become increasingly common after his death. The construct of a purportedly "Jewish" physiognomy is still foreign to this friend of Lavater's. Nor did he subscribe to the phantasmagorical notion of the "masked Jew" who tries to hide his true identity. Still, he always designates Jews as such whenever he mentions them in his correspondence. He observes their participation in cultural life with the awareness that a fundamental change is underway, which cannot but impact social relationships within the artistic community. "Mr. Frisch is the Jews' painter; in fact, he often has just social dealings with them,"[69] he writes in one letter to his aristocratic confidante.

That Frisch acquired a reputation as "the Jews' painter" is hardly surprising, given his many surviving portraits of the prominent Jewish men and women of Berlin. Besides the portraits mentioned earlier, his output from the

Nr. 117 Friedrich Georg Weitsch (1758–1828): Porträt David Friedländer (1750–1834)
ca. 1795
Öl auf Papier (Grisaille)
The Israel Museum, Jerusalem

ses Vergnügens: zur Schadloshaltung wünsche ich bald, das Bildniß dieser lieben Frau von Ihrer Meister Hand gemahlt, hier zu sehen [...]".[71]

Leider ist Darbes' Porträt von Sara Levy nicht überliefert. Doch schuf er in diesen Jahren neben dem Gemälde der Büste Moses Mendelssohns unter anderem die Porträts Miriam und Daniel Itzigs und Isaak Daniel Itzigs.

Auch die übrigen Porträts der Maskilim entstanden in den Jahren um 1790 oder später, etwa Hartwig Wessely 1791 von Löwe und Berger, Salomon Maimon 1792 von Wilhelm Arndt, Marcus Herz 1795 von Friedrich Georg Weitsch, Abraham Abramson 1802 von Johann Georg Rosenberg und Lazarus Bendavid 1806 von Moses Samuel Löwe.

Der allgemeine Aufschwung der bildenden Künste in Berlin durch die Reform der Akademie der Künste 1786 hat zu dieser Blüte der Porträtkultur ebenso beigetragen wie der Wohlstand sowie das Luxus- und Repräsentationsbedürfnis in Teilen der Berliner Jüdischen Gemeinde. Doch ebenso mögen dabei das Bewusstsein für einen kulturellen Wandel, das Bedürfnis, diesen im Bild festzuhalten, und der Wunsch, sich gegenseitig einer offenen Haltung gegenüber diesem Wandel zu versichern, eine Rolle gespielt haben.[72]

Im Hinblick auf eine jüdische Porträtkultur knüpft Mendelssohns erstes Bildnis noch an die Traditionen der Rabbinerporträts und eine bereits bestehende jüdische Porträtkultur außerhalb Berlins an. Die darauffolgenden Porträts von Rode, Graff und Chodowiecki stehen hingegen am Beginn der Berliner jüdischen Porträtkultur und haben hier sicher zusätzlich als Katalysator gewirkt.

Doch wie verhielten sich Tradition und observante Lebensweise zu dieser Entwicklung? Führte letztere zu einer Übertretung der religiösen Gebote? Mendelssohn selbst hat dafür

1780s includes a portrait of Rahel Levin and her brother as children, a portrait of the cantor Aaron Beer and, quite in keeping with our topic, a series of illustrated scenes from Lessing's play "Nathan the Wise". That said, there were few alternatives at the time. "At present, Berlin is quite stripped bare of good portrait painters" wrote Chodowiecki in 1784 to Anton Graff, who had since moved to Dresden. "There is no-one left who paints anything tolerable except Frisch, and he paints very slowly."[70]

Chodowiecki's reference to sociable interaction between Frisch and his Jewish clients is interesting to note. While the sorts of intercultural friendships Mendelssohn had formed with Lessing, Nicolai, and Abbt were still groundbreaking in the 1750s and 1760s, they had since become far more common. But evidently not to the degree that they did not rate a mention.

Of course, Anton Graff enjoyed greater renown as a portrait artist than Frisch and he, too, received a great many commissions during the 1780s, particularly from members of the Itzig and Friedländer families, whom he rendered in silverpoint. He also created painted portraits of Marcus Elieser Bloch, Dorothea Veit-Schlegel, and Henriette Herz, but not until after 1790. The commissions were apparently so numerous that he had to refer a part of this clientele to his colleague Johann Friedrich August Darbes, who had recently returned to Berlin:

"The letter's bearers" writes Graff on July 4th, 1786, in a letter of introduction to Darbes, "are Mr. and Madame Levi [the salonière and rediscoverer of Bach, Sara Levy, I.B.]; the lady is a daughter of Mr. Itzig: this is enough to know that they are honest people [...]. I have painted the husband, and was supposed to paint the wife also; but the recently begun portrait of my Duchess [of Courland] and other works urgently in need of completion rob me of this pleasure. To

EINFÜHRUNG

O. NR. JOHANN GOTTFRIED
SCHADOW (1764–1850):
BÜSTE SALOMON VEIT
(1751–1827)
ca. 1795
Gips
JMB (Foto: Jens Ziehe)

durch die Inschrift auf dem Sockel seiner Büste eine Antwort gegeben, in der zweimal auf sein Judentum hingewiesen wurde: auf seine Geburt „von jüdischen Ältern" und auf seine Lebensweise, die „den Gesetzen der Väter getreu" sei.⁷³

Für observante Betrachter der Büste bedeutete dies: Das Anfertigen einer Porträtbüste steht nicht im Gegensatz zu den Geboten. Eine Begründung dafür gab Mendelssohn in seinem Kommentar zum Dekalog. Dass Malerei und Relief vom sogenannten Bilderverbot nicht berührt waren, darüber herrschte unter den Rabbinern weitgehender Konsens. Mendelssohn hingegen ging einen Schritt weiter. Er vertrat die Auffassung, dass nicht die Zwei- oder Dreidimensionalität eines „Bildes" das Entscheidende sei, sondern die Funktion, dass es sich allein um ein Bilderverehrungsverbot handelte. So übersetzt er das Wort „pessel" nicht als „gehauenes Abbild", sondern frei und in der Bedeutung enger mit „Götzenbild" und ergänzt – ebenso frei – das Verb „verehren" um den prä-

make up for this, I should wish soon to see the likeness of this dear lady painted here by your own master's hand [...]."⁷¹

Unfortunately, no historical information survives as to whether Darbes actually painted a portrait of Sara Levy. But the works he created during this period, besides his painting of Moses Mendelssohn's bust, include portraits of Miriam and Daniel Itzig and of Isaac Daniel Itzig.

All the remaining portraits of the maskilim came into being around 1790 or in the following years. They include a portrait of Hartwig Wessely from 1791 by Löwe and Berger; one of Salomon Maimon from 1792 by Wilhelm Arndt; of Marcus Herz from 1795 by Friedrich Georg Weitsch; of Abraham Abramson from 1802 by Johann Georg Rosenberg; and of Lazarus Bendavid from 1806 by Moses Samuel Löwe.

The general invigoration of the visual arts in Berlin that resulted from the reform of the Academy of Arts in 1786 was as much a contributor to this flourishing of portrait culture as the growing prosperity and appetite for luxury and

zisierenden Zusatz „gottesdienstlich". Er übersetzt also, wie Christoph Schulte es pointiert ausdrückte, nicht im Sinne eines Bilderverbots, sondern eines Götzenbilderverbots. Der Kampf gegen den Götzendienst war für ihn ein zentrales Anliegen.[74]

Sich von einem Künstler in Form eines „gehauenen Abbilds" porträtieren zu lassen, blieb davon unberührt. In dieser Auffassung folgten ihm nicht nur die jüdischen unter den zwanzig Auftraggebern seiner Büste, sondern auch die Vertreter der Jüdischen Freischule, in deren Räumen die Büste aufgestellt wurde. Dennoch: Büsten blieben unter den Berliner jüdischen Porträts eine Ausnahmeerscheinung bis zu der, die Johann Gottfried Schadows um 1795 von Salomon Veit, dem Schwager der Mendelssohn-Tochter Brendel, anfertigte.[75]

Der Unterschied zwischen Funktion und Gestalt des „Bildes", zwischen „Götzenbildern" und dekorativen Skulpturen, war jüdischen Berlinern jedoch schon lange vertraut. Schon in den 1760er-Jahren ließ Veitel Heine Ephraim Putti an der Fassade seines Palais in der Poststraße anbringen und auch sein Garten am Schiffbauerdamm war mit Skulpturen geschmückt. Seine „reizendste Partie", so berichtet Friedrich Nicolai, sei „eine von den schattigsten Spaziergängen umgebene Wiese. Hier stehen auch sechs, zehn bis zwölf Fuß hohe Statuen nach Schlüters Erfindung, welche auf die Brustgeländer, auf dem Dache des Schlosses, haben sollen gesetzt werden. Es sind: Merkur, Juno, Bacchus, Flora, Leda und Venus."[76]

Mit seinem Kommentar zum zweiten Gebot und seiner Auslegung, dieses Verbot beziehe sich auf die Verehrung, nicht auf die Verfertigung von Bildwerken, stand Mendelssohn also nicht am Beginn einer Entwicklung: Er bestätigte eine Unterscheidung, die in der kulturellen Praxis bereits vollzogen worden war.

status among sections of Berlin's Jewish community. But what may also have played a role was a desire to accept the ongoing cultural transformation, to record this transformation visually, and to affirm one's open-mindedness vis-à-vis one's peers.[72]

As regards Jewish portrait culture, Mendelssohn's first portrait still harks back to the traditions of rabbinical portraiture and the practices that had already become established in other Jewish communities outside of Berlin. His subsequent depictions by Rode, Graff, and Chodowiecki, however, inaugurated—and surely helped to encourage—a culture of Jewish portraiture that was unique to Berlin.

Yet how could this development be reconciled with Jewish tradition and religiously observant living? Might it not entail a violation of religious precepts? Mendelssohn's view that it did not conflict with his deeply felt Jewish identity is made clear by the proudly affirmative inscription on the pedestal of his bust, which proclaims that he was born "of Jewish parents" and lived in a manner "true to the laws of his forefathers."[73]

So the bust's message to the perspicacious observer is clear: the creation of a portrait bust does not contravene the Commandments. Mendelssohn explained why in his commentary on the Decalogue. At the time, there was already widespread agreement among the rabbinate that painting and relief were exempt from the ban on "graven images". Mendelssohn went a step further, however. He took the view that it was the function of an image that mattered, not its two- or three-dimensionality, and that the only thing forbidden was to worship an image. Thus, he took the liberty of translating the Hebrew word pessel not as "graven image" but as "idol", which has a far narrower meaning. He was also bold enough to narrow down the meaning of

the verb "to worship" by adding the adverb gottesdienstlich ("in a sacral manner"). As Christoph Schulte incisively put it, he was translating the Second Commandment not as a ban on images, but as a ban on idol-worship. The fight against idolatry was something Mendelssohn took very seriously.[74]

Thus, having oneself portrayed by an artist in the form of a "graven image" was not covered by the Biblical injunction. The many Jews among the twenty clients who commissioned busts of Mendelssohn obviously concurred with this view, as did the representatives of the Jewish Free School, on whose premises the bust was displayed. But for all that, relatively few Jewish Berliners chose to have themselves portrayed in bust form. One notable exception is Salomon Veit, the brother-in-law of Mendelssohn's daughter Brendel, who had his likeness sculpted by Johann Gottfried Schadow around 1795.[75]

The difference between the form and function of an "image" and between "idols" and decorative sculpture was already long familiar to Jewish Berliners. Back in the 1760s, Veitel Heine Ephraim had had the façade of his palatial town house on Poststraße decorated with putti, and had placed works of sculpture in his garden along Schiffbauerdamm. The garden's "most charming part", according to Friedrich Nicolai, was "a meadow surrounded by shaded walkways. This is where six statues after designs by Schlüter, ten- to twelve-feet high, are located, which were originally to be placed along the rooftop balustrade of the royal palace. They are of Mercury, Juno, Bacchus, Flora, Leda, and Venus."[76]

Mendelssohn was not breaking new ground with his comment on the Second Commandment and his interpretation that it referred to the veneration rather than the creation of visual images. He was merely confirming a distinction that had already been implemented in cultural practice.

Nr. 247 Izhar Patkin
(geb. 1955): Moses.
Aus der Installation
„Judenporzellan"
1998
beschichtetes Papier,
geheftet, verklebt, mit
Acrylfarbe besprüht
JMB (Foto: Roman März)

EINFÜHRUNG

Quellenverzeichnis

[1] Siegmund Salfeld: Bilder und Büsten Mendelssohns. Eine Kunstnotiz; in: Populär-wissenschaftliche Monatsblätter zur Belehrung über das Judenthum für Gebildete aller Confessionen. Organ des Mendelssohn-Vereins in Frankfurt Jg. 6, 1886, H. 1, S. 10–14; Albert Wolf, Das jüdische Berlin gegen Ende des 18. Jahrhunderts in Abbildungen und Medaillen, in: Gedenkbuch zur Erinnerung an David Kaufmann, Markus Brann, Ferdinand Rosenthal (Hg.), Breslau 1900, S. 629–653; Moses Mendelssohn Ausstellung, Preußische Staatsbibliothek, Jüdische Gemeinde zu Berlin (Hg.), Karl Schwarz, Moritz Stern (Bearb.), Berlin 1929; Führer durch die Moses Mendelssohn Gedächtnis-Ausstellung, Ludwig Grote, Paul Wahl (Hg.), Dessau 1929.

[2] Herrmann M. Z. Meyer: Moses-Mendelssohn-Bibliographie. Mit einigen Ergänzungen zur Geistesgeschichte des ausgehenden 18. Jahrhunderts, Berlin 1965. Meyer war auch unter den Leihgebern für die Berliner Ausstellung 1929; Gisbert Porstmann: Moses Mendelssohn: Porträts und Bilddokumente, Stuttgart-Bad Cannstatt 1997 (= JubA, Bd. 2).

[3] Richard I. Cohen: Imagining Moses Mendelssohn (1771–2014), Ramat Gan 2014 (Braun Lectures in the History of the Jews in Prussia, 18) (hebr.).

[4] Bernd G. Ulbrich: Das Dessauer Denkmal für Moses Mendelssohn, 1890 bis 1938, Dessau 2008; Holger Jacob-Friesen: Moses Mendelssohn im Bilde. Einige bisher wenig beachtete Darstellungen, in: Mendelssohn-Studien 13, 2003, S. 9–34.

[5] Leah Hochman, The Ugliness of Mendelssohn. Aesthetics, Religion, and Morality in the Eighteenth Century, London 2014; zu den Jubiläen: Martina Steer: Moses Mendelssohn und seine Nachwelt. Eine Kulturgeschichte der jüdischen Erinnerung, Göttingen 2019; allg. zur Rezeptionsgeschichte: Dominique Bourel: Moses Mendelssohn. Begründer des modernen Judentums, Zürich 2007, S. 23–50; David Sorkin: Moses Mendelssohn and the Religious Enlightenment, Berkeley 1996, S. 147–155; ders.: The Mendelssohn Myth and Its Method, in: New German Critique 77, 1999, S. 7–78.

[6] Ein systematischer Katalog ist in digitaler Form geplant.
A systematic digital catalog is planned.

[7] Der Freundschaftstempel im Gleimhaus zu Halberstadt. Katalog der Bildnisse, biografische Notizen, Verzeichnis der Maler, Halberstadt 1911. – Porstmann (wie Anm. 2), S. 18–20, weist auf den Widerspruch hin, dass Gleim das Gemälde bereits im September 1768 erhalten hatte, jedoch rückseitig auf 1769 datierte. Krügers Stich erschien als Frontispiz zum Jahrgang 1768 der Berlinischen Monatsschrift. In der Beschreibung erwähnt Nicolai die Datierung auf 1769.

[8] Brief Johann Georg Hamann an Johann Gottfried Herder vom 28. August 1768, in: Walther Ziesemer und Arthur Henkel (Hg.): Briefwechsel Johann Georg Hamann, Bd. 2, Wiesbaden 1956, S. 419.

[9] Hochman (wie Anm. 5), S. 159 und 174, der ich den Hinweis verdanke, vermutet den Königsberger Maler Johann Gottlieb Becker, der Kant und Herder porträtierte, als Autor.
Hochman (cited in footnote 5), pp. 159 and 174, whom I thank for this information, thinks it might have been the Königsberg painter Johann Gottlieb Becker, who also painted Kant and Herder.

[10] Mark Lehmstedt: Philipp Erasmus Reich (1717–1787). Verleger der Aufklärung und Reformer des deutschen Buchhandels, Leipzig 1989, S. 178; ders.: Die Porträtsammlung Philipp Erasmus Reichs, in: Anton Graff, Selbstbildnis vor der Staffelei, Susanne Heiland (Red.), Leipzig 1986, S. 41–52.

[11] Schon 1771 verlegte Reich dessen „Geheimes Tagebuch. Von einem Beobachter Seiner Selbst"; es folgten 1772 „Von der Physiognomik" und ab 1775 in mehreren Auflagen die „Physiognomischen Fragmente". Zur Beziehung zwischen Fritsch und Reich: Lehmstedt (wie Anm. 10), S. 75–76.

[12] Zit. nach: Lehmstedt (wie Anm. 10), S. 178–179.

[13] Die Stiche nach den Porträts erschienen: Sulzer 1773, Ramler 1774, Spalding 1778.

[14] Porstmann (wie Anm. 2), Abb. 28a und 28b.

[15] Ekhart Berckenhagen: Anton Graff. Leben und Werk, Berlin 1967, S. 272–273, Kat.-Nrn. 994–997, nennt als eigenhändig: die Gemälde in Leipzig, in Berlin/Potsdam (ehem. ausgestellt im Jagdschloss Grunewald), im Mendelssohn-Archiv, sowie ein weiteres im Märkischen Museum. Das heute dort befindliche (Inv.-Nr. VII 60/534 x) wird im Katalog als Kopie angegeben. In der älteren Literatur sind darüber hinaus noch eine Fassung in der Hochdeutschen Israelitengemeinde zu Altona und eine in der Hochschule für die Wissenschaft des Judentums genannt. Der Katalog Moses Mendelssohn. Leben und Werk, Staatsbibliothek Preußischer Kulturbesitz, Berlin 1979, Nr. 152, S. 42 erwähnt „mindestens sechs Repliken wurden jedoch von ihm für die Familie, wie die Vorliegende, und israelitische Gemeinden angefertigt." Weitere Exemplare befinden sich heute im Deutschen Historischen Museum (unklar, ob Replik oder Kopie), in der Familie der Nachfahren Moses Mendelssohns (Kopie) sowie im Jüdischen Museum Berlin eine Kopie von August Theodor Kaselowsky als Leihgabe des Israel Museums, Jerusalem (ursprünglich wohl in der Gesellschaft der Freunde und danach in der Kunstsammlung der Jüdischen Gemeinde, 1954 von der JRSO an das heutige Israel Museum übergeben).
Ekhart Berckenhagen: Anton Graff. Leben und Werk, Berlin 1967, pp. 272-273, catalog numbers 994-997, lists in his catalogue raisonné the

following as being in Graff's own hand: the specimens in Leipzig, in Berlin/Potsdam (formerly displayed at the Jagdschloss in Grunewald) and in the Mendelssohn Archive, as well as another one in the Märkisches Museum. The painting located there today (inventory number VII 60/534 x) is listed as a copy in the catalog. The older literature also mentions a version at the High German Israelite Community in Altona, and at the Higher Institute for Jewish Studies in Berlin. The catalog Moses Mendelssohn. Leben und Werk, Staatsbibliothek Preußischer Kulturbesitz, Berlin 1979, No. 152, p. 42 states that "at least six replicas were created by Graff himself for the family, as is the case with this replica, and for various Jewish communities." Additional specimens today can be found at the Deutsches Historisches Museum (whether this is a replica or copy is unclear), in the hands of the descendants of Moses Mendelssohn (copy), and a copy by August Theodor Kaselowsky is at the Jewish Museum Berlin; this latter is on loan from the Israel Museum, Jerusalem (and was probably once held by the Society of Friends, subsequently in the art collection of the Berlin Jewish Community, and, in the 1950s, was given by the JRSO to what is today the Israel Museum).

[16] Leider war es im Zusammenhang dieses Ausstellungsprojekts nicht möglich, alle vorhandenen Originale in Augenschein zu nehmen und in Zusammenarbeit mit Restauratoren zu prüfen.
Unfortunately, it was not possible, also not in the context of mounting this exhibition, to inspect all existing originals in collaboration with conservators.

[17] Hinweis von Reimar Lacher auf das Symposium der Mendelssohn-Gesellschaft, Januar 2018.

[18] Brandenburgische historische Münzbelustigungen, Johann Jakob Spieß (Hg.), Anspach, 5. Bd. 1774, Taf. IX, S. 101.

[19] Tassilo Hoffmann: Jacob Abraham und Abraham Abramson. 55 Jahre Berliner Medaillenkunst 1755–1810, Frankfurt am Main 1927, S. 19. Für die Verifizierung dieses Belegs danke ich Maximilian Bach.

[20] August Adolph von Hennings an Elise Reimarus, 21. August 1776, zit. nach Meyer Kayserling: Moses Mendelssohn. Sein Leben und seine Werke, nebst einem Anhange ungedruckter Briefe von und an Moses Mendelssohn, Leipzig 1862, S. 243, dem der Originalbrief vorlag.

[21] Heute im Israel Museum, Jerusalem.

[22] Moritz Stern: Ein unbekanntes Porträt Moses Mendelssohns, in: Jüdisches Gemeindeblatt. Organ des Vorstandes der Jüdischen Gemeinde zu Berlin, Jg. 27, 1937, Nr. 35, S. 3.

[23] Erwin Hensler: Nachwort, in: Das Stammbuch Adrian Zinggs, Leipzig 1923, S. 15.

[24] Zit. nach Kayserling (wie Anm. 20), Brief v. 28.08.1776, S. 253.

[25] Moses Mendelssohn's gesammelte Schriften, Bd. 1, Leipzig 1843, S. 37.

[26] Alexander Altmann: Moses Mendelssohn. A Biographical Study, London 1973, S. 328-329.

[27] Hellmut Meyer & Ernst, 17. Dez. 1932, Los-Nr. 1082. In der Bibliografie von Hermann Meyer erwähnt (P 22), der die beiden Porträts – das Gemmenporträt und das realistische Porträt – unterschied, jedoch auf 1784 und 1786 datierte.

[28] Vgl. Angaben im Katalog der Staatsbibliothek.

[29] Aus dem Besitz des mit Margarethe von Mendelssohn verheirateten Bankiers und Unternehmers Paul Kempner, Berlin, danach USA.

[30] Zur Geschichte der Büste: Hermann Simon: Das Berliner Jüdische Museum. In der Oranienburger Straße. Geschichte einer zerstörten Kulturstätte. Teetz 2000, S. 40–46; Porstmann (wie Anm. 2), S. 50–56.

[31] Hinweis von Reimar Lacher auf Symposium der Mendelssohn-Gesellschaft, Januar 2018.

[32] U. a. Ehem: Sammlung Kirstein, Berlin; Museum jüdischer Altertümer, Frankfurt; Sammlung Schwarzschild, Frankfurt, vgl. Mendelssohn-Ausstellung im Museum jüdischer Altertümer, Frankfurt 1929.

[33] Gisbert Porstmann: Moses Mendelssohn und das Porzellan, in: Keramos Nr. 159, 1998, S. 61–68.

[34] Heute Akademie der Künste zu Berlin. Claudia Czok: Schadow, Sokrates und das Judentum. Johann Gottfried Schadow „Sokrates im Kerker", Berlin 2002.

[35] Alle Maßangaben aus jüngerer Zeit beziehen sich wohl auf eine Abbildung, nicht auf das Original. Das Original war zum letzten Mal auf der Mendelssohn-Ausstellung der Staatsbibliothek zu sehen. Eine Farbabbildung publizierte erstmals Kayserling (wie Anm. 20, 2. verm. Aufl. 1888) nach S. 120, weitere erschienen als Frontispiz der Edition der Brautbriefe 1936 und bei Bertha Badt-Strauss: Moses Mendelssohn. Der Mensch und das Werk. Zeugnisse, Briefe, Gespräche, Berlin 1929. Badt-Strauss nennt als Quelle „Jüdische Gemeinde zu Berlin", wobei unklar bleibt, ob sich dies auf das Original oder eine Abbildung bezieht. In der Fotosammlung des Berliner Jüdischen Museums, die sich im Jewish Historical Institute in Warschau erhalten hat, ist das Foto nicht enthalten.
All the references from recent times probably allude to a reproduction, not to the original. The original could last be seen at the Mendelssohn Exhibition mounted by the Prussian State Library. The first color reproduction was published by Kayserling (as cited in footnote 20, second edition 1888) after p. 120. Additional ones were published as the frontispiece of an edition of Mendelssohn's Bridal Letters (Brautbriefe) and by Bertha Badt-Strauss: Moses Mendelssohn. Der Mensch und das Werk. Zeugnisse, Briefe, Gespräche, Berlin 1929. Badt-Strauss states that the source was the "Berlin Jewish Community", but it is unclear whether this refers to

the original or to the reproduction. The photo is not to be found in the photo collection of the Jewish Museum Berlin that has been preserved in the Warsaw Jewish Historical Institute.

[36] Von den bekannten Porträts jüdischer Frauen stammt beispielsweise das Porträt der Miriam Itzig aus dem Jahr 1787, das heute nur in einer späteren Kopie erhaltene Porträt der Madame Kaulla, stammt, der „à la grecque"-Mode des Kleides nach zu urteilen, aus dem letzten Jahrzehnt des Jahrhunderts. Vgl. Ausst.-Kat. From Court Jews to the Rothschilds. Art, patronage, and power 1600–1800, Vivian B. Mann (Hg.), New York, NY 1996, Kat.-Nr. 158, S. 43.
Of the known portraits of Jewish women, that of Miriam Itzig dates from 1787; that of Madame Kaulla, which today survives only in the form of a later copy, stems from the last decade of the century judging from the à la grecque style of the sitter's dress. Cf. the exhibition catalog From Court Jews to the Rothschilds. Art, patronage, and power 1600 – 1800, Vivian B. Mann (ed.), New York, NY 1996, catalog no. 158, p. 43.

[37] Beispiele in: Ausst.-Kat. Jüdische Lebenswelten. Jüdisches Denken und Glauben, Leben und Arbeiten in den Kulturen der Welt, Andreas Nachama u. a. (Hg.), Frankfurt am Main 1991, Kat.-Nrn. 15/45, 15/48, 15/49, 15/53, 15/57.

[38] Richard I. Cohen: Jewish Icons, Berkeley 1998, S. 114–153; Hannelore Künzl: Zur Entwicklung des frühen Rabbinerporträts, in: Michael Graetz (Hg.), Vom Mittelalter in die Neuzeit. Jüdische Städtebilder Frankfurt, Prag, Amsterdam, Heidelberg 1999, S. 31–43; Peter Freimark: Porträts von Rabbinern der Dreigemeinde Altona-Hamburg-Wandsbek aus dem 18. Jahrhundert, in: Peter Freimark, Alice Jankowski, Ina S. Lorenz (Hg.): Juden in Deutschland. Emanzipation, Integration, Verfolgung und Vernichtung, Hamburg 1991, S. 36–57.

[39] Court Jews (wie Anm. 36), Kat.-Nrn. 156, 189, 149 und 150.

[40] Das Gemälde befindet sich heute wieder in der Jüdischen Gemeinde Hamburg. Freimark (wie Anm. 38), S. 55f. Sofern Porträts der Altonaer Portugiesischen Gemeinde existierten, wurden sie, so vermutet Freimark S. 47, beim Stadtbrand 1842 vernichtet.

[41] Max Grunwald: Hamburgs deutsche Juden bis zur Auflösung der Dreigemeinden 1811, Hamburg 1904, Kapitel „Hamburgs Juden in Bild und Karikatur" nennt sieben Porträts, Cohen (wie Anm. 38) vermutet ca. zwanzig.

[42] Den Hinweis verdanke ich Cohen (wie Anm. 38), Abb. 67, S. 124 (verlesen als Dr. F.). Auch Freimark (wie Anm. 38), S. 50–51, diskutiert das Blatt und liest: „Dr. E." und „filta"; Alfred Rubens: Jewish Iconography, Suppl. Vol., London 1982, S. 22 liest „Filter". Exemplare: National Library of Israel, NLI 997003186660405171, und Wolfenbüttel, Herzog August Bibliothek, Inventar-Nr. A 6201.
Ich danke Aubrey Pomerance für Hinweise zur Deutung des Namens.

[43] So auf dem Exemplar des Leo Baeck Instituts, New York, Acc.-Nr. 86.54.

[44] Grunwald 1904 nennt ihn nicht. Auch Freimark konnte nicht feststellen, wer sich hinter dem Namen verbirgt. In der epigrafischen Datenbank (epidat) taucht er nicht auf.
Grunwald 1904 does not mention him. Freimark, too, was unable to determine for whom the name stands. He does not appear in the epigraphical database (epidat).

[45] Fritzsch zeigte Geistliche und Gelehrte meist mit einem Bücherregal im Hintergrund, einem Vorhang, zuweilen mit Fransen und Quasten, an ihrem Schreibtisch stehend, eine Hand auf einem Buch oder in die Seiten geschoben. Vgl. https://www.portraitindex.de/.
Fritzsch mostly depicted clergymen and scholars (like Johann Georg Hagemann, Hermann Wahn, Joachim Johann Daniel Zimmermann, Johann Melchior Goeze, Erdmann Neumeister, Friedrich Wagner or Michael Richey) at their desk with one hand resting on a book or holding it open, with a bookshelf in the background along with a curtain, sometimes with fringes and tassels. Cf. https://www.portraitindex.de/.

[46] Während wir vermuten, dass zumindest einige der vereinfachten Kopien von Pilta ben Schimschons Hand sind, muss offenbleiben, ob sie auf einen konkreten Auftrag zurückgingen oder für noch unbekannte Abnehmer geschaffen wurden.
While we believe that at least some of the simplified copies are from the hand of Pilta ben Schimschon, it remains unclear whether these copies were specifically commissioned or created on spec for buyers yet unknown.

[47] Vgl. Bourel (wie Anm.2), S. 237; Brief v. 4. Mai 1761, in: JubA Bd. 19, S. 2–3 (hebr.), JubA Bd. 20,2, S. 4–6 (dt.).

[48] Shmuel Feiner: Moses Mendelssohn. Ein jüdischer Denker in der Zeit der Aufklärung, Göttingen 2009, S. 23–25, auf dessen Darstellung der Begegnung mit Eybeschütz meine Deutung der Miniatur basiert. Zu jüdischen Künstlern in Hamburg: Iris Firschof: Jüdische Buchmalerei in Hamburg und Altona. Zur Geschichte der Illuminierung hebräischer Handschriften im 18. Jahrhundert, Hamburg 1999.

[49] Zu den Fragen von Kleidung, Haar- und Barttracht vgl. Asriel Schochat: Der Ursprung der jüdischen Aufklärung in Deutschland, Frankfurt 2000, S. 92–104.

[50] Exemplare im Jüdischen Museum Prag, Inv.-Nr. 063.159, https://collections.jewishmuseum.cz/index.php/Detail/Object/Show/object_id/204850
Und im Jewish Historical Institute Warschau, Inv.-Nr. MŻIH B-443/11/11 https://www.delet.jhi.pl/en/library/item/1260425 (21.2.2022)

[51] Samuel Kauder (1830), Abraham Tiktin (um 1850), Samson Raphael Hirsch (um 1850) sowie 1858 eine

Biografie von Jonathan Eybeschütz.

[52] Friedrich Nicolai an Johann Caspar Lavater, 10. März 1770, zit. nach JubA Bd. 7, 340-342.

[53] Meyer Kayserling: Ein ungedruckter Brief Fromet Mendelssohns, in: Allgemeine Zeitung des Judentums, 55. 1891, Heft 9, S. 106.

[54] Wolf (wie Anm. 1), S. 633f.

[55] Cohen (wie Anm. 2), S. 13, Anm. 18, und mit Dank an Richard I. Cohen für weitere Hinweise.

[56] Stadtbibliothek Trier, Nr. 2759. Derselbe Stich mit nachträglich hinzugefügtem Todesdatum: Jewish Historical Institute, Warschau, Inv.-Nr. MZIH B-443/11/21, vgl. Wolf (wie Anm. 1), S. 636.

[57] Briefe Daniel Chodowieckis an die Gräfin Christiane von Solms-Laubach, Charlotte Steinbrucker (Hg.), Strassburg 1928, Brief 32, v. 25. Mai 1786, S. 83. Die Herausgeberin vermerkt das ihr Unverständliche: „im Original folgt hier [nach Mendelssohn] noch ‚von'".

[58] Vgl. von ihm gesammelte Materialien zu Mendelssohn als Teil der Sammlung AR 6793 des Leo Baeck Institute Archive, New York.

[59] Als Rot- und Schwarzdruck mit verschiedenen Adressen.

[60] Gesammelte Schriften (wie Anm. 25), S. 36.

[61] Abb. in: Jüdisches Magazin, Sept. 1929, S. 20.

[62] Abb. in: Ost und West, Jg. 9. 1909, H. 11, Sp. 678. Der Gips befand sich später im Lessing Museum. Die Bronzebüste wurde lt. Meyer (wie Anm. 2) „Ausgeführt 1928 für das Lessing-Museum Berlin. Wurde auch in verkleinertem Format 45 und 27 cm hergestellt."
Illustration in: Ost und West, vol. 9. 1909, issue 11, column 678. The gypsum model was later kept by the Lessing Museum. The bronze bust, Meyer (as cited in footnote 2) reported, was "executed in 1928 for the Lessing-Museum Berlin. It was also cast in smaller format 45 and 27 cm."

[63] Deutsch-jüdische Geschichte in der Neuzeit, Bd. 1: Mordechai Breuer, Michael Graetz: Tradition und Aufklärung 1600–1780, München 1996.
Deutsch-jüdische Geschichte in der Neuzeit, vol. 1: Mordechai Breuer, Michael Graetz: Tradition und Aufklärung 1600 – 1780, Munich 1996.

[64] Schochat (wie Anm. 49), S. 52–72.
Schochat (as cited in footnote 49), pp. 52-72.

[65] Steven M. Lowenstein: The Berlin Jewish community. Enlightenment, Family, and Crisis 1770–1830, New York 1994, S. 43-54.
Steven M. Lowenstein: The Berlin Jewish Community. Enlightenment, Family, and Crisis 1770 – 1830, New York 1994, pp. 43-54.

[66] Dagegen Wolf (wie Anm. 1), S. 646: „In diesem Blatt darf man wohl kaum ein Portrait sehen, da es seine Entstehung nur einem Scherze verdankte, den sich der Stecher mit dem ihm befreundeten Verfasser der «Lettres Juives», dem Marquis D'Argens, machen wollte, zu welchem Zwecke er sich der Namen von dessen fingirten Briefschreibern: «Aaron Moneca» und «Isaac Onis, Craite, ancien Rabbin de Constantinople» bediente."
In contrast Wolf (as cited in footnote 1), p. 646: "This folio can hardly be termed a portrait since its genesis is the result of a joke the engraver intended to enjoy with the author of the «Lettres Juives», the Marquis D'Argens, his friend, for which purpose he used the names of the letter writers he had thought up, «Aaron Moneca» and «Isaac Onis, Craite, ancien Rabbin de Constantinople»."

[67] Vgl. z.B. das Porträt von Ephraim Marcus Ephraim, um 1775, Sammlung des Jewish Museum New York, Inv.-Nr. 1992-59.

[68] Chodowiecki (wie Anm. 57), Brief Nr. 16, vom 12.10.1783, S. 43.

[69] Chodowiecki (wie Anm. 57), Brief Nr. 33, vom 14.06.1786, S. 90.

[70] Briefe Daniel Chodowieckis an Anton Graff, Charlotte Steinbrucker (Hg.), Berlin 1921, Brief Nr. 24, vom 27.12.1784, S. 35.

[71] In Privatbesitz. Ich danke Christoph Frank für diesen Hinweis.

[72] Vgl. Antoine Lilti, Figures publiques. L'invention de la célébrité 1750–1850, Paris 2014.

[73] Zit. nach Porstmann (wie Anm. 2), S. 51.

[74] Christoph Schulte: Die Büste und das Bilderverbot, in: ders: Von Moses bis Moses … Der jüdische Mendelssohn. Studien, Hannover 2020, S. 156–168.

[75] Gipsabgüsse in der Nationalgalerie und im Jüdischen Museum Berlin, Inv.-Nr. 2001/350.

[76] Friedrich Nicolai: Beschreibung der königlichen Residenzstädte Berlin und Potsdam, aller daselbst befindlicher Merkwürdigkeiten, und der umliegenden Gegend, Berlin 1786 (repr. Berlin 1980), S. 931.

Bilderfabrik

Image Factory

In diesem Abschnitt sind die Porträts Moses Mendelssohns, die zu seinen Lebzeiten und kurz nach seinem Tod geschaffen wurden, versammelt. Er umfasst auch Repliken, Kopien, Nachstiche und Abwandlungen sowie Werke, die nicht in der Ausstellung gezeigt werden konnten. Ergänzt werden sie durch eine Auswahl der zahlreichen im 19. Jahrhundert entstandenen Zeugnisse der Mendelssohn-Verehrung.

This section assembles the portraits of Moses Mendelssohn created during his lifetime and shortly after his death. It also includes replicas, copies, engravings and variations, as well as works that could not be shown in the exhibition. They are complemented by a selection of the numerous testimonies venerating Mendelssohn created in the 19th century.

Die Miniaturen

The Miniatures

Die Geschichte der Mendelssohn-Porträts beginnt mit zwei Miniaturen des 38-jährigen Talmudgelehrten und Philosophen und seiner Ehefrau Fromet, geb. Gugenheim. Zum Künstler und den Entstehungszusammenhängen können wir bislang nur Vermutungen anstellen. Bereits von diesem frühen Porträt existieren mehrere Kopien.

The history of Mendelssohn portraits begins with two miniatures of the 38-year-old Talmud scholar and philosopher and his wife Fromet, née Gugenheim. So far, we can only make assumptions about the artist and the contexts of origin. Already this early portrait exists in several copies.

Nr. 28 Dr. P. S. (vermutlich Elimelech Pilta ben Schimschon Rofe): Porträtminiatur Moses Mendelssohn
1767
Tempera auf Elfenbein,
7,5 × 6 cm
Privatbesitz, Berlin
(Foto: Manfred Claudi)

Im Jahr der Veröffentlichung des „Phädon" porträtiert ein unbekannter Künstler Mendelssohn als Miniatur. Es entstehen mehrere Kopien. Das heute verlorene Gegenstück zeigt Fromet.
In the same year "Phaedon" is published, an unknown artist creates a miniature portrait of Mendelssohn, of which multiple copies are made. A matching portrait of Fromet, whereabouts currently unknown, was also created.

Nr. 206 Replik oder Kopie nach Dr. P. S. (vermutlich Elimelech Pilta ben Schimschon Rofe): Porträtminiatur Moses Mendelssohn
1767
Tempera auf Elfenbein,
7,5 × 6 cm
Mendelssohn-Gesellschaft, Berlin (Dauerleihgabe aus dem Nachlass Mary Gilbert)
(Foto: Manfred Claudi)

BILDERFABRIK

Nr. 207 Replik oder Kopie nach Dr. P. S. (vermutlich Elimelech Pilta ben Schimschon Rofe): Porträtminiatur Moses Mendelssohn
nach 1767
Tempera auf Elfenbein,
6,5 × 4,80 cm
JMB (Foto: Roman März)

Nr. 208 Replik oder Kopie nach Dr. P. S. (vermutlich Elimelech Pilta ben Schimschon Rofe): Porträtminiatur Moses Mendelssohn
nach 1767
Tempera auf Horn oder Elfenbein, 5,5 × 4,6 cm (oval)
JMB (Foto: Jens Ziehe)

Das Porträt von Bernhard Rode

The Portrait by Bernhard Rode

Der Historienmaler und Radierer, befreundet mit vielen Protagonisten der Aufklärung, schuf das erste repräsentative Porträt Mendelssohns. Es entstand im Auftrag des Halberstädter Gelehrten Johann Wilhelm Gleim, der Mendelssohn „wegen seines Phädon" in seine Freundschaftsgalerie aufnahm. Der Kupferstich nach dem Gemälde erschien 1768 als Frontispiz des achten Bandes der von Friedrich Nicolai herausgegebenen Allgemeinen Deutschen Bibliothek.

The historical painter and etcher, a friend of many protagonists of the Enlightenment, created the first representative portrait of Mendelssohn. It was commissioned by the Halberstadt scholar Johann Wilhelm Gleim, who included Mendelssohn in his friendship gallery "because of his Phaedon". The engraving after the painting appeared in 1768 as the frontispiece of the eighth volume of the Allgemeine Deutsche Bibliothek published by Friedrich Nicolai.

NR. 49/50 PORTRÄT
MOSES MENDELSSOHN
1929
Glasnegativ auf Gelantinetrocken-
platte, 18 × 13 cm, und Abzug
24 × 18 cm
SBB PK, Abteilung Handschriften
und Historische Drucke bzw.
Gleimhaus Halberstadt –
Museum der deutschen Aufklärung

Das Gemälde wurde 1929 in der
großen Mendelsson-Ausstellung
gezeigt. 1934 aus der Dauerausstellung des Gleimhauses entfernt,
ist es seit Kriegsende verschollen.
*The painting was shown in the
great Mendelsson exhibition in 1929.
Removed from the permanent exhibition of the Gleimhaus in 1934, it has
been lost since the end of the war.*

NR. 211 JOHANN CONRAD KRÜGER
(1733–1791): PORTRÄT MOSES
MENDELSSOHN
1768
Kupferstich, 14,8 × 8,8 cm
JMB (Foto: Roman März)

Das Porträt von Anton Graff

The Portrait by Anton Graff

Als einer der bedeutendsten Porträtmaler seiner Zeit hat der Schweizer Anton Graff die Bildnisse zahlreicher Politiker, Künstler und Wissenschaftler geschaffen. Von seinem Ölgemälde Mendelssohns entstehen Repliken und Kopien und sehr bald schon, als erste von vielen weit verbreiteten Variationen, ein Kupferstich von Johann Friedrich Bause, der eng mit Graff zusammenarbeitete. Der Dargestellte spottet daraufhin über sich selbst und die Verschönerungs-Arbeit der Kunst: Er sehe sich hier nicht gespiegelt, sondern „wie ich meiner besten Freundin dreist in einem Morgentraume erschienen seyn mag."

One of the most important portrait painters of his time, the Swiss Anton Graff created the portraits of numerous important politicians, artists and scientists. Replicas and copies were made of his oil painting of Mendelssohn, and very soon, as the first of many widespread variations, an engraving by Graff's friend Johann Friedrich Bause. The sitter then mocks himself and the embellishment work of art: he sees himself here not reflected, but "as I may have brazenly appeared to my best friend in a morning dream."

O. NR. ANTON GRAFF (1736–1813): PORTRÄT MOSES MENDELSSOHN
1771
Öl auf Leinwand, 65 × 53 cm
Universität Leipzig, Kunstsammlung
(Foto: Marion Wenzel)

Als der Lavater-Streit in vollem Gange ist, beauftragt der Leipziger Buchhändler Philip Erasmus Reich den Maler Anton Graff mit einem Porträt für seine Freundschaftsgalerie.

At the peak of the Lavater dispute, Leipzig bookseller Philip Erasmus Reich commissioned painter Anton Graff to paint a portrait for his "gallery of friendship". This portrait is disseminated as replicas, copies, and prints.

BILDERFABRIK

Nr. 212 Anton Graff (1736–1813): Porträt Moses Mendelssohn (Replik)
nach 1771
Öl auf Leinwand, 62 × 52 cm
SPSG, Leihgabe des Berliner Senats

Nr. 213 Anton Graff (1736–1813): Porträt Moses Mendelssohn (Replik)
nach 1771
Öl auf Leinwand, 54 × 45 cm
SBB PK, Musikabteilung mit Mendelssohn-Archiv

Nr. 214b Anton Graff
(1736–1813) oder Nachfolger:
Porträt Moses Mendelssohn
nach 1771
Öl auf Leinwand, 60,5 × 49,7 cm
Deutsches Historisches Museum
(Foto: Arne Psille)

Nr. 214 Porträt Moses
Mendelssohn
(Kopie nach Anton Graff)
nach 1771
Öl auf Leinwand, 66 × 54,5 cm
Mendelssohn-Gesellschaft, Berlin
(Leihgabe aus Besitz von
Mendelssohn-Nachkommen)

BILDERFABRIK

O. NR. PORTRÄT MOSES
MENDELSSOHN
(KOPIE NACH ANTON GRAFF)
19. Jahrhundert
Öl auf Leinwand, 53 × 45,6 cm
Stiftung Stadtmuseum Berlin
(Foto: Oliver Ziebe, Berlin)

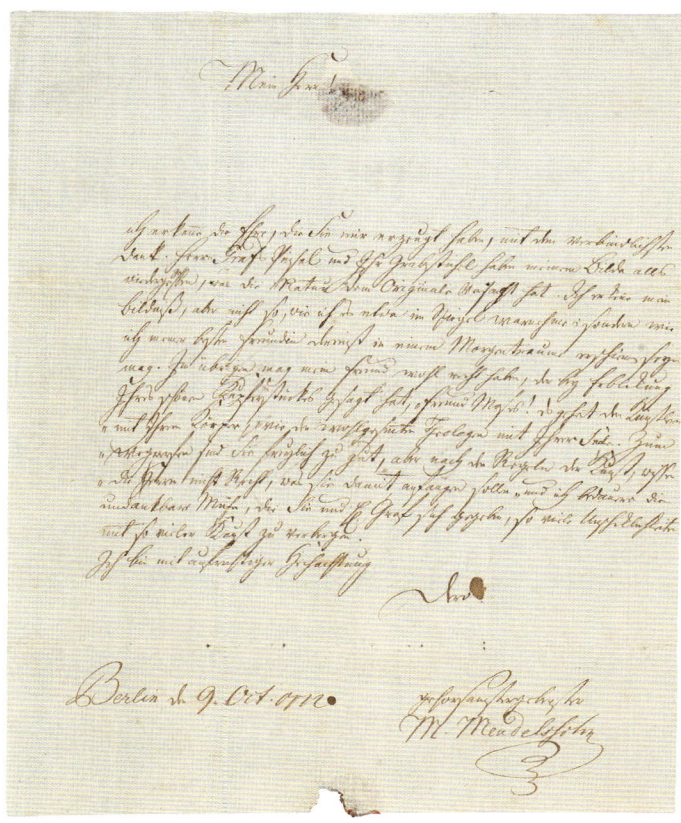

Nr. 215 Moses Mendelssohn (1729–1786): Brief an Johann Friedrich Bause
09.10.1772
Papier, Tinte
Herzog August Bibliothek
Wolfenbüttel

„Mein Herr!
Ich erkenne die Ehre, die Sie mir erzeugt haben, mit dem verbindlichsten Dank. Herrn Grafs Pinsel und Ihr Grabstichel haben meinem Bilde alles wiedergegeben, was die Natur dem Originale versagt hat. Ich erkenne mein Bildniß, aber nicht so, wie ich es etwa im Spiegel warnehme; sondern wie ich meiner besten Freundin dreist in einem Morgentraume erschienen seyn mag. Im übrigen mag mein Freund wohl recht haben, der bey Erblickung Ihres schönen Kupferstückes gesagt hat, «Freund Moses! es gehet den Künstlern mit Ihrem Körper, wie den wohlgesinnten Theologen mit Ihrer Seele. Zum Wegwerfen sind sie freylich zu gut, aber nach den Regeln der Kunst, wissen die Herren nicht Recht, was sie damit anfangen sollen» und ich bedauere die undankbare Mühe, die Sie und Herr Graf sich gegeben, so viele Unschicklichkeiten mit so vieler Kunst zu verbergen.
Ich bin mit aufrichtiger Hochachtung
Dero gehorsamstergebenster
M. Mendelssohn
Berlin den 9. Oct. 1772"

"Dear Sir!
I am most obliged for the distinction you have conferred upon me and send you my heartfelt thanks. Mr. Graf's paintbrush and your own engraving chisel have endowed my likeness with all that which Nature denied to the original version. I do recognize my effigy, but not as I perceive it in the mirror; it seems rather more like a striking vision my closest lady friend may have of me in a morning dream. In all other regards, I must probably second the opinion of a friend who, upon seeing your beautiful work in copper, stated: "Moses, my friend! Your body presents the same challenge to the artist as does your soul to the well-meaning theologian: Although both clearly are too fine to simply discard, these gentlemen, for all their professional skills, hardly know what to make of them;" and I feel sorry for the thankless efforts which you and Mr. Graf have made to conceal so artfully so much that is uncomely.
I remain, most respectfully, your most obedient and devoted
M. Mendelssohn
Berlin, October 9th, 1772"

BILDERFABRIK

Nr. 216 Johann Friedrich Bause
(1738–1814): Porträt Moses
Mendelssohn
(nach Anton Graff)
Leipzig, 1772
Kupferstich, 25 × 18,1 cm
JMB

Nr. 217 Friedrich Jentzen
(1815–1901): Porträt
Moses Mendelssohn
(nach Anton Graff)
Berlin, vor 1870
Lithografie, 36,5 × 23,5 cm
Mendelssohn-Gesellschaft,
Berlin

O. NR. JOHANN ELIAS HAID
(1739–1809): PORTRÄT
MOSES MENDELSSOHN
(NACH ANTON GRAFF)
undatiert
Schabkunstblatt, 22,5 × 14,5 cm
SBB PK, Musikabteilung mit
Mendelssohn-Archiv

O. NR. JOHANN LINDNER
(1839–1906): PORTRÄT
MOSES MENDELSSOHN
(NACH ANTON GRAFF)
München, 1887
Kupferstich
Bayerische Staatsbibliothek,
München

Die Porträts von Daniel Chodowiecki

The Portraits by Daniel Chodowiecki

Kein Künstler hat Mendelssohns Bild selbst so häufig und so unterschiedlich als Zeichner und in Kupferstichen festgehalten, variiert und verbreitet wie der ihm freundschaftlich verbundene Daniel Chodowiecki. Der reformierte Christ schätzt den jüdischen Gelehrten als guten Menschen und Aufklärer, mag aber – ähnlich wie der Theologe Lavater – die Treue des Moses zum Judentum nicht verstehen. Seine Kinder bringt er gelegentlich am Laubhüttenfest in Mendelssohns Haus, um ihnen jüdische Gebräuche zu zeigen. Erstmals scheint er den Philosophen 1773 porträtiert und das verkleinerte Bild nach dem Gegendruck öfters für verschiedene Auftraggeber gezeichnet zu haben. Mendelssohn selbst hat festgestellt, sein Maler Bernhard Rode sei ein „imitateur de la nature embellie", Chodowiecki dagegen „la Nature!"

No artist captured, varied and spread Mendelssohn's image as frequently and variously as an illustrator and etcher as Daniel Chodowiecki, who was on friendly terms with him. The Reformed Christian appreciates the Jewish scholar as a good man and enlightener, but—similar to the theologian Lavater—can not understand Moses' loyalty to the Jewish faith. He occasionally brings his children to Mendelssohn's house on the Feast of Tabernacles to demonstrate Israelite customs to them. He seems to have first painted a portrait of the philosopher in 1773 and, after counterprinting, drew the reduced image more often for various buyers. Mendelssohn himself stated that his painter Bernhard Rode was an "imitateur de la nature embellie," while Chodowiecki was "la Nature!"

NR. 218 DANIEL CHODOWIECKI
(1726–1801): PORTRÄT
MOSES MENDELSSOHN
Berlin, 1773
Rötel, 24 × 21 cm
Privatbesitz, Köln

Nr. 219 Daniel Chodowiecki (1726–1801): Porträt Moses Mendelssohn
Berlin, ca. 1775
Rötel, 31,1 × 25,8 cm
JMB (Foto: Jens Ziehe)

Nr. 220 Daniel Chodowiecki
(1726–1801): Porträt
Moses Mendelssohn
Berlin, 1774
Rötel, 37 × 26,3 cm
SMB PK, Kupferstichkabinett

Nr. 222 Peter Haas (1754 – nach 1804): Porträt Moses Mendelssohn (nach Daniel Chodowiecki)
1774
Kupferstich, 10,9 × 7,90 cm
Nachlass Angelika von Mendelssohn-Siebeck, Berlin

Einzelblatt aus einem Tableau in „Das Basedowische Elementarwerk. Ein Vorrath der besten Erkenntnisse zum Lernen, Lehren, Wiederholen und Nachdenken", 1774. Mendelssohn war an diesem Großprojekt des Dessauer Reformpädagogen Johann Bernhard Basedow beratend beteiligt.
Single page from a tableau in: "The Basedow Elementary Work. A reservoir of the best knowledge for learning, teaching, repeating and reflection" (1774). Mendelssohn was involved in this major project of the Dessau reform pedagogue Johann Bernhard Basedow in an advisory capacity.

o. Nr. Daniel Chodowiecki (1726–1901): Porträt Moses Mendelssohn
undatiert
Fotografie einer verschollenen Zeichnung, 8 × 6,5 cm
SBB PK, Musikabteilung mit Mendelssohn-Archiv

Chodowiecki entwickelt ein idealisiertes Porträt auf der Basis einer karikaturenhaften Skizze. Diese Zeichnung wird mit Hilfe des Abklatschverfahrens reproduziert. Sie dient als Vorlage für Abrahams Medaille und einen Kupferstich.
Chodowiecki develops an idealized portrait based on a cartoon-like sketch. The drawing is reproduced using the counterproofing technique. It serves as the basis for Abramson's medallion and a copperplate engraving.

Nr. 223 Jacob Abraham (1723–1800) und Abraham Abramson (1752/54–1811): Medaille mit Porträt Moses Mendelssohns
1774
Silber, geprägt, 4,37 cm Durchmesser
Deutsches Historisches Museum, Berlin

Nr. 130 Moses Samuel Löwe (1756–1831): Moses Mendelssohns Examen am Berliner Thor zu Potzdam (nach Daniel Chodowiecki)
1792
Kupferstich, 11 × 8 cm
SBB PK, Musikabteilung mit Mendelssohn-Archiv

Mendelssohn in der Sammlung und den Schriften Lavaters

Mendelssohn in Lavater's Collection and Writings

Johann Caspar Lavater (1741–1801), ein reformierter Geistlicher aus Zürich, begründet mit seinen 1775 erschienenen „Physiognomischen Fragmenten" eine Modewissenschaft, die breit diskutiert wird. Auf der Suche nach einer universalen Sprache der göttlichen Natur leitete er das Wesen eines Menschen, den Charakter, aus dem Äußeren, den Gesichtszügen, ab. Mendelssohn steht diesen spekulativen Überlegungen kritisch gegenüber.

Doch wie schon in der Frage der Taufe, zu der Lavater Mendelssohn einige Jahre zuvor gedrängt hatte, spielte Mendelssohn als Jude eine zentrale Rolle in Lavaters christlich fundiertem Gedankengebäude. Lavater sammelte unterschiedliche Mendelssohn-Darstellungen. Seine Kommentare zu diesen Bildern schwanken zwischen Idealisierung und Ressentiment.

Johann Caspar Lavater (1741-1801), a Reformed clergyman from Zurich, established a fashionable science that was widely discussed with his "Physiognomic Fragments" published in 1775. In search of a universal language of divine nature, he deduced the essence of a person, his character, from his appearance, his facial features. Mendelssohn is critical of these speculative reasonings.

However, as in the question of baptism, which Lavater had urged Mendelssohn to consider a few years earlier, Mendelssohn as a Jew played a central role in Lavater's Christian-based body of thought. Lavater collected various portrayals of Mendelssohn. His comments on these images oscillate between idealization and antipathy.

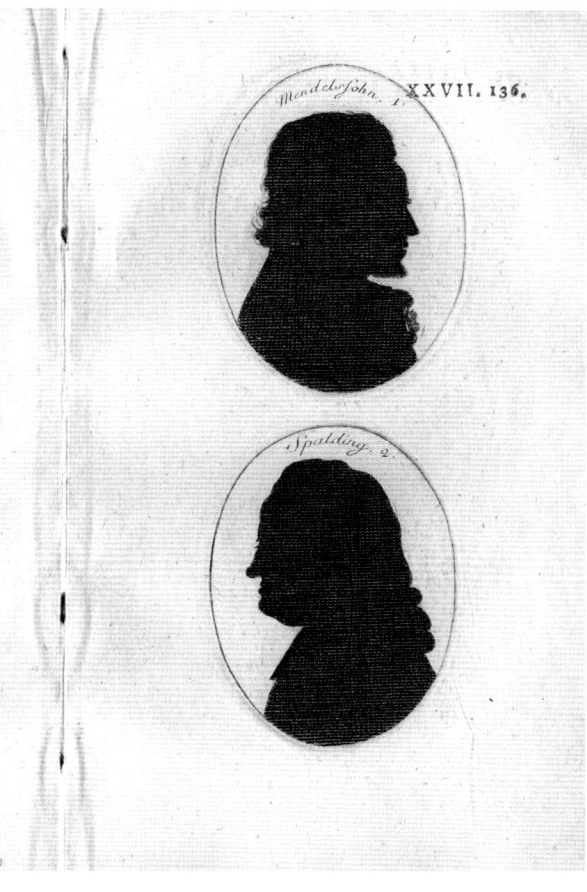

O. NR. PORTRÄT
MOSES MENDELSSOHN
in: Johann Caspar Lavater:
„Physiognomische Fragmente",
Bd. 1, Winterthur
1783
Scherenschnitt
Privatbesitz

Beim Vergleich der Profile „vorzüglicher Menschen" kommentiert Lavater: „Aus der Stirn und der Nase wird man sehr leicht tiefeindringenden, richtigen Verstand herausfinden". Mendelssohns Mund sei „viel feiner" als der des Theologen Spalding.
When comparing the profiles of "excellent people", comments Lavater: "From the the forehead and the nose, it is very easy to discover the deep, penetrating right mind". Mendelssohn's mouth was "much finer" than that of the theologian Spalding.

O. NR. PORTRÄT
MOSES MENDELSSOHN
1775
Scherenschnitt
SBB PK, Musikabteilung
mit Mendelssohn-Archiv

In der 1. Auflage seiner „Fragmente" erkennt Lavater an den Augen dieses Profils „*eine Sokratische Seele! Die Bestimmtheit der Nase [...]. Ja, ich seh ihn, den Sohn Abrahams, der einst noch mit Plato und Moses – erkennen und anbeten wird, den gekreuzigten Herrn der Herrlichkeit!*"
In the 1st edition of his "Fragments" Lavater recognizes from the eyes of this profile "a Socratic soul! The definiteness of the nose [...] Yes, I see him, the son of Abraham, who one day still with Plato and Moses—will recognize and worship, the crucified Lord of glory!" (see No. 184)

NR. 225 PORTRÄT MOSES MENDELSSOHN
Berlin, 1778
Kupferstich, 13,1 × 9,7 cm
Österreichische Nationalbibliothek Wien

Veröffentlicht und kommentiert von Johann Caspar Lavater in Band 4 seiner „Physiognomischen Fragmente", 1778: „Und so unvollkommen dieß zwar sehr ähnliche Bild seyn mag, (besonders scheint mir in der Gegend der Augenbraue eine sehr charakteristische Schärfe zu fehlen) – Nur noch so ein Umriß eines Profils – und keinen Mendelssohnschen Geist! Nur so eine Stirn ohne lichthellen Scharfsinn – so ein Aug unter solcher Augenbraue ohne selbstlebendige Vernunft – so ein Mund ohne Weisheit! – "
Zwischen 1778 und 1811 wurde diese Darstellung in mehreren Variationen publiziert.

Published and annotated by Johann Caspar Lavater in volume 4 of his "Physiognomic Fragments", 1778: "And as imperfect as this very similar picture may be, (especially in the area of the eyebrow a very characteristic sharpness seems to me to be missing)—Only such an outline of a profile—and no Mendelssohnian spirit! Only such a forehead without light-bright acumen—such an eye under such an eyebrow without self-living reason—such a mouth without wisdom!"
Between 1778 and 1811, this depiction was published in several variations.

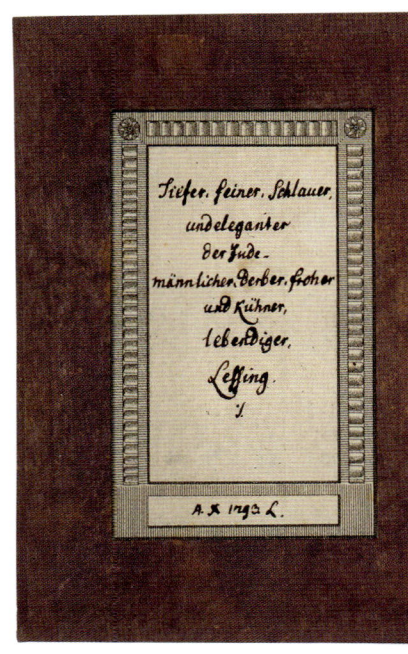

O. NR. CHRISTIAN SCHULE (1764–1816): PORTRÄT MOSES MENDELSSOHN
1811
Punktierstich
Privatbesitz, Berlin
(Foto: Manfred Fuß)

NR. 173 JOHANNES PFENNINGER (1765–1825): GOTTHOLD EPHRAIM LESSING UND MOSES MENDELSSOHN
undatiert
Aquarell, 7,2 × 6,8 cm
Österreichische Nationalbibliothek Wien

Aus der Sammlung Lavaters. Er sah, was er sehen wollte: *„Tiefer, feiner, Schlauer / und eleganter / der Jude / männlicher, derber, froher / und kühner, / lebendiger / Lessing / A. X 1793 L"*
From Lavater's collection. He saw what he wanted to see: "Deeper, finer, cleverer / and more elegant / the Jew / manlier, coarser, more joyful / and bold, / more lively / Lessing / A. X 1793 L"

Das sogenannte Zingg-Porträt

The So-called Zingg Portrait

Der Schweizer Künstler Adrian Zingg, ein Freund Anton Graffs, wurde vor allem als Landschaftsmaler bekannt. Als Mendelssohn mit seinem Freund Hennings Dresden besuchte, wurde er von Zingg „im Profil" gezeichnet. Da dieses Pastell aus der Familie Hennings stammte, wurde es später Adrian Zingg zugeschrieben.

The Swiss artist Adrian Zingg, a friend of Anton Graff, became known primarily as a landscape painter. When Mendelssohn visited Dresden with his friend Hennings, he was drawn "in profile" by Zingg. Since this pastel came from the Hennings family, it was attributed to Adrian Zingg.

Nr. 226 Adrian Zingg (1734–1816) (zugeschrieben): Porträt Moses Mendelssohn
1776
Pastell auf Leinwand, 41 × 35,5 cm
The Israel Museum, Jerusalem
(Foto: Eli Posener)

Aus dem 1936 aufgelösten Lessing-Museum kam das Porträt an das Museum der Jüdischen Gemeinde. Nach Raub durch die NS-Behörden wurde es in den 1950er Jahren dem heutigen Israel Museum übergeben.

The portrait came to the Jewish Community Museum from the Lessing Museum, which was dissolved in 1936. After being looted by the Nazi authorities, it was handed over to today's Israel Museum in the 1950s.

Die Porträts von Johann Christoph Frisch

The Portraits by Johann Christoph Frisch

Johann Christoph Frisch, der Historienmaler und Schüler Christian Bernhard Rodes, porträtiert Moses Mendelssohn zwei Mal: 1778 in Anlehnung an eine antike Kamee und 1783 als natürliches Porträt. Das Gemälde von 1778 sah nur in einer Auktion 1932 das Licht der Öffentlichkeit. Es zeigt Mendelssohn erstmals als antiken Philosophen und prägt das Bild des „Sokrates von Berlin".

Umso lebensnaher und intimer erscheint uns das spätere, das zum beliebtesten aller Mendelssohn-Porträts wurde. Moses' Sohn Joseph bezeichnet es im Vergleich zum Porträt des Anton Graffs als „treffender noch" und stellt fest: „Alle andren Bilder von Mendelssohn, die wir gesehen haben, gezeichnet, gemalt, in Kupfer gestochen, in Stein geschnitten oder in Glas abgedrückt, sind mehr oder weniger Zerrbilder, die von den Zügen des Originals nichts wiedergeben."

Johann Christoph Frisch, the historical painter and student of Christian Bernhard Rode painted two portraits of Moses Mendelssohn: in 1778, based on an ancient cameo, and in 1783 as a natural portrait. The 1778 painting saw the light of day only in an auction in 1932. It shows Mendelssohn for the first time as an ancient philosopher and shapes the image of the "Socrates of Berlin".

The later one, which became the most popular of all Mendelssohn portraits, seems all the more true to life and intimate. Moses' son Joseph describes it as "even more accurate" in comparison to the portrait by Anton Graff, and states: "All other pictures of Mendelssohn that we have seen, drawn, painted, engraved in copper, cut in stone, or printed in glass, are more or less distorted images that reflect nothing of the features of the original."

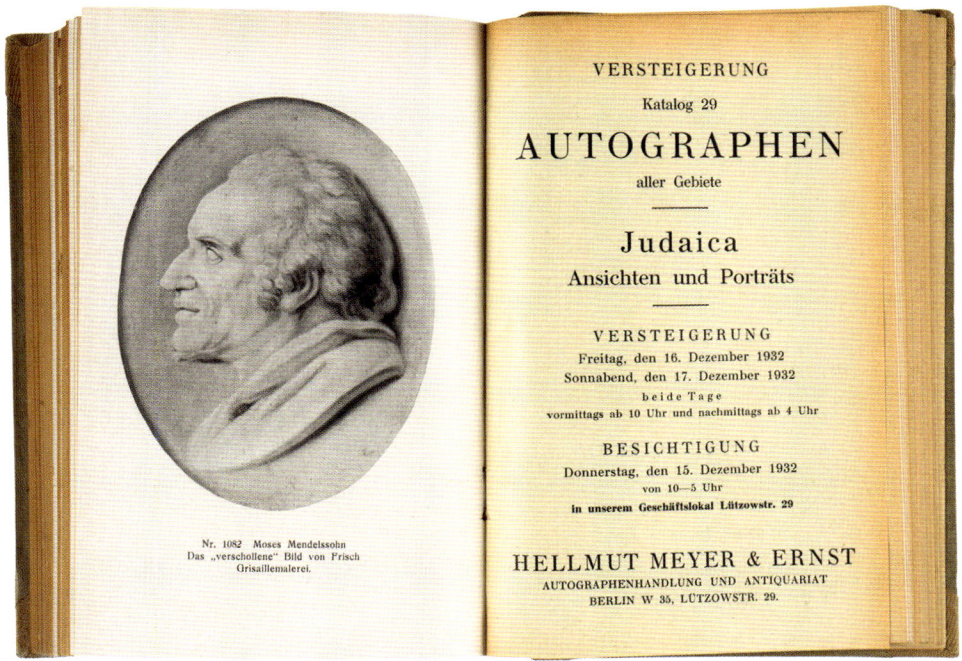

Nr. 236 Johann Christoph Frisch (1738–1815): Porträt Moses Mendelssohn
abgebildet in: Auktionskataloge, Meyer & Ernst, Berlin, 1931/32
Original (Öl auf Leinwand von 1778) verschollen
JMB (Foto: Roman März)

Das heute verlorene Gemälde von Johann Christoph Frisch zeigt Mendelssohn in Anlehnung an antike Kameen (Schmucksteine) und ist zu seinen Lebzeiten sehr populär.
The painting of Mendelssohn by Johann Christoph Frisch, current location unknown, is based on ancient cameo portraiture (engraved gems), a very popular style in his time.

BILDERFABRIK

Nr. 239 Porträt Moses Mendelssohn (nach Johann Christoph Frisch)
nach 1778
Radierung, 12,2 × 19,5 cm
SBB PK, Musikabteilung
mit Mendelssohn-Archiv

Nr. 250 Ring der Stiftung 1791 mit Porträt Moses Mendelssohn
1791
Rotgold, Perlmutt, Glasüberfang,
2 × 1,6 cm (Ringkopf)
Privatbesitz

Sieben jüdische Verehrer Mendelssohns schließen sich zusammen, um sein Aufklärungsvermächtnis zu bewahren. Jeder erhält einen Ring. Der letzte erhaltene befindet sich in Familienbesitz.
Seven of Mendelssohn's Jewish admirers come together to safeguard his Enlightenment legacy. Each of them receives a ring. The last of the seven rings is currently in family ownership.

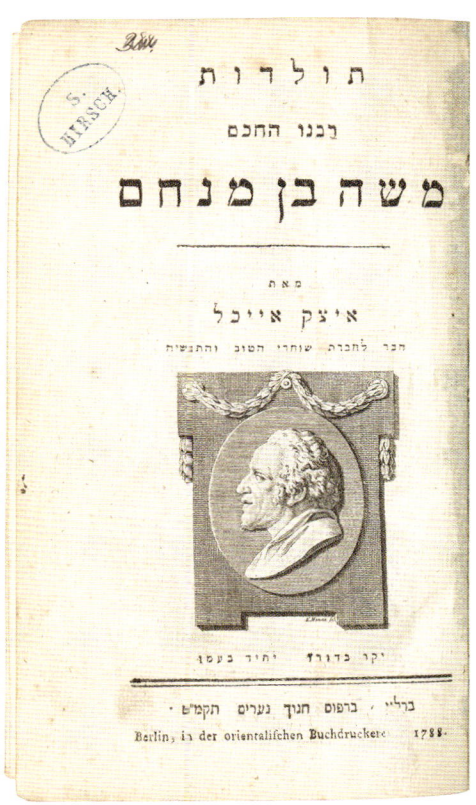

Nr. 237 Eberhard Henne (1759–1828): Porträt Moses Mendelssohn
in: Isaak Abraham Euchel (1756–1804),
Toledot Rabbenu he-chakham
Mosche ben-Menachem
(Das Leben unseres Lehrers des
Weisen Moses Mendelssohn)
Berlin: Orientalische Buchdruckerei,
1788
Kupferstich, Radierung, 13,6 × 8,5 cm
JMB (Foto: Jens Ziehe)

o. Nr. Daniel Berger (1744–1825) Portpät Moses Mendelssohn (nach Johann Christoph Frisch)
1786
Kupferstich
Privatbesitz Berlin

Das griechische Bibelzitat unter Mendelssohns Lebensdaten lautet: „Siehe, ein echter Israelit, an dem kein Falsch ist." (Joh. 1,47)
The Greek Bible passage under Mendelssohn's life dates reads: "Behold, a true Israelite, in whom there s no guile." (John 1:47)

Nr. 238 Moses Samuel Löwe (1756–1831): Porträt Moses Mendelssohn
1784
Kupferstich, 14,5 × 10,3 cm
SBB PK, Musikabteilung mit Mendelssohn-Archiv

Das Blatt erschien 1784 als Frontispiz der Zeitschrift HaMeassef
The print was published as a frontispice of the magazine HaMeassef in 1784.

o. Nr. Moses Samuel Löwe
(1756–1831) und Johann Daniel
Laurens (1772–1835):
Sokrates und Mendelssohn
1819
Kupferstich, 19,5 × 14 cm
Privatbesitz, Israel

BILDERFABRIK

Nr. 227 Johann Christoph Frisch (1738–1815): Porträt Moses Mendelssohn (Original)
Berlin, 1783
Öl auf Leinwand, 60,3 × 52 cm
JMB (Foto: Roman März)

Johann Christoph Frisch, der auch Marcus Elieser Bloch, Marcus Herz und Isaac Daniel Itzig porträtiert, malt das am häufigsten reproduzierte Gemälde im Hochzeitsjahr der Tochter Brendel/Dorothea und dem Erscheinungsjahr von „Jerusalem".

Johann Christoph Frisch, who has also made portraits of Marcus Elieser Bloch, Marcus Herz, and Isaac Daniel Itzig, paints what will be the most frequently reproduced of these portraits in 1783, the same year as the wedding of Mendelssohn's daughter Brendel/Dorothea and the release of "Jerusalem".

Nr. 228 Johann Christoph Frisch (1738–1815): Porträt Moses Mendelssohn (Replik)
Berlin, 1786
Öl auf Holz, 24,2 × 19,3 cm
SBB PK, Musikabteilung mit Mendelssohn-Archiv

BILDERFABRIK

Nr. 229 Johann Christoph Frisch (1738–1815): Porträt Moses Mendelssohn
Berlin, nach ´783
Öl auf Leinwand, 59 × 45,5 cm
SBB PK, Mus kabteilung mit Mendelssohn-Archiv

Nr. 230 Moses Mendelssohn (1729–1786): Albumblatt für den Hofmaler Frisch
08.10.1785
Papier, Tinte
SBB PK, Abteilung Handschriften und Historische Drucke

An Herrn Hofmaler Frisch
Natur, von Vernunft geleitet, begeistert den weisen Künstler, wenn er arbeitet; Vernunft, von Natur geleitet, ergötzt ihn, wenn er ruhet.
Berlin den 8. Oct. 1785
Bey Ueberreichung seiner Morgenstunden, Moses Mendelssohn
To the Court Painter Frisch
Nature, guided by reason, inspires the wise artist when he works; reason, guided by nature, delights him when he rests.
Berlin the 8th of Oct. 1785 while presenting his Morgenstunden, Moses Mendelssohn

BILDERFABRIK

Nr. 209 Vermutlich Moses Samuel Löwe (1756–1831):
1793
Gouache auf Elfenbein, 9 × 6,5 cm
Herzog August Bibliothek
Wolfenbüttel

Nr. 232 Porträt Moses Mendelssohn (nach Johann Christoph Frisch)
ca. 1800
Miniatur auf Pappe, 11,5 × 10 cm
Stiftung Neue Synagoge Berlin –
Centrum Judaicum, Berlin

Nr. 231 Johann Gotthard
Müller (1747–1830): Porträt
Moses Mendelssohn
(nach Johann Christoph Frisch)
Stuttgart, 1786/87
Kupferstich, 29,4 × 20,7 cm
JMB (Foto: Roman März)

o. Nr. Moritz Steinla
(1791–1858): Porträt
Moses Mendelssohn
Gotha, 1821
Stahlstich, 22,8 × 16,7 cm
SBB PK, Musikabteilung
mit Mendelssohn-Archiv

Nr. 177 Johann Gottfried Schadow (1764–1850): Sokrates im Kerker
nach 1786
Feder, in Braun, laviert, aquarelliert, weiß gehöht, 52,9 × 71,2 cm
SMB PK, Kupferstichkabinett

Mendelssohns „Phädon" macht Sokrates zum Vorbild für eine Moralität, die aus Vernunft und Wissen, nicht aus dem Glauben schöpft. Schadow zeigt die Szene, als der gefangene Sokrates seinem Tod entgegensieht, und Mendelssohn im Kreis der Schüler.
In Mendelssohn's Phaedon, Socrates is presented as the paradigm of a morality grounded in reason and knowledge rather than in faith. Schadow depicts the scene in which the philosopher, surrounded by his disciples, awaits death in prison. Mendelssohn can be seen among them.

Die Büste von Jean Pierre Antoine Tassaert

The Bust of Jean Pierre Antoine Tassaert

Der in Antwerpen geborene Jean Pierre Antoine Tassaert lebt seit 1775 als Hofbildhauer in Berlin. Bei ihm bestellen 20 Freunde, darunter der Gründungs- und Förderzirkel der Jüdischen Freischule, eine Büste ihres Mit-Initiators, Ideengebers und Förderers. Das Marmor-Original wird in den Räumen der Schule aufgestellt. Die Sponsoren erhalten jeweils einen Gipsabguss. Es war das erste vollplastische repräsentative Bildnis eines Juden. So ungewöhnlich war diese Ehrung, dass sie weitere Künstler zur Reflexion und zur eigenständigen Auseinandersetzung anregte.

Born in Antwerp, Jean Pierre Antoine Tassaert has lived in Berlin since 1775 as a court sculptor. Twenty friends, including the founding and sponsoring circle of the Jewish Free School, order from him a bust of their co-initiator, idea giver and promoter. The marble original will be placed in the school's rooms. The sponsors each receive a plaster cast. It was the first fully sculptural, representative portrait of a Jew. So unusual was this tribute that it stimulated further artists to reflect and to engage with it independently.

Nr. 233 Joseph Friedrich Darbes (d'Arbes), (1747–1810): Porträt Moses Mendelssohn (nach der Büste von Antoine Tassaert)
Berlin, 1786
Öl auf Leinwand, 61,4 × 43,6 cm
Leo Baeck Institute, New York
(Foto: Roman März)

Ersatz für eine Büste oder künstlerisches Experiment? Die Mendelssohn-Verehrerin Dorothea von Kurland besitzt es und hat es vielleicht auch in Auftrag gegeben. Der Maler steht mit dem kurländischen Adel ebenso in Verbindung wie mit der Berliner jüdischen Oberschicht.

A substitute for a bust or an artistic experiment? This portrait belongs to Mendelssohn's admirer Dorothea of Courland, who may also have commissioned it. The artist paints portraits of the nobility in Courland (in today's Latvia) as well as Berlin's Jewish elite.

Nr. 180 Antoine Tassaert (1727–1788): Büste Moses Mendelssohn
1785
Marmor, 54 × 42 × 27 cm

Mendelssohn ist als antiker Philosoph dargestellt. Der Künstler versucht durch den geöffneten Mund die Unmittelbarkeit einer Gesprächssituation einzufangen. Tassaerts Schüler, Johann Gottfried Schadow, kommentiert dies kritisch.
Mendelssohn is depicted as an ancient philosopher. The artist tries to capture the immediacy of a conversational situation by showing the mouth open. Tassaert's student Johann Gottfried Schadow comments on this critically.

O. NR. BÜSTE MOSES MENDELS-SOHNS AUF IHREM SOCKEL
ca. 1929
Fotografie
Jüdisches Historisches Institut „Emanuel Ringelblum", Warschau

Die von dem Dichter Karl Wilhelm Ramler formulierte Inschrift auf dem Sockel nimmt Bezug auf Sokrates und auf Mendelssohns Treue zum Judentum: Moses Mendelssohn / Geboren in Dessau im Jahr 1729 von jüdischen Ältern. / Ein Weiser wie Sokrates den Gesetzen der Väter getreu / Unsterblichkeit lehrend und unsterblich wie er.

The inscription on the pedestal, composed by poet Karl Wilhelm Ramler, refers to Socrates and Mendelssohn's loyalty to Judaism: Moses Mendelssohn / Born in Dessau in 1729 of Jewish elders. / A sage like Socrates faithful to the laws of the fathers / Teaching immortality and immortal like him.

O. NR. DIE BESCHÄDIGTE BÜSTE VOR DER RESTAURIERUNG
Foto: Andreas Artur Hoferick
2007

Die Büste gelangte seit 1964 in beschädigtem Zustand wieder in den Besitz der Jüdischen Gemeinde und ist seitdem im Foyer des Gemeindehauses in der Fasanenstraße aufgestellt. 2007 wurde sie restauriert.
The bust came back into the possession of the Jewish Community in a damaged condition in 1964 and has been placed in the foyer of the community center in Fasanenstraße since then. In 2007 it was restored.

Nr. 235 Johann Gottfried Schadow (1764–1850): Porträt Moses Mendelssohn mit „Phädon", „Psalmen" und „Jerusalem"
ca. 1786/87
Radierung, 17,8 × 10,5 cm
JMB (Foto: Roman März)

Nr. 234 Jean Joseph François Tassaert (1765–1825): Porträt Moses Mendelssohn (nach Antoine Tassaert)
nach 1786
Kupferstich, 13 × 10,4 cm
JMB (Foto: Roman März)

Mendelssohns Nachleben im Bild

Posthumous Images of Mendelssohn

Pläne für ein Mendelssohn-Denkmal gibt es schon bald nach seinem Tod. Sie scheitern an der Finanzierung und leben in der Fantasie fort. Die Verehrer Mendelssohns stellen sein Bild in christlich inspirierte Apotheosen, Bilderserien jüdischer Gelehrter und Historienszenen. Sie zeigen ihn in repräsentativen Gemälden, intimen Mikrographien und populären Buchillustrationen.

Plans for a monument to Mendelssohn were made soon after his death. They fail due to funding and live on in fantasy. Mendelssohn's admirers place his image in Christian-inspired apotheoses, picture series of Jewish scholars and history scenes. They show him in representative paintings, intimate micrographs, and popular book illustrations.

Nr. 249 David Rosenberg: Ansicht eines zum 100. Geburtstag von Moses Mendelssohn geplanten Denkmals
Brüssel, 1829
Lithografie, 47 × 33,5 cm
JMB (Foto: Roman März)

O. NR. CHRISTIAN RÄNTZ (1751–1794): AUF MOSES MENDELSSOHNS TOD
1786/94
Radierung, 19,9 × 15,4 cm
SBB PK, Abteilung Handschriften und Historische Drucke

Mendelssohn wird im Himmel von den Erzvätern erwartet: Man erkennt Moses an den Gesetzestafeln, Aaron an Priesterstab und -Haube. In der Mitte steht die Patriarchengestalt Abrahams. Auf der zweiten, dichter komponierten Fassung übernimmt das Gedicht die Identifikation der drei Gestalten.

Mendelssohn is awaited in heaven by the archfathers: Moses is recognized by the tablets of the law, Aaron by the priestly staff and hood. In the center there is the patriarchal figure of Abraham. On the second, more densely composed version, the poem takes over the identification of the three figures.

Nr. 178 Christian Räntz (1751–1794): Auf Moses Mendelssohns Tod
1786/94
Radierung, 41 × 25,7 cm
JMB (Foto: Roman März)

Seinen verunsicherten Zeitgenossen bezeugt Mendelssohn die Unsterblichkeit der Seele philosophisch – und verewigt sich durch sein Lebenswerk. Nach seinem Tod wird er selbst als unsterblich imaginiert.

Mendelssohn philosophically proves to his anxious contemporaries that the soul is immortal—and gains immortality himself through his life's work. After his death, he himself is imagined as immortal.

Nr. 210 Vermutlich Otto Christian Sahler (1720–1811):
undatiert
Wachsrelief auf Holz, 17,5 × 15 cm
SBB PK, Musikabteilung mit
Mendelssohn-Archiv

**O. NR. PORTRÄT
MOSES MENDELSSOHN**
undatiert
Öl auf Leinwand, 48 × 38 cm
SBB PK, Musikabteilung
mit Mendelssohn-Archiv

BILDERFABRIK

o. Nr. Heinrich Pollem
(1804–1844): Porträt
Moses Mendelssohn
Detmold, um 1830
Lithographie, 12,5 × 8,2 cm
Bayerische Staatsbibliothek,
München

o. Nr. Rudolf Schellenberg
(1740–1806): Porträt
Moses Mendelssohn
undatiert
Radierung, 7,8 × 7,2 cm
SBB PK, Musikabteilung
mit Mendelssohn-Archiv

Nr. 241 Mikrographische Federzeichnung mit Porträt Moses Mendelssohn
undatiert
Tinte auf Papier, 9,4 × 5,4 cm
Herzog August Bibliothek
Wolfenbüttel

In Anlehnung an Mendelssohns Übersetzung des 21. Psalms:
„Herr Mendelson in Seligkeit. Von den Weisheit Mendelsons zu melden, vergleicht einen tapfren Kriegeshelden. Ewiger Deiner Weisheit frohlockt der Weise. Wie jauchzt er Deines Triumphs. Seines Herzens Wunsch verleihst Du Ihm. Versagtest nicht was seine Lippen flehen. Kamest Ihm mit gebenedeitem Gut zuvor. Um Leben bat er Dich. Dies gabst du Ihm. Langes Leben Menschenalter lang"

Based on Mendelssohn's translation of the 21st Psalm:
"Mr. Mendelson in beatitude. To report of the wisdom of Mendelson compares to a brave war hero. [...] Eternal of Thy wisdom the wise man rejoices. How he rejoices in Your triumph. You grant his heart's desire. Thou didst not deny what his lips plead. You preceded him with blessed goods. For life he asked Thee. This you gave him. Long life, human age, long".

BILDERFABRIK

o. Nr. Demarchi und Colni:
Porträt Moses Mendelssohn
Mailand, 1818
Radierung, 16,2 × 11,6 cm
JMB (Foto: Roman März)

**Nr. 252 Wolf Pascheles
(1814–1857): Porträt
Moses Mendelssohn**
undatiert
Aquatinta, 34,7 × 29,5 cm
Jüdisches Historisches Institut
„Emanuel Ringelblum", Warschau

Nr. 95 Moritz Daniel Oppenheim (1800–1882): Lavater und Lessing bei Moses Mendelssohn
Frankfurt am Main/Hanau, 1856
Öl auf Leinwand, 68,5 × 55,4 cm
The Magnes Collection of Jewish Art and Life, University of California, Berkeley, Gift of Vernon Stroud, Eva Linker, Gerda Mathan, Ilse Feiger and Irwin Straus in memory of Frederick and Edith Straus

Lessing
Mendelssohns Freund. Er war nicht am Streit beteiligt und nicht in Berlin, als er stattfand.
Blickt verächtlich auf Lavater herab und ist empört.

Mendelssohn
Macht eine Geste des kritischen Nachdenkens. Er hält sich zurück, die Füße zusammen - ruhig. Geschäftsbuch, Feder und Manuskript zeigen ihn als Buchhalter und Autor.
Lavater unterbrach die beiden Freunde beim Schachspiel, einem Sinnbild für Logik, Vernunft und Gleichberechtigung.

Lavater
Schwarz gekleidet als Geistlicher. Mit Hut und Wanderstab als Reisender und Gast.
Präsentiert das von ihm übersetzte Buch. In der Widmung fordert er Mendelssohn auf, Argumente gegen das Christentum vorzubringen oder zu konvertieren.
Er greift nach Mendelssohns Arm. Die Geste der Übertretung zeigt seine Anmaßung und wiederholt sich in den gespreizten Beinen.

Fromet und das Haus
Fromet bekommt hier nur eine Nebenrolle. Bescheiden, mit gesenkten Augen, bringt sie den Tee.
Über der Tür ein Segensspruch für die Kommenden und die Gehenden. Wasserbassin, Hängelampe und Gebetstafel zeigen das religiöse Haus; die Bücher und das Bild des Königs, den Gelehrten und preußischen Patrioten.

Hebräische Inschriften
Auf der linken Seite, unter dem Porträt Friedrichs II., ist eine Misrach-Tafel zu sehen, die Osten als Richtung des Morgengebets anzeigt.
Auf der rechten Seite, über der Tür, steht ein Zitat aus dem Deuteronomium: „Gesegnet bist du, wenn du heimkehrst, gesegnet bist du, wenn du ausziehst." (Dtn 28,6)

Lessing
Mendelssohn's friend. He was not in Berlin at the time and did not take an active role in the conflict.
Looks down in contempt and indignance on Lavater.

Mendelssohn
Makes a gesture of critical reflection. He keeps to himself, feet together— quietly.
Account book, pen and manuscript show him as a bookkeeper and an author.
Lavater interrupted the two friends playing chess, serving as a symbol for logic, reason and equality.

Lavater
Dressed in black as a clergyman. With walking stick and hat as a traveler and guest.
Presents the book he translated including the dedication urging Mendelssohn to bring up arguments against Christianity or to convert.
He reaches for Mendelssohn's arm. The gesture of transgression shows his insolence and is repeated in his spreadeagled legs.

Fromet and the house
Fromet only gets a supporting role here. Modestly, with lowered eyes, she brings the tea.
Above the door a blessing for those coming and those going.
Water basin, hanging lamp and prayer board show the religious house, books and the picture of the king the scholar and the Prussian patriot.

Hebrew inscriptions
On the left side, below the portrait of king Frederick II, a misrach plate marks the East, the direction of prayer, used for the morning prayer at home. On the right side, above the door, a quote from the from the Book of Deuteronomy to be seen: "Blessed shalt thou be when thou comest in, and blessed shalt thou be when thou goest out." (Dtn. 28:6)

BILDERFABRIK

O. NR. S. MAIER: LAVATER UND LESSING BEI MOSES MENDELSSOHN (NACH MORITZ DANIEL OPPENHEIM)
Verlag Karlsruhe/St. Petersburg: J. Velten, nach 1856
Druck Paris: Lemercier
Lithographie, 40,3 × 33,2 cm
Mendelssohn-Gesellschaft, Berlin

Aufgrund des großen Erfolgs entstehen für verschiedene Zielgruppen unterschiedliche Stiche nach der Oppenheim'schen Vorlage.
Wer findet die Unterschiede?
Due to the great success, different engravings for different target groups are created after Oppenheim's painting. Who can find the differences?

O. NR. WILHELM AARLAND (1822–1906): LAVATER UND LESSING BEI MOSES MENDELSSOHN (NACH MORITZ DANIEL OPPENHEIM)
1860, publiziert in der „Gartenlaube", Heft 25
Holzstich
Mendelssohn-Gesellschaft, Berlin

Bilder aus dem Leben deutscher Dichter.
Nr. 2.

Mendelssohn, Lessing und Lavater
über Religion disputirend.
Nach dem Originalgemälde des Professor Oppenheim.

Es war im Jahre 1763, kurz nach Beendigung des siebenjährigen Krieges, als ein junger Theolog aus Zürich nach Berlin reiste, um die dortige gelehrte Welt kennen zu lernen. Er selbst war eine hochbegabte Natur voll Poesie, aber auch voll Schwärmerei und Ueberschwänglichkeit, die ihn bei seinem Hange zum Mysticismus und allem Wunderbaren früher oder später auf gefährliche Abwege führen mußte. Schon damals genügte ihm nicht das vorhandene Christenthum, er sehnte sich nach einem unmittelbaren Verkehr mit der überirdischen Welt und schrieb seinem Gebete die Kraft zu, Wunder zu thun. Er war von einem gewissen geistlichen Hochmuth nicht frei zu sprechen, den er freilich unter sanften Formen und einer liebenswürdigen Persönlichkeit geschickt verbarg. In den Nebenstunden beschäftigte er sich mit physiognomischen Studien, denen er eine große Wichtigkeit beilegte. Zu diesem Zwecke verfehlte er selten, die berühmten Männer seiner Zeit in Gesellschaft eines Freundes, des Malers Füßli, aufzusuchen, um ihre Silhouetten aufzunehmen und ihre Züge in oft mehr poetischen, als wahren Ausdrücken zu schildern. Oft verführte ihn dabei seine Freundschaft oder die Vorliebe für sein System, dem gesunden Menschenverstande zu widersprechen. Trotz dieser Schwächen war er aber eine der hervorragendsten Erscheinungen des achtzehnten Jahrhunderts, mit dem er die Liebe zur Menschheit, den Drang nach Freiheit, aber auch die Sucht nach dem Wunderbaren und Abenteuerlichen theilte. Dieser Mann hieß Johann Kaspar Lavater.

In Berlin machte der christliche Theolog die Bekanntschaft des jüdischen Philosophen Moses Mendelssohn, er besuchte ihn

BILDERFABRIK

O. NR. LOUIS KATZENSTEIN (1824–1907): BEIM SCHACHSPIEL
1861
Öl auf Leinwand, 93 × 76 cm
Museumslandschaft Hessen Kassel,
Neue Galerie, Städtischer Kunstbesitz

Der Kassler Künstler nimmt Oppenheims Gemälde auf und deutet es um: Mendelssohn spricht deutlicher, Lavater bleibt konzilianter, Lessing gemäßigter, das Haus bürgerlicher.

The Kasse׳ artist takes Oppenheim's painting and reinterprets it: Mendelssohn speaks more clearly, Lavater remains more conciliatory, Lessing more moderate, the house more bourgeois.

Nr. 131 Izsó (Isidor) Köves (1853–1917): Moses Mendelssohn vor Friedrich dem Grossen
1930
Fotografie des um 1880/90 entstandenen Gemäldes
Jüdisches Historisches Institut „Emanuel Ringelblum", Warschau

Der ungarische Künstler inszeniert eine legendäre Begegnung in Sanssouci, die vielfach patriotisch ausgeschmückt wurde, aber nie stattgefunden hat.

The Hungarian artist stages a legendary encounter in Sanssouci, which was often patriotically embellished, but never never took place.

Objektverzeichnis

List of Objects

Nr. 110 Jakob Liepmann (1803–1865): Stillleben mit Porträt Moses Mendelssohn
1823
Öl auf Leinwand
The Israel Museum, Jerusalem, Bequest of Mrs. S.B. Dimson, London (Foto: Eli Posener)

„Wir träumten von nichts als Aufklärung"

So wie es war, kann es nicht weitergehen. Noch bleibt vieles, wie es ist. Das 18. Jahrhundert ist der Anfang vom Ende einer alten Zeit. Naturkatastrophen und Religionskriege erschüttern Glaubenssätze. Rationale Argumente fallen ins Gewicht. Aufklärung – Licht an! – wird zum Programm. Hüter religiöser Tradition lassen sich ungern infrage stellen. An der Macht sind Monarchen. Bürgerrechte sind begrenzt; von Menschenrechten redet vorerst keiner. Doch es kommt etwas in Bewegung.

Moses Mendelssohn reist als Teenager nach Berlin. Mit seinen Freunden wird er zum Motor der Berliner Aufklärung, für die Juden zum Brückenbauer. Gegen Betonköpfe und Fakten-Verdreher setzt er auf die Kraft der Vernunft.

"We dreamed of nothing but enlightenment"

It cannot go on the way it used to be, but plenty of it persists. The eighteenth century marks the beginning of the end for an age that is set in its ways. Natural disasters and religious wars are shaking the foundations of faith. Rational arguments are gaining sway. All eyes now fall on the Enlightenment—the clarity of sunrise! The guardians of religious traditions do not tolerate being questioned. Monarchs reign supreme. Civil rights are restricted and human rights not even invented yet. But change is in the air.

Moses Mendelssohn travels to Berlin as a teenager. Together with his friends, he will become the engine of the Berlin Enlightenment and a bridge-builder for the Jews. Defying die-hards and distorters of facts, he champions the power of reason.

Auf den folgenden Seiten sind die Objekte der Moses-Mendelssohn-Ausstellung „Wir träumten von nichts als Aufklärung" aufgeführt, ausgenommen die in der „Bilderfabrik" (Raum 7) versammelten Mendelssohn-Porträts und jene vereinzelten, die in anderen Themenbereichen zu sehen sind. Die Exponate sind, soweit sie nicht bereits in der „Bilderfabrik" gezeigt wurden, regulär in der Reihenfolge des Gangs durch die Ausstellungsräume aufgelistet: Raum 1 *Von Dessau nach Berlin; Der „Jude von Berlin"*; Raum 2 *Dialog & Netzwerk;* Raum 3 *Aufklärung & Verdunkelung; Religion; Übersetzung & Pädagogik;* Raum 4 *Menschenrechte;* Raum 5 *Ästhetik & Freundschaft;* Raum 6 *Bestimmung des Menschen;* Raum 7 *Judenporzellan; Was wird aus Moses Mendelssohn?* Raum 8 *Filme.*

Bei Objekten, deren Urheber (Maler, Fotograf, Kupferstecher usw.) im Verzeichnis nicht genannt wurde, ist dieser unbekannt.

The following section lists the objects in the Moses Mendelssohn exhibition "We dreamed of nothing but enlightenment", with the exception of the Mendelssohn portraits gathered in the "Bilderfabrik" (Room 7) and those isolated ones that can be seen in other chapters (status at the time of the editorial deadline). The exhibits are listed according to the tour through the exhibition rooms: Room 1 **From Dessau to Berlin; The "Jew of Berlin";** *Room 2* **Dialogue & Networks;** *Room 3* **Enlightenment Versus the Shadows; Religion; Translation & Education;** *Room 4* **Human Rights;** *Room 5* **Aesthetics & Friendship;** *Room 6* **Destiny of Man;** *Room 7* **Jewish Porcelain; What is Moses Mendelssohn's Legacy?** *Room 8* **Films.**

For objects whose creator (painter, photographer, engraver etc.) is not mentioned in this list, the author is unknown.

Von Dessau nach Berlin

From Dessau to Berlin

Wer von sonstwo in Preußens Residenz einwandert, hat erst mal nichts zu melden. Zwischen Dessau und Berlin gibt es Verbindungen – und Hickhack.

Moses, geboren 1729, ist der Jüngste von Dreien. Vater Mendel ist Dessaus Synagogendiener und Lehrer. Die Vorfahren der Mutter sind große Gelehrte bis zur 20. Generation. In der Talmudschule des Rabbi Fränkel lernt Moses Tag und Nacht. Hier kriegt sein Körper den ersten Knacks, sein Verstand den Kick. Er entdeckt die Texte des Maimonides 500 Jahre zuvor: Lust an der Logik, am freien Denken.

Sollten junge Bildungsmigranten unbegleitet einwandern? Als David Fränkel zum Oberrabbiner nach Berlin berufen wird, folgt ihm der 14-jährige Moses. Das Hallesche Tor wird für ihn zum Portal in eine neue Welt.

Any outsider who migrates to the Prussian capital begins as a nobody. Dessau and Berlin have connections—but also frictions.

Moses, born in 1729, is the youngest of three children. His father, Mendel, serves as the sexton at Dessau's synagogue. His ancestors on his mother's side have been great scholars for twenty generations. Moses studies night and day at Rabbi David Fränkel's Talmudic school, where he first struggles with his sickly body and stimulates his sharp mind. Encountering 500-year-old writings by Maimonides, he delights in their logic, their free-thinking spirit.

Should young students migrate for the sake of their education, even unaccompanied? When Fränkel is appointed Chief Rabbi of Berlin, the 14-year-old Moses follows him there. Hallesches Tor, the city's southern gate, becomes a portal to a new world.

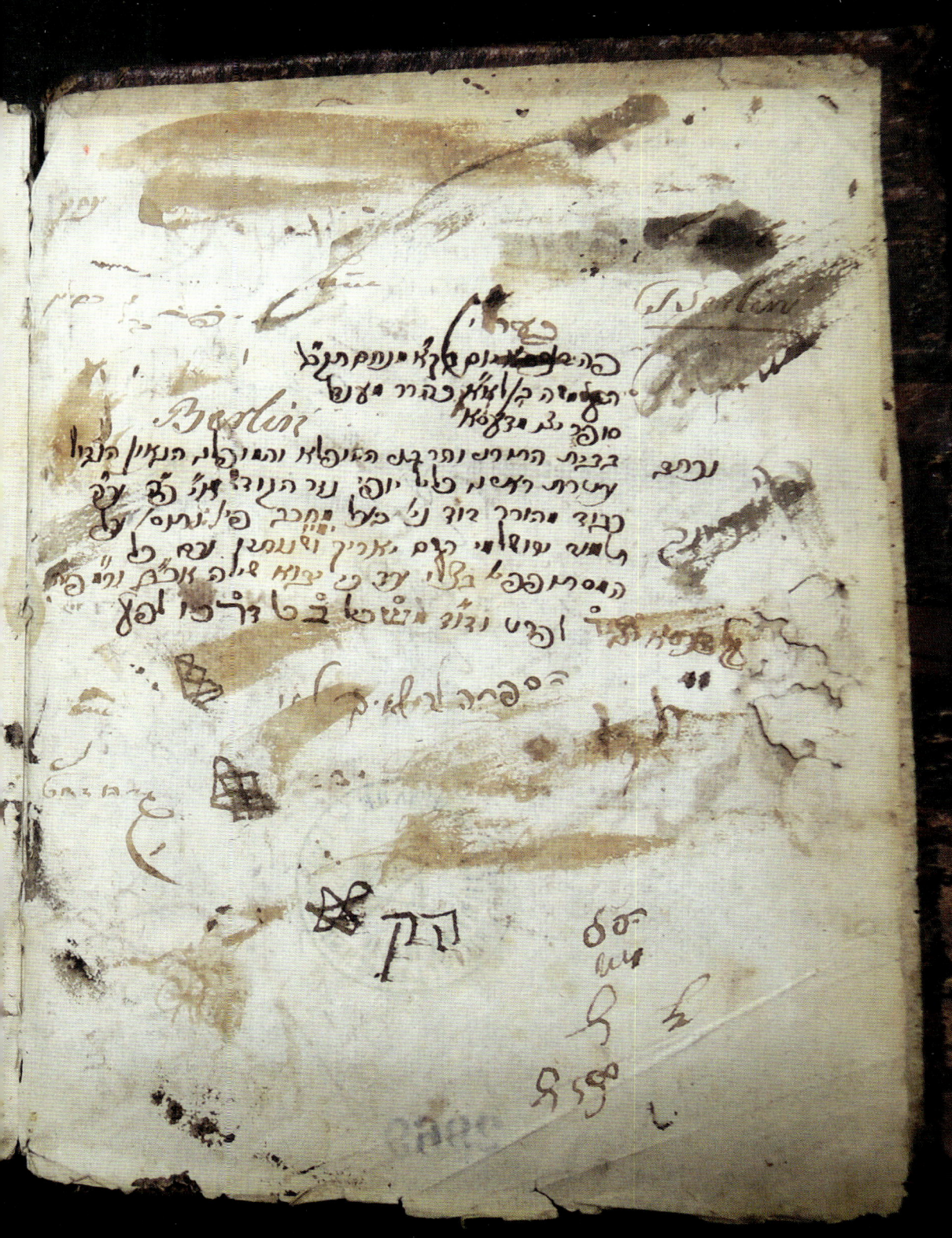

OBJEKTVERZEICHNIS

Nr. 16 Isaak Ben Scheschet (1326–1408): Scheelot u-teschuwot (Responsen)
Riva, 1559
Jüdisches Museum Prag

Nr. 2 Stadt Dessau. Gesamtansicht über die Mulde mit Hospitalkirche, Neuem Schloss, Pfarrkirche und Rathaus
Zerbst, 1710
Kupferstich
JMB
Dessau ist die Residenzstadt des Fürstentums Anhalt. Nach dem Dreißigjährigen Krieg reformiert der Fürst sein Land. Juden sind Teil der Wirtschaftspolitik.
Dessau is the capital of the principality of Anhalt. After the Thirty Years' War, the ruling prince decides to reform his realm. Jews are part of his economic policy.

Nr. 4 Moses Mendelssohns Geburtshaus in Dessau
ca. 1800
Öl auf Leinwand
Privatbesitz, Köln
Das Haus gehört einem christlichen Seifensieder.
The house belongs to a Christian soap maker.

Nr. 3 Ansicht der Alten Synagoge in Dessau
Ca. 1900
Fotografie
Museum für Stadtgeschichte Dessau
Eine junge Gemeinde, ähnlich wie die Berliner. Hof und Leipziger Messe bestimmen die Wirtschaft, Rabbiner David Fränkel und eine hebräische Druckerei das intellektuelle Leben.
A young Jewish community like that of Berlin. Its economic cornerstones are the prince's court and the Leipzig fair. Rabbi David Fränkel and a Hebrew printing house shape its intellectual life.

Als zwölfjähriger Schüler will Moses dem verehrten Rabbi David Fränkel ein wertvolles Buch zu schenken, die „Responsen des Rabbi Isak ben Scheschet" von 1559. Die Ortsangabe seiner Widmung wird er später in Berlin, wohin er dem Lehrer nachgereist ist, vor der Geschenkübergabe korrigieren. So könnte man sein ältestes erhaltenes Schriftstück verstehen. Die Widmung von 1740/42 lautet:

„Hier zu Berlin, am zweiten des Trostmonats Aw [5]502
Der geringe Moses, Sohn meines Herrn Vaters, des ehrwürdigen Rabbi Mendel Sofer, sein Hort und Erlöser beschütze ihn! Aus Dessau Berlin. Geschrieben im Hause des Thora-beflissenen, des rabbinischen Gelehrten, des ausgezeichneten und hervorragenden, des grossen Gaon, der Krone unseres Hauptes, des Kranzes der Schönheit, des Diadems der Heiligkeit, des Israel Liebenden, der Zierde des Geschlechts, Säule des Exils, unseres ehrwürdigen Lehrers, des Rabbi David, es leuchte sein Licht, des Verfassers des Kommentars und der Glossen zum Jerusalemischen Talmud, Gott verlängere seine Tage und Jahre in Gemeinschaft mit allen, die sich in seinem Schatten bergen, bis der Erlöser kommt, des Vorsitzenden des Gerichtshofs und Haupts der Akademie am Orte, der heiligen Gemeinde Dessau, mögen Zion und Jerusalem wiedererbaut werden, im Jahre ,Und David war verständig in allen seinen Wegen' nach der kleinen Zeitrechnung.
Dieses Buch gehört mir."

Twelve-year-old Moses plans to give his teacher, the esteemed Rabbi David Fränkel, a valuable book as a gift: the Responsa of Rabbi Isaak ben Sheshet, published in 1559. Later, after following his teacher to Berlin, he crosses out and corrects the place of his inscription before giving the gift. The dedication, from 1740/42, reads:

*"Here in Berlin, on the 2nd of Av, the month of comfort, [5]502
The humble Moses, son of the honorable Rabbi Mendel the scribe—may his Rock preserve him and give him life! From Dessau Berlin. Written in the home of the Torah-devoted rabbinic scholar, the extraordinary and remarkable, the great genius, the crown of our head, the wreath of beauty, diadem of holiness, lover of Israel, grace of his generation, pillar of Exile, our honorable teacher, Rabbi David may his light shine, the author of the commentary and glosses to the Jerusalem Talmud, may God lengthen his days and years in the company of all who dwell in his shadow until the Messiah shall come, the Senior Judge of the Court and Head of the Academy in this town, the sacred community of Dessau, may Zion and Jerusalem be rebuilt, in the year "David was prudent in all his undertakings" according to the Lesser Era.
This book belongs to me."*

Nr. 5 Moses Mendelssohns Geburtshaus in Dessau, Strassenansicht
ca. 1900
Fotografie
Museum für Stadtgeschichte Dessau

Nr. 6 Moses Mendelssohns Geburtszimmer in Dessau
ca. 1929
Fotografie
Jüdisches Historisches Institut „Emanuel Ringelblum", Warschau

Nr. 8 Grabstein von Moses Mendelssohns Vater Mendel Heymann in Dessau
ca. 1929
Fotografie
Jüdisches Historisches Institut „Emanuel Ringelblum", Warschau

Nr. 9 Grabstein von Moses Mendelssohns Schwester Jente Heymann in Dessau
ca. 1929
Fotografie
Jüdisches Historisches Institut „Emanuel Ringelblum", Warschau

Nr. 10 Viktor Weiss (1913–1966): Dessauer Marsch auf Berlin
Berlin, 1932
Karikatur aus einer Berliner Zeitung
Druckgrafik
SBB PK, Musikabteilung mit Mendelssohn-Archiv

Nr. 13 Porträt David Fränkel (1704–1762)
undatiert
Fotografie
Jüdisches Historisches Institut „Emanuel Ringelblum", Warschau

Der Lieblingsschüler des Talmud-Herausgebers David Fränkel studiert die Tora, den mittelalterlichen Religionsphilosophen Maimonides und den Interpreten-Chor der jüdischen Tradition.
As the star pupil of Talmud publisher David Fränkel, Moses studies the Torah, medieval religious philosopher Maimonides, and the numerous commentators of Jewish tradition.

Nr. 14 Moses Maimonides (1135/38–1204): Mischne-Tora
Jeßnitz: Yisrael bar Avraham, 1739
SBB PK

Der „Jude von Berlin"

The "Jew of Berlin"

Preußen braucht nützliche Zuwanderer. Aber wer hat Bleiberecht? Für Juden gilt: Nur Wohlhabende sollen bleiben, nicht die Armen. Moses will lernen. Der Bettelstudent erobert sich den Bildungskanon und die Sprachen des Abendlandes.

Sein Brotberuf als Buchhalter in einer Seidenfabrik schützt ihn vor Ausweisung. Er gewinnt Freunde bei den Gelehrten. Erste Texte erscheinen anonym, später unter „Moses Mendelssohn". Seine intellektuelle Karriere erregt Aufsehen. Man bewundert diesen Ausnahme-Juden, den „juif à Berlin".

Der Philosoph wird zu einer Instanz fortschrittlichen Denkens. Seine Ehe mit der Hamburger Kaufmannstochter Fromet macht beide zu Stammeltern einer einflussreichen Familie.

Prussia needs useful immigrants. But who will be granted residency? When it comes to Jews, the "right to stay" is reserved for the wealthy, not the poor. Moses wants to learn. The starving student masters the classic canon and Western European languages.

His day job as a bookkeeper at a silk factory protects him from eviction. Meanwhile, he befriends some of the local scholars. He publishes early writings, first anonymously and later under the name Moses Mendelssohn. His career as an intellectual turns heads. People marvel at this unusual Jew, this "Jew from Berlin."

The philosopher becomes a luminary of progressive thought. His marriage to Fromet, the daughter of a Hamburg businessman, is the foundation of the influential Mendelssohn dynasty.

zu Nr. 43

OBJEKTVERZEICHNIS

Nr. 43 Tora-Vorhang
Berlin, 1774–75
Seide, Leinen, bestickt
JMB
Der Tora-Vorhang war ein Geschenk Moses Mendelssohns an das kleine Berliner Bethaus, das er besuchte. Die Seide dafür stammte vermutlich von Fromets Hochzeitskleid. Der Anlass der Schenkung ist nicht bekannt.
Moses and Fromet Mendelssohn donated this Torah curtain to the small Berlin prayer house Moses frequented. Its silk likely came from Fromet's wedding dress. The occasion of the donation is unknown.

Inschriften zu den Darstellungen auf dem Querbehang: Zwei Bundestafeln – Goldener Leuchter – Goldener Altar – Schaubrot – Kupfernes Waschbecken
Inschrift auf dem Vorhang: Krone der Tora – Das spendeten der gelehrte R. Moses, sein Fels und Erlöser möge ihn schützen, Sohn des Rabbiner R. Menachem Mendel s.[eligen] A.[ngedenkens] aus Dessau – und seine Ehefrau Frau Fromet, sie möge leben, Tochter unseres Lehrers R. Abraham s.[eligen] A.[ngedenkens] Gugenheim – 535 nach der kleinen Zeitrechnung
Text on the valance: Two Tablets of the Covenant—Golden candle holder—Golden altar—Showbread ("Bread of the Presence")—Copper wash basin—
Text on the curtain: Crown of the Torah—This was donated by the learned R. Moses, may his rock and savior protect him, son of Rabbi R. Menachem Mendel of blessed memory, from Dessau.—and by his wife Ms. Fromet, [long] may she live, daughter of our teacher R. Abraham, of blessed memory, Gugenheim.—In the year 535 according to the Jewish calendar

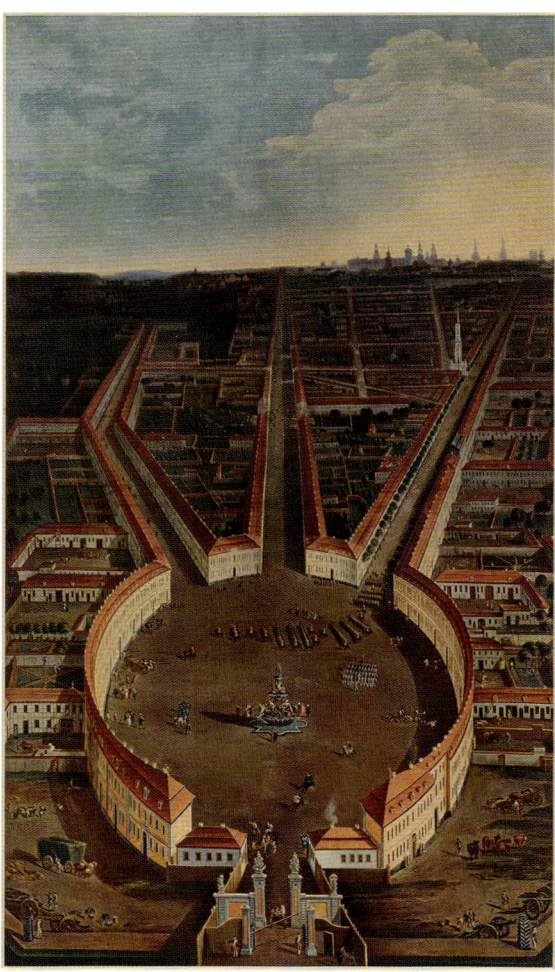

Nr. 12 Dismar Degen (ca. 1690–1753): Friedrichstadt
um 1735
Fotografie des im Zweiten Weltkrieg verlorengegangenen Originals
SMB, Kunstbibliothek
(Foto: Dietmar Katz)

Über alte und neue Sprachen, Geistes- und Naturwissenschaften erschließt sich dem Selfmade-Gelehrten die Mehrheitskultur, unterstützt von seinen Mentoren Aaron Gumpertz, Israel Samosz und Abraham Kisch.
Through ancient and modern languages, the humanities, and the natural sciences, the self-taught scholar absorbs the majority culture with the help of his mentors Aaron Gumpertz, Israel Samoscz, and Abraham Kisch.

Nr. 18 Johann Gustav Reinbeck (1682–1741): Betrachtungen über die in der Augspurgischen Confession enthaltene und damit verknüpfte Göttliche Wahrheiten
Berlin/Leipzig: Haude, 1740
SBB PK, Abteilung Handschriften und Historische Drucke

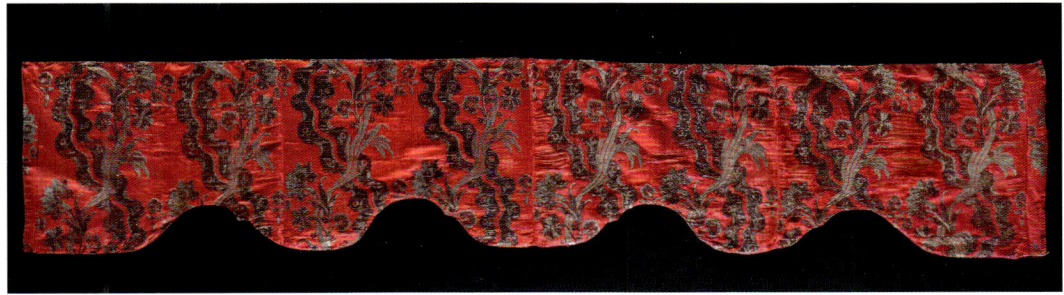

**Nr. 19 John Locke (1632–1704):
De Intellectu Humano.
In Quatuor Libris**
London: A. & J. Churchil, 1701
SBB PK, Abteilung Handschriften
und Historische Drucke

**Nr. 20 Christian Wolff
(1679–1754): Vernünfftige
Gedancken von den Kräfften
des menschlichen Verstandes
und ihrem richtigen Gebrauche**
Halle: Renger, 1719
SBB PK, Abteilung Handschriften
und Historische Drucke

**Nr. 21 Yonah Ben-Eliyahu
Landsofer (1678–1712): Scheelot
u-teschuwot meil zedaka**
Prag, 1756
Universitätsbibliothek Leipzig
Ein hebräischer Euklid-Kommentar
für mathematische Studien.

**Nr. 22 Carl Traugott Fechhelm
(1748–1819): Blick vom Schlossplatz in die Königstrasse**
Berlin, 1788
Öl auf Leinwand
Stiftung Stadtmuseum Berlin
Das Gemälde zeigt im Vordergrund
Alt-Cölln mit Schloss und Militär.
Jenseits der Brücke sieht man die
Bürgerhäuser der Königstraße in
Alt-Berlin, wo die jüdische Bevölkerung hauptsächlich wohnte.
*In the foreground, the painting
shows Old Cölln, where the palace
and soldiers are located. The Jewish
population mostly resides in Old
Berlin, which can be seen across the
bridge, including the townhouses on
Königstraße.*

„Gestern sind unsere kijjumim
[Niederlassungsrechte] be-esras
ha-Schem [mit Gottes Hilfe] accordirt
worden. Nun mehr sind Sie so gut als
R. Mausche Wesel ein preußischer
Unterthan, und müssen die preußische Partey ergreifen. Sie werden
also auf gut preußisch alles glauben,
was zu unserm Vorteil ist. Die Russen,
die Türken, die Amerikaner stehen
uns alle zu Dienst und erwarten nur
unsern ersten Wink. Unsere Münz wird
noch besser werden als Banco, die
ganze Welt wird Sicherheit in Berlin
suchen, und unsere Börs wird
berühmt seyn, von dem Schloßplatz
bis an unser Haus. Dieses alles
müssen Sie glauben, denn Sie haben
kijjumim b- Berlin."
Moses Mendelssohn an seine
Verlobte Fromet Gugenheim in
Altona, 26. März 1762

*"Yesterday, our kiyyumim [residency
rights] were approved, with God's
help. From now on, you are, just as
much as R. Mausche Wesel, a Prussian
subject, and must take the Prussian
side. Hence, in good Prussian fashion,
you will believe that everything is in
our favor. The Russians, the Turks, the
Americans are all at our service and
merely await our first signal. Our mint
will grow even superior to Banco, the
entire world will seek out stability in
Berlin, and our stock exchange will be
famed all the way from the Palace
Square to our house. You must believe
all of this, for you have kiyyumim
be-Berlin [residency in Berlin]."*
Moses Mendelssohn to his fiancée
Fromet Gugenheim in Altona, March
26th, 1762

**Nr. 23. Lambrequin. Querbehang
einer Fensterdraperie**
Vermutlich Seidenmanufaktur
Bernhard Isaak
Berlin, ca. 1765
Seide, Metallfäden
SPSG, Neues Palais
Aus der Kammer vor der Bibliothek
in der Wohnung Friedrichs II. im
Potsdamer Neuen Palais; wahrscheinlich in der Manufaktur Bernhard
Isaaks angefertigt.
*From the chamber adjoining the
library in Frederick II's apartments
at the New Palace in Potsdam; mostly
likely produced at Bernhard Isaak's
manufactory.*

Vom Lehrer für die Söhne eines
Seidenfabrikanten zum erfolgreichen
Textilkaufmann. Der ungeliebte Beruf
raubt dem Denker Zeit, aber sichert
seiner Familie die Existenz in Berlin.
*After tutoring a silk manufacturer's
sons, he becomes a successful
textile merchant himself. His unloved
profession eats up the thinker's time,
but secures his family's livelihood in
Berlin.*

**Nr. 24 Johann Karl Gottfried
Jacobsson (1725–1789):
Schauplatz der Zeugmanufakturen in Deutschland**
Berlin: Mylius, 1755
DHM Berlin

**Nr. 25 Schutzbrille Moses
Mendelssohns mit Etui**
zweite Hälfte des 18. Jahrhunderts
Horn, Glas, Leder, beschichtet
und geprägt
LBI New York

OBJEKTVERZEICHNIS

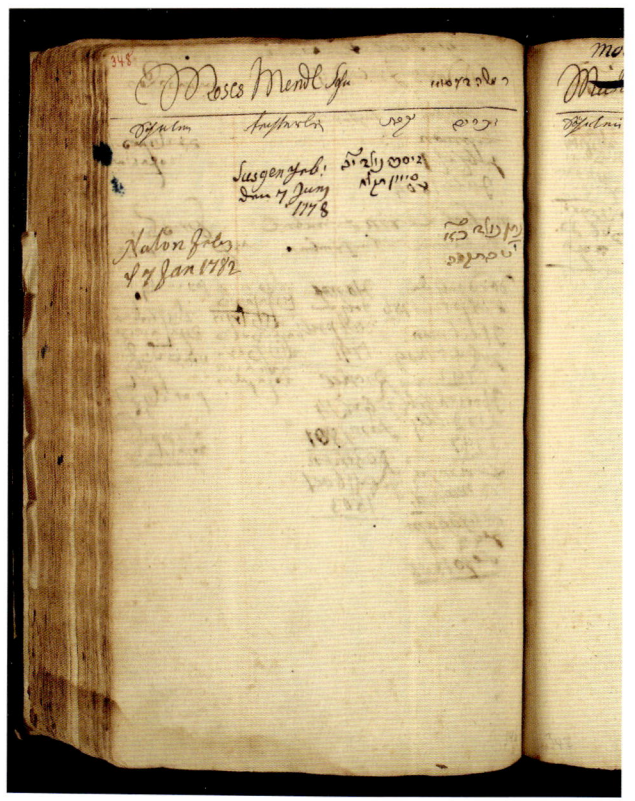

ZU NR. 37

**NR. 26 KLADDE DER SEIDEN-
MANUFAKTUR BERNHARD ISAAK
WITWE UND SÖHNE**
Berlin, 1734
Papier, Tinte
SBB PK, Musikabteilung mit
Mendelssohn-Archiv

**NR. 29 PORTRÄT FROMET MENDELS-
SOHN MOSES MENDELSSOHN,
BRAUTBRIEFE**
Berlin: Schocken, 1936
JMB

**NR. 30 JOSEPH FRIEDRICH AUGUST
D'ARBES (1747–1810): PORTRÄT
BRENDEL/DOROTHEA VEIT,
GEB. MENDELSSOHN (1764–1839),
SCHRIFTSTELLERIN UND LITERATUR-
KRITIKERIN**
1798
Pastell
Mendelssohn Gesellschaft, Berlin

**NR. 31 LUDWIG BUCHHORN
(1770–1856): PORTRÄT SIMON VEIT
(1754–1819), KAUFMANN UND
BANKIER (NACH JOHANNES VEIT)**
Berlin, 1811/50
Stahlstich
JMB

Nr. 32 Porträt Abraham Mendelssohn
undatiert
Scherenschnitt
SBB PK, Musikabteilung mit
Mendelssohn-Archiv

Nr. 33 Porträt Joseph Mendelssohn (1770–1848), Bankier
undatiert
Grisaille, Öl auf Karton
Nachlass Angelika von
Mendelssohn-Siebeck

Nr. 34 Georg Friedrich Raschke (1772–1849): Porträtminiatur Nathan Mendelssohn (1781–1852), Mechaniker und Instrumentenbauer
undatiert
Miniatur auf Elfenbein
Mendelssohn Gesellschaft, Berlin

Nr. 35 Porträt Recha Meyer, geb. Mendelssohn (1767–1831)
undatiert
Öl auf Leinwand
Privatbesitz, Köln

Nr. 36 Porträt Mendel Meyer (gest. 1831), Kaufmann
undatiert
Öl auf Leinwand
Privatbesitz, Köln

Nr. 37 Geburtsregister der Jüdischen Gemeinde zu Berlin. Eintragungen für Susgen (geb. 1778) und Nathan (1781–1852) Mendelssohn
Berlin, 1782
Papier, Tinte
LBI

Nr. 38 Hypothekenvertrag von Moses und Fromet Mendelssohn
Berlin, 1765–1789
Papier, Tinte, Siegel
LBI

Berlin, 20. April 1762

„Liebste Fromet! Ihr Schreiben min Chaul hamaued Peßach [aus den Peßach-Zwischenfeiertagen] habe gestern erhalten. Die Post-Sekretärs wissen vermuthlich nit, wie viel an unsern Briefen gelegen ist. Sie glauben, es wären nur gemeine Handelsgeschäfte, die aufgeschoben werden können. [...]

Indeßen liebe Fromet! Ist gar nit ratsam, jaum tauw kaan [hier das Wochenfest] zu halten, weil die hauzoaus [Ausgaben] gar zu stark wären. Mein Kind! So lang mir die Zeit währt, bevor ich das Glück habe Dich die Meinige zu nennen, so müssen wir doch so viel möglich trachten, hauzoaus zu menagiren [mäßigen], bifrat [besonders] für unsere Eltern, die mehr Kinder sche-jichju w'ßaarechno jomim [sie mögen am Leben bleiben und ihre Tage seien lang] zu besorgen haben. Wenn Sie achar jaum tauw imjirze ha-Schem mischom [nach dem Feiertag, so Gott will, von dort] abreisen, und einen Schabbos zu Havelberg halten, so kommen Sie ungefähr chazi Ssiwon [Mitte des Monats Siwan, Anfang Juni] hierher, [...]

Sie werden sagen, ich denke wie ein Bulgar, immer zu menagiren, niehmals auf die Empfindungen des Herzens. Nein, mein Kind! Sie werden finden, daß mein Herz noch immer so beschaffen ist, wie im vorigen Jahr, als ich Ihnen solches in dem wüsten Garten-Häuschen zu erkennen gegeben. [...]"

Berlin, April 20th, 1762

"Dearest Fromet! I received your letter from the middle days of Passover week. The postal secretaries presumably do not know how much was depending on our letters. They assumed these were only ordinary business dealings that could be put off. [...]

Nevertheless, dear Fromet! It is not at all advisable to spend the festival here because the cost would be much too high. My child! For all the time I must bide before I have the joy to call you mine, we must devote as much thought as possible to economizing our costs, especially for our parents, who have more children to care for—may they live and have long days. If you depart after the holiday, God willing, and spend Shabbos in Havelberg, you will arrive here by roughly mid-Sivan [early June], [...]

You will say I think like a Bulgar, always economizing, and never about the sentiments of the heart. No, my child! You will find that my heart is still as it was when I revealed it to you in the deserted garden pavilion."

Nr. 39 Brief Moses Mendelssohns an Brief an Fromet Gugenheim
20.04.1762
Papier, Tinte
SBB PK, Musikabteilung mit
Mendelssohn-Archiv
Moses und Fromet kommen durch Liebesheirat zusammen. Sie agieren gemeinsam – eine innige Partnerschaft. Schon in den Briefen des Verlobungsjahres diskutieren sie über Gott und die Welt.

Moses and Fromet marry for love. They act as a couple—a very close partnership. In the letters they exchange during their engagement, they are already discussing major spiritual and worldly questions.

OBJEKTVERZEICHNIS

Berlin 18. Juli 1777

„Lieber Mausche leb! Ich hoffe daß Dir mein Schreiben, munter und vergnügt in Königsberg finden wird […]
　Donnerstag beim Aufstehen, waren schon viele gute Freunde bei mir die sich erkundigt haben, wie ich die Nacht geschlafen habe. Nach Mittag kam Herr Lessing und holte mich, mit Brendel und Reikel, zum Cafè bei seiner Frau ab, Professor Engel war auch da. Wir tranken also da Café, und rudelten dabei auf die deutsche und französische Truppe. Ein jeder behauptete, daß es ihm recht wäre von solch elende Aktörs sich amusieren zu lassen. Was meinst Du wol, lieber Mausche, was wir nach dem Café taten? Wir Frauen-Zimmer gingen nach die französischen Komödie, die Manns-Leute nach die deutsche. Und das schönste is, wir amusieren uns beider Seiten. Ich werde mir sogar Mühe geben öfter mit die Kinder hin zu gehen […] Brendel hat die Komödie ziemlich verstanden. Und Reikel wird sich nun Mühe geben sie verstehen zu lernen, wenigsten sizt sie doch heute schohn mit ein französisch Buch in der Hand. Ja, lieber Mausche, nun Visite angenommen Visite gegeben, in der Komödie gewesen. Und bei allen dem lange Weile, die ich doch gar nit empfinde wenn Du bei mir bist, Du mags mir es glauben daß es die drei Tage die erste vergnügte Stunde is, die ich mich hier mit Dir unterhalte. […]"

Berlin, July 18th, 1777

"Dear Mausche live! I hope that my letter will find you cheerful and in good spirits in Königsberg. [...]
　By the time I awoke on Thursday, there were already many good friends there inquiring how I had slept. In the afternoon, Mr. Lessing came and fetched me, along with Brendel and Reikel, to have coffee with his wife; Professor Engel was there too. And so, we drank coffee, and chatted about the German and French troupes. Everyone claimed to be amenable to entertainment by such wretched actors. And what do you think we did after coffee, dear Mausche? We ladies went to see the French comedy, and the men saw the German one. And the best thing was that both sides were entertained. I would even make an effort to take the children there more often. (…) Brendel understood the comedy fairly well. And Reikel will now do her best to learn how to understand it, at least today she is already sitting with a French book in her hand. Yes, dear Mausche, I had a visitor, paid a visit, and saw the comedy. And for all the boredom I never feel when you are with me, you must believe that during these three days, this hour that I chat with you here, is the first cheerful one."

O. NR. PORTRÄT FROMET MENDELSSOHN, GEB. GUGENHEIM (1737–1812)
aus dem Stammbuch Herz Homberg
Scherenschnitt
Mendelssohn-Gesellschaft, Berlin

NR. 40 BRIEF FROMET MENDELSSOHNS AN MOSES MENDELSSOHN
18.07.1777
Papier, Tinte
SBB PK, Musikabteilung mit Mendelssohn-Archiv

NR. 41 BESUCHERBUCH DER HERZOGLICHEN BIBLIOTHEK WOLFENBÜTTEL MIT EINTRAG MOSES UND FROMET MENDELSSOHNS VOM 21.12.1777
1769–1786
Papier, Tinte
Herzog August Bibliothek Wolfenbüttel

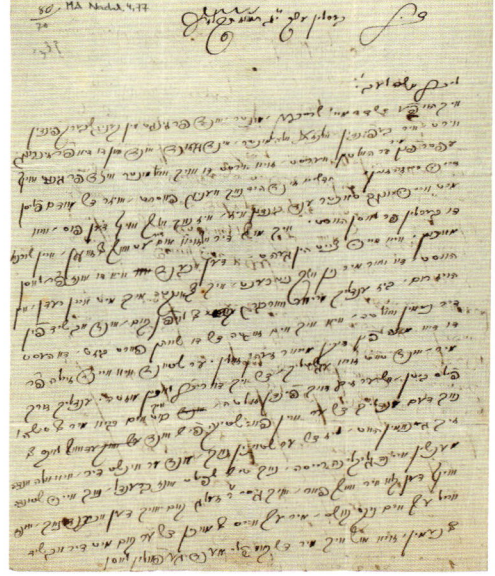

Dialog & Netzwerk

Dialogue & Networks

Bürger verschaffen sich Gehör. Jenseits der Fürstenhöfe entsteht eine neue Öffentlichkeit: in Cafés, Gelehrtenclubs und Publikationen. Der Meinungsaustausch überschreitet Landes- und Standesgrenzen. Im Idealfall zählt das Argument, nicht, wer es vorbringt.

Wie redet man mit Andersdenkenden? Mendelssohn wird zum Dialog-Profi. Er schreibt Bücher in Gesprächsform, als Briefwechsel. Die andere Ansicht denkt er mit. Als Zeitschriftenautor, Redakteur und Gastgeber für Debattierer aus unterschiedlichsten Milieus. Er verteidigt die Meinungsvielfalt, moderiert den Konsens der Vernünftigen – und erlebt utopische Momente der Verständigung.

Civilians are making themselves heard. Outside royal and princely courts, new public spaces are emerging in cafés, scholarly societies, and publications. The exchange of ideas crosses national and estate lines. Ideally, what matters is the argument, not who makes it.

How do you talk to people you disagree with? Mendelssohn becomes an expert at dialogue. He writes books structured as conversations, as exchanges of letters. He considers the opposing viewpoint—as a magazine contributor, an editor, and the host of debaters from various backgrounds. He defends the diversity of opinions, helps the rationalists reach consensus—and takes part in utopian moments of mutual understanding.

Nr. 46 Joseph Friedrich August d'Arbes (1747–1810): Porträt Elisa von der Recke (1754–1833)
Berlin, 1784
Öl auf Leinwand
Stiftung Stadtmuseum Berlin
Dichterin, Halbschwester der Herzogin Dorothea von Kurland, Verehrerin Mendelssohns.
Poet, half-sister of Duchess Dorothea of Courland, admirer of Mendelssohn.

Nr. 47 Joseph Matthias Grassi (1757–1838): Porträt Dorothea von Kurland (1761–1821)
undatiert
Öl auf Leinwand
Lindenau-Museum Altenburg
(Foto: Bertram Kober)
Herzogin und Diplomatin, Verehrerin Mendelssohns.
Duchess and diplomat, admirer of Mendelssohn.

Nr. 48 Daniel Chodowiecki (1726–1801): Porträt Agnes Sophie Schwarz, geb. Becker (1754–1789)
1791
Radierung
JMB
Baltische Schriftstellerin, Freundin Elisa von der Reckes und Mendelssohns im letzten Lebensjahr.
Baltic author, friend of Elisa von der Recke, and of Mendelssohn during the year before his death.

Nr. 51 Daniel Chodowiecki (1726–1801): Gesellschaft in der Gartenlaube
undatiert
Aquarell, Feder
Akademie der Künste Berlin, Kunstsammlung
Geistes- und Naturwissenschaftler, Künstler, Publizisten und Staatsbeamte begegnen einander (halb-)öffentlich oder sehr privat. In der Baumannshöhle und im Gelehrten Kaffeehaus beim Billardspiel, in der Montags- und der Mittwochsgesellschaft, in Gärten und Lauben am Rande der Stadt lernt man, sich zu verständigen, und debattiert.
Humanities scholars, scientists, artists, writers, journalists, and civil servants meet in public, semi-public, and very private spaces. They converse, debate, and learn the art of civil discourse at the Baumann's Cavern wine hall, over billiards at the Learned Coffeehouse, at meetings of the Monday and Wednesday Societies, and in gardens and pavilions on the city's outskirts.

OBJEKTVERZEICHNIS

Nr. 52 Der „Freundschaftstempel" in Gleim's Geburtshause zu Halberstadt (nach Carl Jordan (1826–1907)
1862
Stahlstich
Gleimhaus, Museum der deutschen Aufklärung, Halberstadt
Eine neue Freundschaftskultur: Mit wem man Briefe schreibt, wessen Bücher man begeistert liest, dessen Bild möchte man stets um sich haben.
The enthusiasts of a new 'Culture of Friendship' surround themselves with pictures of the people they exchange letters with and those who write the books they so eagerly read.

Nr. 53 Saal eines öffentlichen Kaffeehauses
1770
Federzeichnung
Staatliche Kunstsammlungen Dresden, Kupferstich-Kabinett

Nr. 54 Anton Graff (1736–1813): Porträt Friedrich Nicolai (1733–1811)
1795
Öl auf Leinwand
Universität Leipzig, Kustodie Kunstsammlung
Buchhändler und Verleger, beständigster Freund Mendelssohns, Partner für zahlreiche publizistische Projekte.
Bookseller and publisher, longstanding friend of Mendelssohn, his partner in numerous journalistic and publishing projects.

„Ich besuche Hrn. Nicolai sehr oft in seinem Garten. (Ich liebe ihn wirklich, theuerster Freund! Und ich glaube, daß unsere Freundschaft noch dabei gewinnen muß, weil ich in ihm Ihren wahren Freund liebe.) Wir lesen Gedichte; Herr Nicolai liest mir seine eigenen Ausarbeitungen vor; ich sitze auf meinem kritischen Richterstuhl, bewundere, lache, billige, tadele, bis der Abend hereinbricht. Dann denken wir noch einmal an Sie, und gehen, mit unsrer heutigen Verpflichtung zufrieden, von einander..."
Mendelssohn an Lessing, 2. August 1756
"I visit Mr. Nicolai quite often in his garden. (I love him genuinely, dearest friend! And I believe our own friendship must further benefit from that, for in him I love a true friend of yours.) We read poetry; Mr. Nicolai reads me his own drafts aloud; I sit on my critical judge's bench, admiring, laughing, affirming, criticizing, until night falls. Then we think of you once again, and part ways, satisfied with our day's duty..."
Moses Mendelssohn to Gotthold Ephraim Lessing, August 2nd, 1756

Nr. 55 Johann Heinrich Tischbein d. Ä. (1722–1789): Jugendbildnis Gotthold Ephraim Lessing (1729–1781)
ca. 1755
Öl auf Leinwand
SMB, Alte Nationalgalerie
Dichter und Aufklärer, im „Dreigestirn" mit Nicolai und Mendelssohn dessen wichtigster Vertrauter, Inspirator und Mitstreiter. Das Porträt gelangte aus der Lessing-Familie über Mendelssohns Freunde Marcus Herz und David Friedländer an die Nationalgalerie.
Poet and Enlightenment thinker. Alongside Mendelssohn and Nicolai, the principle member of the "Three Stars" group and the chief confidant, muse, and ally of the other two. The portrait passed from the Lessing family to Mendelssohn's friends Marcus Herz and David Friedländer before entering the Nationalgalerie's collection.

Nr. 56 Johann David Schleuen (1711–1774): Porträt Thomas Abbt (1738–1766)
Bückeburg, 1766
Kupferstich
JMB
Philosoph, enger Freund und Dialogpartner Mendelssohns.
Philosopher, close friend and debate partner of Mendelssohn's.

Nr. 57 Moses Mendelssohn (1729–1786): Briefumschlag mit Siegelabdruck

12.06.1767
Papier, Wachs
Niedersächsisches Landesarchiv,
Abteilung Bückeburg
Übersetzungsexperimente, Diskurs-
beiträge, rastlose Korrespondenz.
Die jüdische Tradition von Diskussion
und Kommentar entwickelt Mendelssohn weiter.
*Through his experiments in translation,
contributions to intellectual discourse,
and correspondence, Mendelssohn
extends the Jewish tradition of discussion and commentary.*

NR. 58 MOSES MENDELSSOHN
(1729–1786): „VOTUM ZU MÖHSENS
VORTRAG ÜBER AUFKLÄRUNG"
in: Vorträge der Berliner
Mittwochsgesellschaft
Bern, 1787
SBB PK, Abteilung Handschriften
und Historische Drucke

NR. 59 JOHANN GEORG MÜCHLER
(1724–1819): BESCHÄFTIGUNGEN
DES GEISTES UND DES HERZENS.
ZWEYTER BAND
Berlin: J.C. Klüter, 1756
SBB PK
Als teambegabter Publizist entwickelt
Mendelssohn seinen bewunderten,
eleganten Stil – für moralische
Wochenschriften, Literaturjournale
und Aufklärungsforen.
*As a journalist with a penchant for
drawing the best out of his collabora-
tors, Mendelssohn hones his esteemed
elegant style in articles for weekly
ethics magazines, literary journals,
and forums of Enlightenment thought.*

NR. 68 MOSES MENDELSSOHN
(1729–1786) UND TUVIA (TOBIAS)
BOCK (HRSG.): KOHELET MUSAR
Berlin, 1755
Universitätsbibliothek Leipzig

NR. 64 FRIEDRICH NICOLAI
(1733–1811) UND MOSES MENDELS-
SOHN (1729–1786) (HRSG.):
BIBLIOTHEK DER SCHÖNEN WISSEN-
SCHAFTEN UND DER FREYEN
KÜNSTE, BAND 3
Berlin, Dyck: 1758
SBB PK, Abteilung Historische Drucke

NR. 63 JOHANN GEORG MÜCHLER
(1724–1819) (HRSG.): DER
CHAMÄLEON. EINE MORALISCHE
WOCHENSCHRIFT
Berlin: Birnstiel, 1759
Württembergische Landesbibliothek
Stuttgart

NR. 66 FRIEDRICH NICOLAI
(1733–1811) (HRSG.): BRIEFE DIE
NEUESTE LITTERATUR BETREFFEND,
BAND BD. VI
Berlin und Stettin: Nicolaische
Verlagsbuchhandlung, 1760
SBB PK, Abteilung Handschriften
und Historische Drucke

NR. 67 FRIEDRICH NICOLAI
(1733–1811) (HRSG.): ALLGEMEINE
DEUTSCHE BIBLIOTHEK, BAND 1.1
Berlin und Stettin: Friedrich Nicolai:
1765
SBB PK

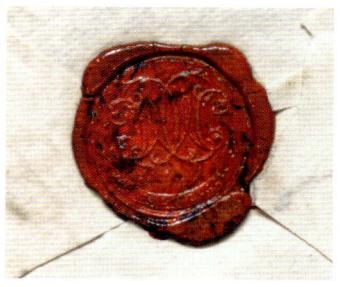

NR. 61 ISAAK EUCHEL (1756–1804)
UND GESELLSCHAFT ZUR
FÖRDERUNG DER HEBRÄISCHEN
SPRACHE (HRSG.): HAMEASSEF
(DER SAMMLER), BAND 1
Königsberg: Kanter, 1783/84
JMB

NR. 60 JOHANN ERICH BIESTER
(1749–1816) UND FRIEDRICH GEDIKE
(1754–1803) (HRSG.): BERLINISCHE
MONATSSCHRIFT, BAND 5
Berlin: Haude & Spener, 1785
JMB

Aufklärung & Verdunkelung

Enlightenment Versus the Shadows

Eine verwirrende Informationsflut erreicht immer mehr Leute. Oft steht das neue Wissen gegen das alte. Die Wissenschaft sagt: Vernunft + Erfahrung = Erkenntnis. Doch wie stoppt man Fake News? Die Aufklärer bekämpfen Aberglauben, Verschwörungstheorien und Esoterik.

    Mendelssohn ist Mathematiker, Metaphysiker, Psychologe, Literaturwissenschaftler. Das System des Rationalismus bricht er auf für ein komplexes Menschenbild. Es gibt zwei Werkzeuge zur Vervollkommnung des Menschen: die Fertigkeiten der Alltagspraxis, die Kultur, und die Fähigkeit zur Vernunft, die Aufklärung. Das Wagnis des Selber-Denkens ist kein Selbstzweck.

A bewildering flood of information reaches more and more people. Often the new knowledge conflicts with old beliefs. Science says: reason + experience = truth. But how can fake news be stopped? The Enlightenment thinkers battle against superstition, conspiracy theories, and esotericism.

    Mendelssohn is a mathematician, metaphysician, psychologist, and literary scholar. He opens up the rationalist system to embrace a complex conception of humanity. There are two tools for achieving human fulfillment. The first involves day-to-day practical skills: culture. And the second is the gift of reason: the Enlightenment. Thinking for oneself, however brave, is not the goal.

zu Nr. 90

OBJEKTVERZEICHNIS

Nr. 69 Gipsformerei Staatliche Museen zu Berlin: Büste des Immanuel Kant (1724–1804) (nach Emanuel Bardou)
1789 (Original)
Deutsches Historisches Museum Berlin
Metaphysiker, berühmter Aufklärer („Kritik der reinen Vernunft"), den sein Briefpartner Mendelssohn in Königsberg besucht. Dieser bewundert den „Alleszermalmer", Kant die Kommunikationskunst des Kollegen: „So glücklich … ist nur ein Mendelssohn."
Metaphysician and renowned Enlightenment thinker (author of "Critique of Pure Reason"). His correspondent Mendelssohn visits him in Königsberg. Mendelssohn affectionately calls Kant the "all-crusher." Kant, in turn, is impressed with his counterpart's artful communication: "Few are so happy… only a Mendelssohn."

Nr. 70 Johann Christoph Frisch (1738–1815): Porträt Marcus Herz (1747–1803)
1779
Öl auf Leinwand
Israel Museum, Jerusalem
Der Kant-Schüler, Arzt und Freund Mendelssohns schreibt über Medizin und Psychologie, Ästhetik und Experimentalphysik.
Herz, pupil of Kant, a physician, and a friend of Mendelssohn, writes about medicine, psychology, aesthetics, and experimental physics.

Nr. 72 Johann Christoph Frisch (1738–1815): Porträt Marcus Elieser Bloch (1723–1799)
1775/80
Öl auf Leinwand
Israel Museum, Jerusalem
Mitgründer der Berlinischen Gesellschaft Naturforschender Freunde, Verfasser der zwölfbändigen „Allgemeinen Naturgeschichte der Fische", Freund und Hausarzt Mendelssohns.
Co-founder of the Berlin Society of Naturalist Friends, author of the twelve-volume "General Natural History of Fish", Mendelssohn's friend and primary physician.

zu Nr. 72

Nr. 71 Daniel Chodowiecki (1726–1801): Titelillustration zu „Ueber die frühe Beerdigung der Juden"
Berlin, 1787
Radierung
Herzog August Bibliothek Wolfenbüttel
Birgt die frühe Beerdigung nicht die Gefahr, Lebendige zu begraben? Im Jahrzehnt nach Mendelssohns Tod verschärft sich an dieser Frage der Gegensatz zwischen Reformern und Traditionalisten, zwischen Obrigkeit und Gemeinden.
Does the Jewish practice of early burial increase the risk of someone being buried alive? During the decade after Mendelssohn's death, this question heightens the tensions between reformers and traditionalists, government authorities and communities.

zu Nr. 70

**Nr. 73 Fischpräparat
„Langflossen-Fledermausfisch"
aus der Sammlung von Marcus
Elieser Bloch (1723–1799)**
1781
Trockenpräparat
Museum für Naturkunde, Berlin
Die Erforschung der Natur steht nicht im Widerspruch zur jüdischen Tradition. Die neuen Erkenntnisse sind dennoch eine Herausforderung. Ob es gelingt, beide zu verbinden?
Investigating nature is compatible with Jewish tradition, but the new scientific insights pose a challenge. Can the two be reconciled?

**Nr. 74 Friedrich Wilhelm Schmidt
(1756–1798) (nach Johann Conrad
Krüger): Trachinus Draco –
Das Petermännchen**
aus: Marcus Elieser Bloch's Naturgeschichte der Fische Deutschlands
ca. 1775–1782
Kupferstich, koloriert
JMB

**Nr. 75 Anton Graff (1736–1813):
Porträt Johann Georg Ritter
von Zimmermann (1728–1795)**
Berlin, ca. 1772/73
Öl auf Leinwand
SMB PK, Gemäldegalerie
Schweizer Arzt und Autor, seit 1768 am Hof in Hannover. Philosophiert mit Mendelssohn, berät ihn als Patienten, wandelt sich zum Aufklärungsgegner.
Swiss physician, author, and official at the royal court in Hanover from 1768 onwards. He philosophizes with Mendelssohn, advises him as a patient, but later opposes the Enlightenment.

**Nr. 76 Moses Samuel Löwe
(1756–1831): Porträt Friedrich
Nicolai (1733–1811) mit Vignette**
Berlin, ca. 1806
Öl auf Leinwand
Stiftung Stadtmuseum Berlin
Die Allegorie unter seinem Porträt zeigt ihn als Kämpfer gegen die Mächte der Finsternis.
The allegorical scene beneath his portrait shows him fighting the forces of darkness.

**Nr. 77 Daniel Chodowiecki
(1756–1831): Minerva von den
drei Grazien umgeben**
Leipzig, 1790
Radierung
Minerva, die Göttin der Weisheit, blickt auf zum lichtumfluteten Sinnbild der Schönheit. Die strahlende Gestalt der Toleranz, der junge Morgen der Aufklärung, sie stehen für den Beginn des Neuen.
Minerva, the goddess of wisdom, gazes at the luminous embodiment of Beauty. The radiant figure of Tolerance, and the dawn of Enlightenment—they all represent the beginning of something new.

**Daniel Chodowiecki (1756–1831):
Nr. 78 Toleranz
Nr. 79 Aufklärung**
Göttingen, 1791
Radierungen
Herzog August Bibliothek, Wolfenbüttel

NR. 80 Johann Rudolph Holzalb
(1723–1806): Vorstellung der
berühmten Aerostatischen
Luftkugel welche sich den
1 Decemb[er] 1783 Mittags um
1 Uhr 40 Minute in die Höhe
erhoben ob einem derer Bassins
in dem Königlichen Garten der
Tuilleries zu Paris
nach 1783
Radierung, teilweise koloriert
Zentralbibliothek Zürich
Mendelssohn schreibt am 26. Dezember 1783 im Zirkular der Mittwochsgesellschaft über den Pionierflug des Heißluftballons: Wahrscheinlich führe „Montgolfiers Entdeckung zu großen Umwälzungen". Man müsse sie fördern, auch wenn ihre positiven Auswirkungen nicht garantiert seien.
On December 26th, 1783, Mendelssohn writes about the very first flight of a hot-air balloon in the Wednesday Society's circular. He predicts Montgolfier's discovery would likely lead to "great upheavals." It deserves support, he writes, even if positive effects could not be guaranteed.

„Wir mißbilligen das geschehene Böse. Ist es ohne unser Verschulden geschehen, so hat die Vorstellung davon vielmehr einen starken Reuz für uns. Das im Erdbeben untergegangene Lissabon reizte unzehlige Menschen, diese Verwüstung in Augenschein zu nehmen."
Moses Mendelssohn, 1761
"We deplore the evil that has been done. If it has happened through no fault of our own, the idea of it has a strong attraction for us. Lisbon, which perished in the earthquake attracted countless people to take a look at this devastation." Moses Mendelssohn, 1761

NR. 81 François-Philippe Charpentier (1734–1817):
Die Zerstörung Lissabons
Paris, nach 1755
Radierung, koloriert
SMB PK, Museum Europäischer Kulturen
Ein Erdbeben, ein Großbrand und ein Tsunami zerstören am 1. November 1755 Lissabon, fordern bis zu 100.000

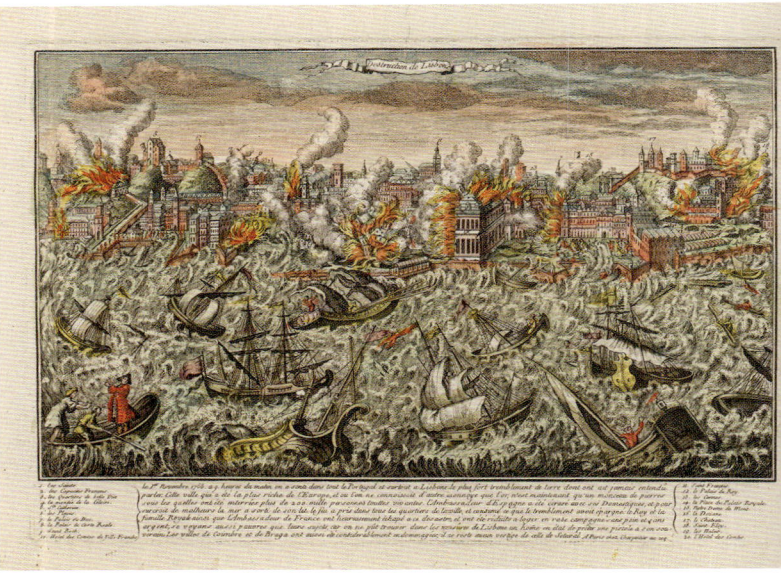

Todesopfer. Angesichts dieser verheerenden Katastrophe diskutieren europaweit nicht nur Aufklärer und Religionskritiker Gottes Gerechtigkeit oder Gleichgültigkeit.
On November 11th, 1755, a combined earthquake, wildfire, and tsunami destroyed the city of Lisbon, claiming as many as 100,000 lives. This devastating catastrophe sparks discussions across Europe about God's justice or indifference, and not just among Enlightenment thinkers and critics of religion.

„Gesezt ein Gottesleugner, und ein wahrer Naturalist hätten durch einen freywilligen Tod das grosse und schreckliche Erdbeben verhüten können. Wie hätten sie sich in einem so critischen Falle verhalten?"
Moses Mendelssohn, 1756
"Suppose a God-denier and a true naturalist could have prevented the great and terrible earthquake through one voluntary death. How would they have acted in such a critical case?" Moses Mendelssohn, 1756

NR. 82 Daniel Chodowiecki
(1756–1831): Eine Schulmeisterstube
1791
Radierung
Herzog Anton Ulrich-Museum, Braunschweig

Daniel Chodowiecki (1756–1831):
NR. 83 Der Geisterbeschwörer
NR. 84 Pater Gassner,
Exorzierung eines Mädchens
NR. 85 Der Magnetiseur
NR. 86 Kartengukkerei
in: Karl Knoblauch, Taschenbuch für Aufklärer und Nichtaufklärer auf das Jahr 1791
Berlin, 1790
Radierungen
Gleimhaus Halberstadt – Museum der deutschen Aufklärung
Erscheinungsformen der „Schwärmerei": Die Vorherrschaft der Vernunft wird in Frage gestellt.
Assorted displays of "sentimentality," calling into question the supremacy of reason.

NR. 87 Friedrich Georg Weitsch
(1758–1828): Porträt Friedrich
Jacobi (1743–1819)
1799
Öl auf Leinwand

Berlin den 1. Sept. 1784

„Wir träumten von nichts als Aufklärung, und glaubten durch das Licht der Vernunft die Gegend so aufgehellt zu haben, daß die Schwärmerey sich gewiß nicht mehr zeigen werde. Allein wie wir sehen, steiget schon, von der andern Seite des Horizonts, die Nacht mit allen ihren Gespenstern wieder empor. Das Fürchterlichste dabey ist, daß das Uebel so thätig, so wirksam ist. Die Schwärmerey thut, und die Vernunft begnügt sich zu sprechen.
   Der Lord Shaftesbury glaubte, Witz und Laune seyen die kräftigsten Gegenmittel wider den Fortgang des schädlichen Aberglaubens. Allein bloßer Scherz vertreibet das Vorurtheil nur zum Scheine. Aus Furcht verspottet zu werden, sucht man höchstens seine Albernheit zu verheimlichen. Man spottet wohl selbst mit, wo dieser Ton herrschet, und ist in seinem geheimsten Schlafgemache, wie ich Beyspiele gesehen, nichts desto weniger verführter und verführender Schwärmer.
   Der beste Ton ist, wie mich dünkt, der den Sie gewählt haben. Sie lassen dem gesunden Menschenverstand die Laune zur Seite gehen; Sie geben der Vernunft ihre Nahrung und lassen auch die Einbildungs- und Dichtungskraft nicht darben. Man denkt und empfindet, bedauert, lacht und bewundert, nachdem der Gegenstand es erfordert. […]"

Berlin, September 1st, 1784

"We dreamed of nothing but Enlightenment and believed that the light of reason would so illuminate the land that zealousness would never again show its face. But as we can see, from beyond the horizon, night is ascending once again with all its ghosts. Most frightening of all is that evil is so active, so potent. Zealousness takes action, and reason contents itself with speech.
   Lord Shaftesbury believed that wit and humor were the most powerful antidotes to the advancement of pernicious superstition. On its own, a simple joke only dispels prejudice superficially. At most, a person seeks to conceal his own foolishness for fear of being mocked. And indeed, he joins in the mocking wherever that tone holds sway, yet in his most private bedchamber—and I have seen examples of this—he remains no less of a misguided and misguiding zealot.
   The best tone, it seems to me, is the one you have chosen. You let common sense being joined by humor; you feed reason its fill and do not let starve the forces of imagination and poetic inspiration. A person thinks and feels, regrets, laughs, and marvels as the object necessitates."

As a popular philosopher and metaphysician, Mendelssohn concerned himself with basic questions of existence, with the Enlightenment and its enemies, and with the boundaries between faith and reason.

Nr. 89 Moses Mendelssohn (1729–1786): Ueber die Frage: was heisst aufklären?
in: Berlinische Monatsschrift, Band 4
Berlin: Haude & Spener, 1784
JMB

Nr. 90 Joseph Rose & Sons: Englische Taschenuhr von Moses Mendelssohn Repoussé-Doppelgehäuse-Spindeluhr
undatiert
Metall, Glas
Mendelssohn-Gesellschaft, Berlin
(Foto: Bernhard Thévoz)
„Man kann sich alle Federn, Räder und Triebwerke einer Uhr vorstellen, ohne an den Grund zu gedenken, warum diese Gefässe mit einander verknüpft sind." Moses Mendelssohn, 1755
"A person can imagine all the springs, gears, and workings of a clock without fundamentally considering why these vessels are interconnected."
Moses Mendelssohn, 1755

Nr. 91 Moses Mendelssohn (1729–1786): Brief an den Arzt Johann Georg Zimmermann
Berlin, 01.09.1784
Papier, Tinte
Gottfried Wilhelm Leibniz Bibliothek – Niedersächsische Landesbibliothek, Hannover

Stadtmuseum Düsseldorf
Der Philosoph stellt Lessing posthum als „Spinozisten" = Atheisten dar. Jacobi zwingt Mendelssohn, seinen Freund zu verteidigen und löst eine Debatte über die Existenz Gottes aus, den „Pantheismus-Streit".
The philosopher portrays Lessing posthumously as a "Spinozist," that is, an atheist. Jacobi forces Mendelssohn to defend his friend, triggering a debate over the existence of God that became known as the "Pantheism Controversy."

Nr. 88 Moses Mendelssohn (1729–1786): Abhandlung über die Evidenz in Metaphysischen Wissenschaften
Berlin: Haude & Spener, 1764
SBB PK, Abteilung Handschriften und Historische Drucke
Der Popularphilosoph und Metaphysiker Mendelssohn beschäftigt sich mit Grundfragen der Existenz, mit Aufklärung und der Reaktion auf ihre Verächter, mit den Grenzen zwischen Glauben und Vernunft.

Nr. 92/93 Moses Mendelssohn (1729–1786): Philosophische Schriften, Erster und Zweyter Theil
Berlin, Christian Friedrich Voß: 1777
Privatbesitz, Berlin

Nr. 94 Moses Mendelssohn (1729–1786): Ueber Wunder u wunderbar, Notizen zu einem Essay
undatiert
Papier, Tinte
SBB PK, Musikabteilung mit Mendelssohn-Archiv

Notiz zu einem Essay: Ueber Wunder u[nd] wunderbar

„[…] Seltenheit ist nicht hinreichend eine Begebenheit zum Wunder zu machen. Durchgang der Venus. Pabst zu Wien. – Ausnahme von den Nathurgesetzen scheinet nicht nothwendig. Einwirkung freyer Wesen hebt die Naturgesetze nicht auf. […] Absichten in der Natur sind im Allgemeinen sichtbar, im Besonderen aber versteckt. Die gemeinsamen Eigenschaften der Dinge haben eine solche Schiklichkeit zu bestimmten Endzweken, daß die Absicht bey der Anlage und Einrichtung derselben nicht zu läugnen ist. Das Einzelne hingegen […] das Schiksal eines jeden Menschen; so wie jede besondere Naturbegebenheit; […] giebt keine solche Absicht deutlich zu erkennen. […]

Sichtbare Absicht im Einzelnen ist Wunder, in so weit sie die Mitwirkung übermenschlicher Wesen zu erkennen giebt. Daher ihre Seltenheit, ihr scheinbarer Widerspruch mit den Gesetzen der Natur.

Was können Wunder beweisen? – Sie können den Willen eines übermenschlichen Wesens zu erkennen geben […] aber keine Lehren.

Jede Einwirkung Gottes in den Lauf der Natur war kein Wunder; in so weit sie keine besondere Absicht zu erkennen geben würde.

Das Wunderbare hat Reitz für den Menschen, weil er gern mit höheren Wesen in Verbindung stehet.
Ausnahmen von den Naturgesetzen können als solche nicht ergötzen. […]"

Notes for a paper: On miracles and miraculous

"Rarity does not suffice to make a phenomenon a miracle. The passage of Venus. Pope in Vienna.—An exception to the laws of Nature does not seem necessary. The influence of individuals with free will does not invalidate the laws of Nature. […] Intentions in Nature are visible in general, but concealed in specific. The common attributes of things are so expedient toward certain ultimate ends that the intentionality behind their conception and features is undeniable. On an individual level, by contrast […] each human being's destiny, as with any specific natural phenomenon; […] does not clearly reveal such intentionality.

Visible intentionality on an individual level is a miracle, insofar as it reveals the involvement of superhuman entities. Hence the rarity [of such events], their apparent contradiction with the laws of Nature.

What can miracles prove?—They can reveal the will of a superhuman entity […] but not any lessons.

Each of God's interventions in the course of Nature was not a miracle insofar as it did not reveal a specific intentionality. Humans are drawn to the miraculous, for they like having a connection to higher entities.
Yet exceptions to the laws of nature cannot, as such, regale."

Religion

Religion

Religion ist out und in. Die Konfrontation mit verschiedenen Konfessionen erschüttert nach dem 30-jährigen Krieg Wahrheitsmonopole. Ein verheerendes Erdbeben in Lissabon weckt Zweifel an der himmlischen Gerechtigkeit.

Mendelssohn verteidigt klassische Gottesbeweise und das Ritualgesetz. Als Vermittler zwischen Judentum und deutscher Kultur stellt er sich gegen die Gemeindeführer: Sie möchten Tradition und Abgrenzung fixieren. Zugleich berät er jüdische Gemeinden bei Konflikten mit der Obrigkeit.

Besitzt eine Religion die Wahrheit? Soll man konvertieren? Mendelssohn verbindet natürliche Religion, Offenbarungsglauben und Philosophie. Für ihn ist der jüdische Glaubenskern identisch mit der universalen Vernunftreligion.

Religion is having a slump and a heyday at the same time. In the aftermath of the Thirty Years' War, different religions and denominations are coming face to face, leaving cracks in their monopoly on truth. A devastating earthquake in Lisbon casts further doubts on divine justice.

Mendelssohn defends the traditional proof of God and ritual laws. As an intermediary between Judaism and German culture, he is at odds with community leaders, who want to preserve tradition and separation. But he also advises Jewish communities when conflicts arise with the authorities.

Does one religion possess the truth? Should people convert? Mendelssohn merges philosophy, natural religion, and belief in divine revelation. As he sees it, the core of Jewish faith is identical with universal rational religion.

zu Nr. 109

Nr. 100 Johann Caspar Lavater (1741–1801): Zueignungsschrift der Bonnetischen philosophischen Untersuchung der Beweise für das Christenthum. Auf Kosten guter Freunde
1770
Mendelssohn-Gesellschaft, Berlin/ Leihgabe Sammlung Dopfer

Nr. 101 Moses Mendelssohn (1729–1786): Das Dasein Gottes a priori erwiesen
Berlin, undatiert (vermutlich 1778)
Papier, Tinte
SBB PK, Abteilung Handschriften und Historische Drucke

Nr. 102 Moses Mendelssohn (1729–1786): Morgenstunden oder Vorlesungen über das Daseyn Gottes
Berlin, Christian Friedrich Voß: 1785
JMB
Mendelssohn argumentiert: Das Judentum missioniert nicht und beansprucht keine Ausschließlichkeit. Jeder, der die grundlegenden Gebote einhält, hat Anteil an der kommenden Welt und der ewigen Seligkeit.
Mendelssohn argues that Judaism is not a missionary religion and makes no claim on exclusivity. Anyone who follows the basic commandments has a share in the World to Come and eternal life.

Nr. 136 Johann Christoph Frisch (1738–1815): Nathan und der Tempelherr
1798
Öl auf Leinwand
Lessing-Museum Kamenz
Schon bei der Uraufführung des Schauspiels wird die Figur des Nathan mit Mendelssohn identifiziert. Im Gegensatz zur Figur im Stück bedeutet für Mendelssohn Toleranz nicht die Ununterscheidbarkeit der Religionen.
The character of Nathan is identified with Mendelssohn at the play's premiere already. But unlike the figure in the play, Mendelssohn does not construe tolerance as minimizing the differences between religions.

Nr. 98 Moses Mendelssohn (1729–1786): Brief an den Herzog Ferdinand von Braunschweig (Abschrift)
Januar 1770
Papier, Tinte
Geheimes Staatsarchiv
Preußischer Kulturbesitz, Berlin

Brief an den Erbprinzen von Braunschweig, aus der ältesten erhaltenen Abschrift

„Nach der Lehre des N. T. (wenigstens wie das in öffentlichen Lehrbüchern erklärt wird) muß ich 1) eine dreieinige Gottheit 2) die Menschwerdung einer Person dieser Gottheit, 3) das Leiden derselben, nachdem sie sich ihrer göttlichen Majestät entäußert hat, 4) die Genugthuung und Befriedigung der ersten Person in der Gottheit durch das Leiden und den Tod der erniedrigten zweyten Person [...] glauben. [...] Wenn ich diese Lehren im alten Testamente fände, so müßte ich dieses verwerfen [...]

Daß ein Unschuldiger die Schuld eines Andern trage, und wenn er sie auch freiwillig übernehme, kann, meinen Begriffen nach, in dem Staate Gottes von dem allergerechtesten Wesen nicht zugelassen werden. [...]

Von der Erbsünde weiß die gesunde Vernunft nichts und das A. T. eben so wenig. [...]

Der Stifter der christlichen Religion hat niemals mit ausdrücklichen Worten gesagt, daß er das mosaische Gesetz aufheben u[nd] die Juden davon dispensiren wolle. [...] Man räume mir also ein, daß ich mich auf keine Weise von dem Mosaischen Gesetze befreyen kann. [...]

Wie unaussprechlich elend wäre das Schicksal der Menschen, wenn von der Auslegung dunkler Stellen in einem Buche, das vor undenklichen Zeiten, in einer fremden, jetzt todten Sprache für eine bestimmte Nation in Asien geschrieben worden, die ewige Glückseligkeit des ganzen menschlichen Geschlechts abhängen sollte! [...]
Berlin 23. Januar 1770"

Letter to the hereditary prince of Brunswick, from the oldest surviving copy

"According to the teachings of the New Testament (at least as explained in the published textbooks), I am expected to believe 1) in a tripartite divinity, 2) that one person of this divinity took human form, 3) that this same person suffered after relinquishing his divine majesty, and 4) that first person in the divinity was gratified and satisfied by the suffering and the death of the humiliated second person. [...] Were I to find these teachings in the Old Testament, I would be compelled to repudiate it. [...]

For an innocent person to bear another's guilt, even if he assumed it voluntarily, will not be permitted, in my view, in the City of God by the most righteous Supreme Being.. [...]

Common sense knows nothing of heritable sin; no more does the Old Testament. [...]

The founder of the Christian religion never said in explicit terms that he intended to revoke the Mosaic law and grant the Jews a dispensation from it. [...] One must therefore acknowledge that I cannot, in any fashion, release myself from the Mosaic Laws. [...]

How unspeakably wretched the fate of humanity would be if the eternal happiness of the entire human race were to depend on the interpretation of obscure passages in a book written many ages ago in a foreign, now dead tongue, for a particular people in Asia! [...]
Berlin January 23rd 1770"

Nr. 99 Moses Mendelssohn (1729–1786): Brief an Johann Caspar Lavater
Berlin, 15.01.1771
Zentralbibliothek Zürich

Nr. 96 Martin Gottlieb Klauber (1742–1801): Porträtbüste des Theologen Johann Caspar Lavater (1741–1801)
Schweiz, vor 1774
Terracotta
Zentralbibliothek Zürich
Für den Schweizer Theologen ist die Bekehrung der Juden zum Christentum die Voraussetzung für die Wiederkehr von Jesus.
The Swiss theologian posits the Jews' conversion to Christianity as a precondition for the Second Coming of Jesus.

Moses Mendelssohn an Lavater, 15. Januar 1771

„*Es ist ein eingewurzeltes Vorurtheil Ihrer Glaubensgenossen, daß die Juden alle unaufhörlich die Religion der Christen und den Stifter derselben lästern, und daraus läßt sich […] im gemeinen Leben manches rechtfertigen, das so irreligiös als vernünftig ist. Es ist aber Ihrer nicht anständig, würdigster Menschenfreund! dergleichen Vorurtheile, die noch Ueberresten der alten Barbarey sind, nur zu begünstigen zu scheinen, und den Religionshaß, den wir immer mehr und mehr einzuschläfern suchen sollten, auch nur durch bloße Rednerfiguren aufzuwecken. […]*

Als die Stärkern noch, um der Religion Willen, Blut vergossen, blieb den Schwächern kein ander Vergöltungsmittel, als, wie man zu sagen pflegt, Schnipgen in der Tasche zu schlagen, das heißt, bei verschlossenen Thüren die Religion ihrer Widersacher zu lästern. So wie auf der einen Seite der Verfolgergeist,; so weichet auf der andern Seite der Haß […] nunmehr ist es die Pflicht aller guten Menschen, den alten Zwist zur Vergessenheit zu befördern. […]
Berlin d. 15. Jan. 1771"

Moses Mendelssohn to Lavater, January 15th, 1771

"*It is a deep-rooted prejudice of your coreligionists that all Jews continually slander the Christian religion and its founder, this prejudice rather conveniently allows much to be explained […] as it justifies much in common life that is as irreligious as it is irrational. But it is not proper for you, most worthy friend of humanity, even to appear to encourage such prejudices, which are remnants of the old barbarism, and to awaken, even with mere figures of speech, the religious hatred that we should now more and more be putting to sleep. […]*

When the more powerful spilled blood for the sake of religion, the weaker had no other means of retaliation than underhand tricks such as slandering the religion of their opponents behind closed doors. Just as on one side the spirit of persecution, on the other side hatred will abate […] henceforth it is the duty of all good people to help see to it that the old quarrel is forgotten."
(Translation as cited in Jonathan M. Hess: Germans, Jews, and the Claims of Modernity; New Haven/CT: Yale UP 2002, p. 102f. Original translation of final sentence.)

Übersetzung & Pädagogik

Translation & Education

Wer in seiner Blase bleibt, verpasst zu viel. Gegen Scheuklappen, mit denen sich Konfessionen und Milieus voneinander abschotten, hilft Bildung – so hoffen die Aufklärer.

Als Lernender erschließt sich Mendelssohn die Welt. Als Übersetzer verbindet er Welten. Seine in vielen Editionen verbreitete Tora-Übertragung bringt jiddisch-sprachigen Kindern und Erwachsenen Hochdeutsch bei. Sein Kommentar erschließt den Text und schlägt die Brücke zwischen Tradition und modernem Wissen.

Kann man durch Erziehung alles erreichen? Kinder sollen beides lernen: traditionell-jüdischen und modern-praktischen Stoff. Als Berater von Reformschulen in Dessau und Berlin setzt Mendelssohn auf das Potential kommender Generationen.

To live in a bubble is to miss out. Education helps break down the blinders that religions and communities use to segregate themselves—or so Enlightenment thinkers hope.

As a learner, Mendelssohn takes in the world. As a translator, he brings worlds together. His translation of the Torah, distributed in many editions, teaches Yiddish-speaking children and adults Standard German. His commentary makes the text accessible and builds a bridge between tradition and modern knowledge.

Is education the gateway to all achievements? In Mendelssohn's opinion, children should learn both traditional Jewish subjects and modern, practical ones. As an advisor to reformed schools in Dessau and Berlin, Mendelssohn sets great store in the potential of future generations.

Kurze Anweisung zum Lesen.

1) Das kleine deutsche Alphabeth.

a, b, c, d, e, f, g, h, i, k, l, m, n, o, p, q, r, s, ß, t, u, v, w, x, y, z.

2) Das große deutsche Alphabeth.

A, B, C, D, E, F, G, H, J, K, L, M, N, O, P, Q, R, S, T, U, V, W, X, Y, Z.

Zusammengezogene Zeichen sind.

ä, ch, ck, ff, ö, ss, st, ü, tz.

Das geschriebene deutsche Alphabeth.

a, b, c, d, e, f, ff, g, h, i, k, l, ll, m, n, o, p, q, r, s, ss, ß, st, t, ä, ö, ü, v, w, x, y, z.

A, B, C, D, E, F, G, H, J, K, L, M, N, O, P, Q, R, S, T, U, V, W, X, Y, Z.

OBJEKTVERZEICHNIS

Nr. 104 J. Nathan (?): Porträt Raphael Cohen (1722–1803)
undatiert
Mezzotinto
Jüdisches Historisches Institut „Emanuel Ringelblum", Warschau
Der Altonaer Rabbiner will alle Leser von Mendelssohns Bibelübersetzung mit einem Bann belegen. Mendelssohns Gegenstrategie: Er gewinnt den dänischen König als Subskribenten.
The rabbi of Altona intends to issue a ban prohibiting Jews from reading Mendelssohn's bible translation. Mendelssohn's counter-strategy: he obtains the King of Denmark's support as a subscriber.

Nr. 105 Markus Klauber: Porträt Ezechiel Landau (1713–1793)
undatiert
Kupferstich, Radierung
Österreichische Nationalbibliothek, Wien
Rabbiner und halachische Autorität in Prag. Lehnt Mendelssohns Bibelübersetzung ab, akzeptiert aber weltliche Bildung.
Rabbi and halakhic authority in Prague. He rejects Mendelssohn's bible translation, but allows for secular education.

Nr. 106 Johann Balzer: Porträt Jonathan Eybeschütz (1896–1764) (nach Wilhelm Kleinhardt)
1770
Kupferstich
JMB
Rabbiner und Kabbalist in Altona. Mendelssohn besucht ihn 1761 und erhofft von ihm eine Bestätigung als Rabbiner. Eybeschütz reagiert ausweichend.
Rabbi and kabbalist in Altona. Mendelssohn visits him in 1761, hoping for his recognition as a rabbi. Eybeschütz demurs.

Nr. 108 vermutlich Johann F. A. Krüger (1754–1807): Porträt Hirschel Loebel (1721–1800)
1772–1799
Öl auf Leinwand
United Synagogue. Jewish Museum London

Berliner Oberrabbiner. Kooperiert mit Mendelssohn für das Buch „Ritualgesetze der Juden" (1778), approbiert seine Tora-Übersetzung.
Berlin's Chief Rabbi. Collaborates with Mendelssohn on the book „Ritual Laws of the Jews" (1778) and approves his Torah translation.

Nr. 109 A. B. Golbin: Inneres der Berliner Synagoge Heidereuthergasse (nach Anna Maria Werner)
ca. 1720
Kupferstich
SMB PK, Kupferstichkabinett
Im Hinterhof und dennoch repräsentativ: Das Vorlesepult in der Mitte des Raumes, der Tora-Schrein in prächtigem Barock. Die königliche Familie kommt zur Besichtigung.
In the backyard and yet imposingly grand. The bimah, a platform for the cantor and Torah readings, stands at the center of the sanctuary; the Torah ark is designed in magnificent baroque style. The royal family arrives for an official visit.

Nr. 112 Kilian Ponheimer (1757–1828): Porträt Naftali Herz Homberg (1749–1841)
1823
Kupferstich
Österreichische Nationalbibliothek, Wien
Hauslehrer bei Mendelssohns, Schulreformer. Drängt auf die Modernisierung jüdischer Bildung. Verfasst den Kommentar zu Deuteronomium für die Pentateuch-Übersetzung.

Private tutor to the Mendelssohn family, school reformer. Agitator for the modernization of Jewish education. Writes the commentary on Deuteronomy for the Pentateuch translation.

Nr. 97 Tora-Krone (Keter)
vermutlich Berlin, 1912
Silber, teilvergoldet
JMB
Die Offenbarung der Tora am Berg Sinai ist Grundlage des Judentums. Nach jüdischer Überlieferung sind die schriftliche Tora und ihre Kommentare und Auslegungen, die mündliche Tora, untrennbar und verbindlich.
The gift of the Torah on Mount Sinai is the foundation of Judaism. According to Jewish tradition, the written Torah is inseparable from the oral Torah, which consists of its commentary and interpretations. Both are binding.

Nr. 113 Franciscus Sansom: Porträt Salomon ben Joel Dubno (1738–1813) (nach Schabracq)
1791
Punktiermanier, Reproduktion
Rijksmuseum Amsterdam
Hebräischer Dichter, Hauslehrer bei Mendelssohns. Beteiligt an der Pentateuch-Übersetzung. Verfasst die grammatischen Teile des Pentateuch-Kommentars.
Hebrew poet, private tutor to the Mendelssohn family. Involved in Pentateuch commentary. Writes the grammatical parts of the Pentateuch commentary.

Nr. 114 Daniel Berger (1744–1825): Porträt Hartwig Wessely (1725–1805)
1791
Kupferstich
Herzog August Bibliothek, Wolfenbüttel
Hebraist, Schriftsteller, Kaufmann, Bildungsreformer. Verfasst den Kommentar zu Leviticus für die Pentateuch-Übersetzung.
Hebraist, writer, merchant, education reformer. Writes the commentary on Leviticus for the Pentateuch translation.

zu Nr. 97

Nr. 115 Moses Samuel Löwe (1756–1831): Porträt Lazarus Bendavid (1762–1836)
1806
Radierung
Herzog August Bibliothek, Wolfenbüttel
Philosoph, Mathematiker, zweite Generation der jüdischen Aufklärer. Ab 1802 Direktor der Jüdischen Freischule.
Philosopher, mathematician, second-generation Jewish Enlightenment thinker. Director of the Jewish Free School, from 1802.

Nr. 116 Daniel Berger (1744–1825): Porträt Isaac Daniel Itzig (1750–1806) (nach Anton Graff)
1789
Kupferstich
Gleimhaus, Museum der deutschen Aufklärung, Halberstadt
Unternehmer, Bürgerrechtsaktivist, Mäzen der Haskala, Mitgründer der Jüdischen Freischule und der Orientalischen Buchdruckerei.
Businessman, civil rights activist, patron of the Haskalah (Jewish Enlightenment), co-founder of the Jewish Free School and the Oriental Book Printing House.

OBJEKTVERZEICHNIS

Nr. 117 Georg Friedrich Weitsch (1758–1828): Porträt David Friedländer (1750–1834)
Berlin, ca. 1795
Öl auf Papier
Israel Museum, Jerusalem
Seidenfabrikant und Aktivist für die Gleichberechtigung der Juden, Mitgründer der Jüdischen Freischule.
Silk manufacturer and activist for Jews' rights, co-founder of the Jewish Free School.

Nr. 118 Moses Mendelssohn (1729–1786): Alim li-terufah (Medizinische Blätter)
Amsterdam: Abraham Proops, 1777/78
SBB PK, Musikabteilung mit Mendelssohn-Archiv

Nr. 123 Moses Mendelssohn (1729–1786): Sefer netiwot ha-schalom (Buch der Wege des Friedens). Die fünf Bücher Mose mit deutscher Übersetzung und Kommentar
5 Bände
Berlin: Georg Friedrich Starke, 1780–1783
JMB

Nr. 126 David Friedländer (1750–1834): Lesebuch für jüdische Kinder. Zum Besten der Jüdischen Freyschule
Berlin: Voß & Sohn, 1779
Universitätsbibliothek Rostock
Friedländer entwirft im Lesebuch Lese- und Schreibübungen, Mendelssohns Beiträge sind Erzählungen und Fabeln, Grundartikel des Judentums und die „Andachtsübung eines Weltweisen".
Friedländer composes reading and writing exercises for the reader. Mendelssohn contributes stories and fables, articles about the foundations of Judaism, and "A Philosopher's Devotional Exercises."

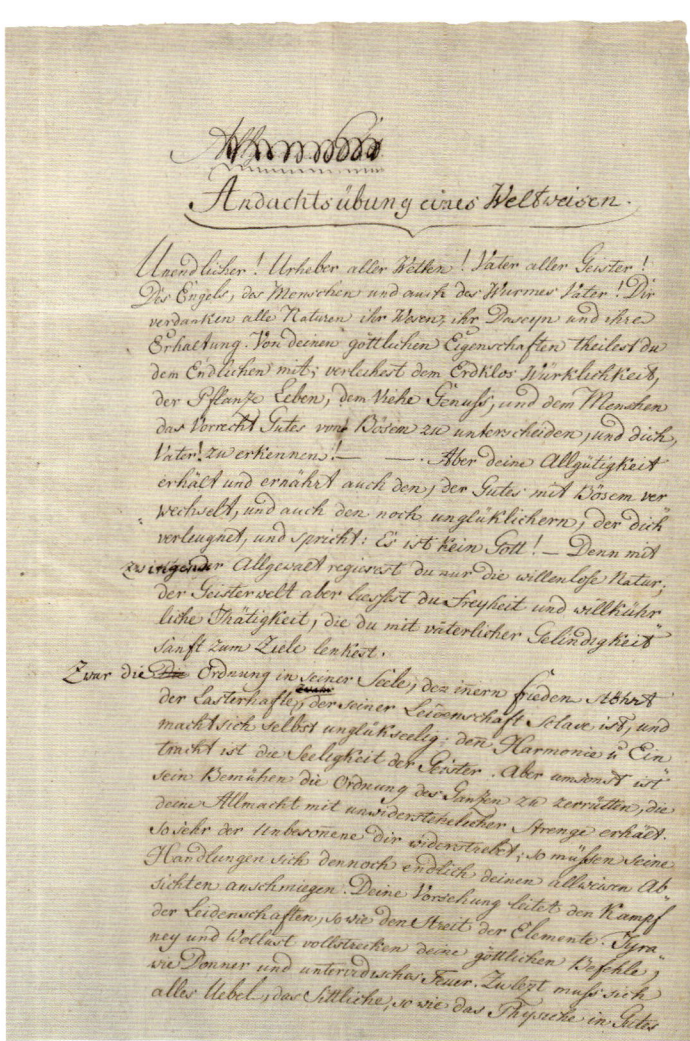

Nr. 127 Moses Mendelssohn (1729–1786): Andachtsübung eines Weltweisen
Berlin, 1779
Manuskript, Reproduktion
Historical Society of Pennsylvania, Philadelphia

Menschenrechte

Human Rights

Die Juden, das unterdrückte, aber auserwählte Volk, sollen Rechte haben wie alle andern. Jeder soll gleich sein vor dem Gesetz; alle sind unendlich verschieden. Aber muss man für die Gleichberechtigung seine Traditionen aufgeben?

    Menschenduldung = Toleranz ist ein erster Schritt. Mendelssohn verteidigt das jüdische Ritualgesetz, denn es widerspricht nicht den staatlichen Gesetzen. Er plädiert für Gewissensfreiheit und für die Trennung von Staat und Religion.

    13 nordamerikanische Staaten proklamieren „unveräußerliche Rechte wie die auf Leben, Freiheit und das Streben nach Glück". Mit preußischen Reformern setzt sich Mendelssohn „für die bürgerliche Verbesserung der Juden" ein.

The Jews—the long-oppressed Chosen People—ought to have rights just like everyone else. Everyone is entitled to equality under the law; everyone has countless differences. But do equal rights require abandoning one's own traditions?

    Tolerance for others is the first step. Mendelssohn defends the Jewish ritual laws, which in his view do not conflict with government laws. He advocates freedom of conscience and a separation between state and religion.

    Thirteen North American states declare "unalienable Rights" including the rights to "Life, Liberty and the pursuit of Happiness." Mendelssohn joins Prussian reformers in calling "for a civil improvement of the Jews."

ZU NR. 133

Nr. 128 Porträt Johann Georg Hamann (1730–1788)
1840/50
Stahlstich
SBB PK, Abteilung Handschriften und Historische Drucke
Gefühlsphilosoph, Aufklärungsgegner und Polemiker gegen Kirchenkritik Mendelssohns, mit dem er in freundschaftlichem Kontakt steht.
A philosopher of feeling and an opponent of the Enlightenment, Hamann polemicizes against Mendelssohn's criticism of the church but is on friendly terms with him.

Nr. 129 Eberhard Henne (1759–1828): Porträt Johann David Michaelis (1717–1791)
1788
Radierung
JMB
Theologe und Orientalist, scharfer Gegner jüdischer Emanzipation, zugleich im kollegialen Austausch mit Mendelssohn.
Theologian and orientalist. Although a fierce opponent of Jewish emancipation, he engages in a collegial exchange of ideas with Mendelssohn.

Nr. 133 François Lonsing (1739–1799): Porträt Honoré Gabriel Riqueti, Marquis von Mirabeau (1749–1791)
1790
Öl auf Leinwand
Musée des Beaux-Arts, Bordeaux
Politiker und Publizist, durch Mendelssohn inspiriert zum Einsatz für die Gleichberechtigung der Juden in der französischen Nationalversammlung.
A politician and journalist, Mirabeau is inspired by Mendelssohn to fight for Jewish equality in the French National Assembly.

Nr. 134 Georg Adolf Schöner (1774–1841): Porträt Christian Wilhelm von Dohm (1751–1820)
1801
Öl auf Leinwand
Museen der Stadt Regensburg
Jurist im preußischen Staatsdienst, erster Publizist für die Judenemanzipation in Zusammenarbeit mit Mendelssohn.
Jurist in the Prussian civil service, first journalist to support Jewish emancipation, collaboration with Mendelssohn.

Nr. 138 nach Johann Gottfried Schadow (1764–1850): Friedrich II., König von Preussen (1712–1786)
1804
(Gipsabguss nach historischer Form)
SMB PK, Gipsformerei
Friedrich benutzt Juden für seine Wirtschaftspolitik: um Warenexport zu organisieren, Manufakturen zu betreiben und durch Sondersteuern die Staatskasse zu füllen. Nur die Wohlhabenden dürfen bleiben. Die Armen werden ausgewiesen, viele werden zu Bettlern.
King Frederick exploits Jews for his economic policy: to organize the export of goods, to run manufactories, and to fill the state coffers through special taxes. Only the wealthy are allowed to stay. The poor are expelled and many become beggars.

OBJEKTVERZEICHNIS

Nr. 135 Johann Christoph Frisch (?) (1738–1815): Porträt Fanny von Arnstein (1758–1818)
undatiert
Kreide, Bleistift
Jüdisches Historisches Institut „Emanuel Ringelblum", Warschau
Wiener Salonière, sozial engagiert für Juden und Christen, politisch einflussreich. Von ihrem Verwandten Mendelssohn gerühmt als „irdisches Bild" der Toleranz-Göttin Minerva.
Viennese salonière, socially active in support of Jews and Christians, politically influential. Moses Mendelssohn, to whom she is related, praises her as the "earthly image" of Minerva, goddess of tolerance.

Nr. 139 Honoré Gabriel Riqueti, Graf von Mirabeau (1749–1791): Sur Moses Mendelssohn, sur la reforme politique des Juifs et en particulier sur la révolution tentée en leur faveur en 1753 dans la grande Bretagne
London, 1787
SBB PK, Musikabteilung mit Mendelssohn-Archiv
Thesen und Debatten zu Toleranz und Bürgerrechten: Mendelssohn inspiriert die Diskussion.
Theses and debates regarding tolerance and civil rights, inspired by Mendelssohn.

Nr. 140 Christian Wilhelm Dohm (1751–1820): Ueber die bürgerliche Verbesserung der Juden. Erster Theil
Berlin und Stettin: Friedrich Nicolai, 1783
JMB

Nr. 141 Christian Wilhelm Dohm (1751–1820): Brief an Moses Mendelssohn
März 1782
Papier, Tinte
SBB PK, Abteilung Handschriften und Historische Drucke

Nr. 142 Gotthold Ephraim Lessing (1729–1781): Nathan der Weise. Ein Dramatisches Gedicht, in fünf Aufzügen
1779, JMB

Nr. 143 Moses Mendelssohn (1729–1786): Johann Jacob Rousseau, Bürgers zu Genf Abhandlung von dem Ursprunge der Ungleichheit unter den Menschen
Berlin: Christian Friedrich Voß, 1756
SBB PK, Musikabteilung mit Mendelssohn-Archiv

Nr. 144 Moses Mendelssohn (1729–1786): Jerusalem oder über religiöse Macht und Judentum
Berlin: Maurer, 1783
Mendelssohn-Gesellschaft, Berlin
„Schicket euch in die Sitten und die Verfassung des Landes, in welches ihr versetzt seid; aber haltet auch standhaft bei der Religion eurer Väter. Traget beider Lasten so gut ihr könntet!"

"Comply with the customs and the civil constitution of the countries in which ye are transplanted, but, at the same time, be constant to the faith of your forefathers. Bear both burdens as well as ye may"

Nr. 146 Moses Mendelssohn (1729–1786): Rettung der Juden. Als ein Anhang zu des Hrn. Kriegsraths Dohm Abhandlung Ueber die bürgerliche Verbesserung der Juden. Menasseh Ben Israel, aus dem Englischen übersetzt nebst einer Vorrede von Moses Mendelssohn
Berlin und Stettin: Friedrich Nicolai, 1782
JMB

Nr. 147 Gotthold Ephraim Lessing (1729–1781): Die Juden

In: G. E. Lessings Schriften, Vierter Theil
Berlin: Christian Friedrich Voß, 1754
Privatbesitz, Berlin

Mit seiner Verteidigung dieser Komödie beginnt die Zusammenarbeit zwischen Mendelssohn und Lessing.

Mendelssohn's defence of this comedy marks the beginning of the collaboration between him and Lessing.

Nr. 148 Johann Georg Hamann (1730–1788): Golgatha und Scheblimini! Von einem Prediger in der Wüsten

Riga: Hartknoch, 1784
SBB PK, Abteilung Handschriften und Historische Drucke

Mendelssohns Plädoyer für die Gleichberechtigung der Religionen im Staat. Johann Georg Hamann wendet sich gegen dessen naturrechtliche Basis. Johann David Michaelis formuliert den Gegensatz von „Deutschen" und „Juden". Im Theater und in Frankreich werden Mendelssohns Ideen aufgenommen.

Mendelssohn calls for the equality of religions within the state. Johann Georg Hamann opposes how Mendelssohn bases his appeal in natural law. Johann David Michaelis formulates the idea of an opposition between "Germans" and "Jews". Mendelssohn's ideas find an echo in the theater and in France.

Nr. 149 Johann David Michaelis (1717–1791): Orientalische und Exegetische Bibliothek, Erster Theil

Frankfurt am Main: Garbe, 1771–1773
SBB PK

o. Nr. Revidiertes General-Privilegiums und Reglement vor die Judenschaft im Königreiche Preussen (1750)

Berlin, 1756
Druck
Bayerische Staatsbibliothek, Bamberg

Auf Bitten der Judenschaft wurde das verschärfte Reglement im Jahr seines Erlasses noch nicht veröffentlicht.

Christian Dohm an Mendelssohn, März 1782

„P.P.

Sehn Sie hier meinen ersten Gegner, dessen Äußerungen Sie wohl so wenig befremden werden, als mich. Nur wegen des ersten Eindrucks können sie der guten Sachen nachtheilig seyn. Sollte das, was von Eisenmenger gesagt wird, gegründet seyn? Ich werde im Archiv nachsehen, wo sich das, was K. Friedr. I. deshalb gethan haben soll, finden muss. Ich höre, dass auch mehrere unserer Theologen nicht mit meiner Schrift zufrieden sind; aber ihr Beyfall war auch nicht das Ziel, das ich zu erreichen strebte.
Dohm"

Christian Dohm to Mendelssohn, March 1782

"P.P.

*See here my first opponent, whose statements are bound to disconcert you as little as they do me. Only as a result of the first impression could they be a disadvantage to the good cause. Should what is being said about Eisenmenger be substantiated? I will check the archive, where I am sure to find what K[aiser] Fr[ederick] I is said to have done as a result. I hear that several of our theologians are also displeased with my treatise; but their applause was not the goal I sought to achieve.
Dohm"*

Mirabeau sollte später preußische Judengesetze als „eines Kannibalen würdig" kritisieren.

At the request of the Jewish community, the more oppressive regulations were not yet published in the year of their enactment. Mirabeau later criticized Prussia's anti-Jewish edicts as "worthy of a cannibal".

Ästhetik & Freundschaft

Aesthetics & Friendship

Kopf oder Bauch, das ist hier die Frage. Steuern Gefühle den Verstand oder umgekehrt? Die Idee des „Moral Sense" kommt nach Deutschland: Der Mensch soll vernunftgeleitet dem Gesetz des Herzens folgen.

Das Individuum wird wichtiger. Wer jetzt wahre Beziehungen sucht, sieht in den kalkulierten Kontakten der Karrieristen bei Hofe kein Modell mehr für Lebensqualität. Mendelssohn lebt den neuen Freundschaftskult. Seine Ehe entsteht – unkonventionell – aus einer Liebesheirat.

Mendelssohn publiziert „Briefe über die Empfindungen". Um Schönheit wahrzunehmen, reicht die Ratio nicht: Seine Kunsttheorie analysiert, wie uns Malerei, Musik, Theater im Innersten bewegen.

Head or gut? That is the question. Do emotions influence our thoughts or the other way around? The notion of "moral sense" arrives in Germany: humans ought to follow their hearts, guided by reason.

The individual gains importance. People seeking genuine relationships no longer see noblemen's calculated connections as a worthy model. Mendelssohn lives by the new cult of friendship. Unconventionally, he marries for love.

Mendelssohn publishes "Letters on Feeling". We cannot appreciate beauty on a purely rational level: His theory of art analyzes the profound ways that paintings, music, and theater move us.

zu Nr. 151

Nr. 150 Giacomo Zoffoli: Laokoon-Gruppe
ca. 1780/90
Bronze
Royal Collections, Stockholm
Am Todeskampf des antiken Helden und seiner Söhne stellen sich Fragen nach der künstlerischen Darstellung von starken Gefühlen. Lessings kunsttheoretische Schrift „Laokoon" entsteht aus Diskussionen mit Mendelssohn und Nicolai über Sinnlichkeit und Mitleid, und wie Bildhauerei und Dichtung auf uns wirken.
The depiction of the ancient hero and his sons during the agonies of death raises questions about the artistic representation of strong feelings. Lessing's treatise on art theory, Laocoön, emerges from discussions with Mendelssohn and Nicolai about sensualism, empathy, and how sculpture and poetry affect us.

Nr. 151 Jan van Huijsum (1682–1749): Blumenstrauss mit Schnecken
ca. 1724
Öl auf Leinwand
Herzog Anton Ulrich-Museum, Braunschweig
An einer „Rose von Huysum" erkennen wir laut Mendelssohn den Geist des Künstlers, dessen Vollkommenheit uns mehr Vergnügen bereitet als die bloße Ähnlichkeit der gemalten Blume. Er sieht die gemalte Blume wohl bei seinem Besuch in Braunschweig.
According to Mendelssohn, a single "rose by Huysum" allows us to recognize the artist's spirit, whose perfection gives us more pleasure than the painted flower's resemblance to the real one. He probably sees the painted flower during his visit to Brunswick.

Nr. 152–160 Daniel Chodowiecki (1726–1801): Illustrationen zu Shakespeares „Hamlet"
Berlin, 1778
Radierungen
Herzog Anton Ulrich-Museum, Braunschweig
Anhand seiner Übersetzung des Monologs „Seyn oder Nichtseyn" und im „Briefwechsel über das Trauerspiel" analysiert Mendelssohn die Bühneneffekte Mitleid und Erhabenheit. Das Berliner Hamlet-Gastspiel von J. F. Brockmann reißt ihn vor Begeisterung „völlig hin".
In "Correspondence on Tragedy" Mendelssohn analyzes sympathy and the sublime as effects of theater. He draws in particular on his own translation of Shakespeare's "To Be or Not to Be" monologue. He is "completely enraptured" by J. F. Brockmann's performance of Hamlet in Berlin.

William Hogarth (1697–1764):
Nr. 162 Analysis of Beauty, Plate I (Analyse der Schönheit)
Nr. 161 Analysis of Beauty, Plate II (Analyse der Schönheit)
London, 1753
Radierung und Kupferstich
Herzog August Bibliothek Wolfenbüttel
Die Kupferstiche in Hogarths Buch regen Mendelssohn zu Reflexionen über antike Schönheit und „Satyre in der Mahlerey" an.
Mendelssohn is inspired to reflect on ancient beauty and "satire in painting" by the engravings in Hogarth's book.

Nr. 163 Moses Mendelssohn (1729–1786): Psalm 65. Über den Tempel, die Zuflucht bei Gott, Natur, Ernte, Jahreszeiten, Schöpfung und Naturgewalten
Berlin, ca. 1780
Papier, Tinte
SBB PK, Musikabteilung mit Mendelssohn-Archiv
Zehn Jahre dauert Mendelssohns Übersetzung der Psalmen, einige werden von Zeitgenossen vertont.

Musik verbindet und verwandelt nach Mendelssohns Ansicht die Nachahmung von Leidenschaften, Widersinnigem und sinnlicher Lust zur „Zauberkraft der Harmonie".
It takes Mendelssohn ten years to complete his translation of the Psalms, some of which are set to music by contemporaries. In his view, music combines and transforms human passions, discordance, and sensuous pleasure into the "magical power of harmony."

NR. 164 JOHANN FRIEDRICH REICHARDT (1752–1814): DER 65STE PSALM (DER SEELEN RUHE IST ES, GOTT) NACH MOSES MENDELSOHNS ÜBERSETZUNG
ca. 1800
Papier, Tinte
Bibliothek der Hansestadt Lübeck
„Göttliche Tonkunst! Du bist die eintzige, die uns mit allen Arten von Vergnügen überraschet! Welche süsse Verwirrung von Vollkommenheit, sinnlicher Lust und Schönheit! Die Nachahmungen der menschlichen Leidenschaften; die künstliche Verbindung zwischen den widersinnigsten Uebellauten: Quellen der Vollkommenheit! Die leichten Verhältnisse in den Schwingungen: eine Quelle der Schönheit! Die mit allen Saiten harmonische Spannung der nervigten Gefässe: eine Quelle der sinnlichen Lust!"
"Divine art of sound! You are the only one who surprises us with all kinds of pleasure! What sweet confusion of perfection, sensuous pleasure, and beauty! The imitations of human passions, the artful combination of discordant tones: sources of perfection! The simple proportions of vibrations: a source of beauty! The tensions of the vessels of the nerves harmonizing with every string: a source of sensuous pleasure!"

NR. 165 MOSES MENDELSSOHN (1729–1786): VERSUCH, EINE VOLLKOMMEN GLEICHSCHWEBENDE TEMPERATUR DURCH DIE CONSTRUCTION ZU FINDEN
In: Friedrich Wilhelm Marpurg, Historisch-Kritische Beyträge zur Aufnahme der Musik, Band V
Berlin, Lange: 1761
SBB PK, Musikabteilung mit Mendelssohn-Archiv

NR. 166 MOSES MENDELSSOHN (1729–1786): VERSUCH, EINE VOLLKOMMEN GLEICHSCHWEBENDE TEMPERATUR DURCH DIE CONSTRUCTION ZU FINDEN
In: Friedrich Wilhelm Marpurg, Historisch-Kritische Beyträge zur Aufnahme der Musik, Band V
Berlin, Schütz: 1761
Akademie der Künste, Berlin

NR. 168 MOSES MENDELSSOHN (1729–1786): ÜBER DIE EMPFINDUNGEN
Berlin: Christian Friedrich Voß, 1755
SBB PK, Abteilung Handschriften und Historische Drucke
Sinnlicher Ausdruck der Vollkommenheit: In der Diskussion zwischen Mendelssohn, dem Ästhetikprofessor Sulzer und Lessing entwickeln sich Grundlagen einer Wissenschaft vom Schönen.
The sensuous expression of perfection: this and other foundations of aesthetics emerge in the discussions among Mendelssohn, Lessing, and the aesthetics professor Johann Georg Sulzer, and Lessing.

„In den Regeln der Schönheit, die das Genie des Künstlers empfindet, und der Kunstrichter in Vernunftschlüße auflöset, liegen die tiefsten Geheimnisse unserer Seele verborgen."
"The deepest secrets of the soul lie hidden among the rules of beauty, which the genius of the artist feels and from which the critic of art derives rational inferences."

NR. 169 MOSES MENDELSSOHN (1729–1786): BETRACHTUNGEN ÜBER DIE QUELLEN UND DIE VERBINDUNGEN DER SCHÖNEN KÜNSTE UND WISSENSCHAFTEN
In: Friedrich Nicolai (Hrsg.), Bibliothek der schönen Wissenschaften und der freyen Künste
Leipzig: Christian Friedrich Dyck, 1757
SBB PK, Abteilung Handschriften und Historische Drucke

OBJEKTVERZEICHNIS

Nr. 170 Gotthold Ephraim Lessing (1729–1781): Laokoon oder über die Grenzen der Mahlerey und Poesie. Erster Theil
Berlin: Christian Friedrich Voß, 1766
SBB PK, Abteilung Handschriften und Historische Drucke

Nr. 171 Moses Mendelssohn (1729–1786): Rezension des Buchs von Christian Gottlieb von Murr „Anmerkungen über Herrn Lessings Laokoon, nebst einigen Nachrichten die deutsche Literatur betreffend"
In: Friedrich Nicolai (Hrsg.), Allgemeine deutsche Bibliothek, Band 11, 1. Theil
Berlin: Friedrich Nicolai, 1770
SBB PK

Nr. 172 Johann Georg Sulzer (1720–1779): Allgemeine Theorie der Schönen Künste in einzeln, nach alphabetischer Ordnung der Kunstwörter auf einander folgenden, Artikeln abgehandelt, Theil 1
Leipzig: Weidemanns Erben und Reich, 1771
SBB PK, Abteilung Handschriften und Historische Drucke

Nr. 174 Daniel Chodowiecki (1726–1801): Die Freundschaft
Göttingen, 1783
Radierung
Herzog Anton Ulrich-Museum, Braunschweig
Aus dem Zusammenspiel von Vernunft und Empfindung sollen wahrhaftige, beständige, vertrauensvolle Beziehungen entstehen. Mendelssohn mit seinem sozialen Talent praktiziert diese neue Idee in seinem nahen Umfeld und im erweiterten Kreis.
The goal is to establish truthful, enduring, and trusting relationships on the basis of the interaction between reason and feeling. With the help of his social skills, Mendelssohn puts the new ideas into practice in his immediate and extended circle.

Nr. 175 Andreas Ludwig Krüger (1743–1822): Der Freundschaftstempel im Park von Schloss Sanssouci
1780
Radierung
JMB

Bestimmung des Menschen

Destiny of Man

Ist der homo sapiens eine Maschine? Funktioniert der Deal zwischen Körper und Seele? Ist mit dem Tod alles vorbei? Gehört Freitod zur Autonomie?

Mendelssohns Bestseller zur unsterblichen Seele begegnet den Fragen verunsicherter Zeitgenossen. Für ihn ist jeder von Gott bestimmt, es gilt, eigene Handicaps zu überwinden. Selbstvervollkommnung durch Tugend macht glücklich und verändert die Gesellschaft zum Guten.

Mendelssohn stottert, hat einen Buckel und ist häufig krank. Dass in seiner Person Unsterbliches und Fragilität so drastisch verbunden erscheinen, verstört und fasziniert. Wie er Behinderung und Diskriminierung in Brillanz verwandelt: Das trägt bei zur Ausstrahlung seines Lebenswerkes.

Is homo sapiens a machine? Do body and soul have a workable arrangement? Is death the end? Is suicide an exercise of free will?

Mendelssohn's bestselling book on the immortal soul addresses the questions of his troubled contemporaries. As he sees it, God dictates each person's lot in life, and it is up to individuals to rise above their own challenges. Self-fulfillment through good deeds brings happiness and changes society for the better.

Mendelssohn stutters, has an abnormally curved spine, and is often ill. The radical link between his immortality and his fragility is both fascinating and disconcerting. His brilliance in the face of disability and discrimination is a further credit to his life's work.

Nr. 181 Daniel Chodowiecki (1726–1801): Die Gleichheit aller Stände im Grabe
Berlin, 1770
Radierung
JMB
Im Verhältnis zur Schöpfung und angesichts des Todes sind Menschen unterschiedlicher Religionen alle gleich.
In their relationship with creation and in the face of death, people of different religions are equal.

Nr. 182 Daniel Chodowiecki (1726–1801): Titelkupfer zu Lehre vom richtigen Verhältnisse des Menschen zu den Schöpfungswerken, und die durch öffentliche Einführung derselben allein zu bewürkende algemeine Menschenbeglükkung, hg. v. Franz Heinrich Ziegenhagen
1791
Radierung
Herzog Anton Ulrich-Museum, Braunschweig

Nr. 183 William Pether (1738–1821): Drei Männer betrachten die Figur des Gladiators (nach Joseph Wright of Derby)
1769
Mezzotinto, Radierung
SMB PK, Kupferstichkabinett
Mendelssohn erwähnt den „bewunderungswürdigen Borghesischen Fechter" (Borghese Gladiator), das antike Vorbild für Derbys Gemälde, in einer Laokoon-Rezension (Nr. 171).
Mendelssohn mentions the "admirable Borghese swordsman" (Borghese Gladiator), the ancient model for Derby's painting, in a Laocoon review (no. 171).

Nr. 184 Profilsilhouetten von Friedrich Gottlieb Klopstock, Friedrich A. Klockenbring, Johann Andreae und Moses Mendelssohn aus der Sammlung Lavater
1783
Radierung
Österreichische Nationalbibliothek Wien

Nr. 185 Christian von Mechel (1737–1817): Stufenfolge von dem Frosche bis zum Apollo-Profile
Basel, 1797
Radierung, koloriert
Österreichische Nationalbibliothek Wien
Woraus besteht der Mensch? Was ist seine Bestimmung? Mendelssohn sagt: Seine gottbestimmte Vervollkommung beginnt im Mutterleib und hört mit dem Tod nicht auf. Er sei „zur Unsterblichkeit geschaffen", könne sich „wahre Zernichtung" nicht vorstellen. Was ist dann das Verhältnis zwischen Körper und Seele?
What Is the nature of man? What is man's vocation? Mendelssohn's answer: human perfection, ordained by God, begins in the womb and does not end with death. Men are "created for immortality" and cannot imagine "true annihilation." What, then, is the relationship between body and soul?

Nr. 188 G. Rauscher (?): Muskelmann aus Weichholz (Kopie des Écorché von J. P. Houdon)
vor 1866
Weichholz
Germanisches Nationalmuseum, Nürnberg – Leihgabe der Friedrich von Praun'schen Familienstiftung

Nr. 189 Aderlasskasten mit Schröpfköpfen und Aderlassdarstellung
1746–1755
Holz, Glas, Metall, textiles Gewebe
Deutsches Hygiene-Museum Dresden, Sammlung Schwarzkopf

Nr. 190 Badermesser mit 8 Klingen
1701–1750
Holz, Messing, Stahl
Deutsches Hygiene-Museum Dresden, Sammlung Schwarzkopf

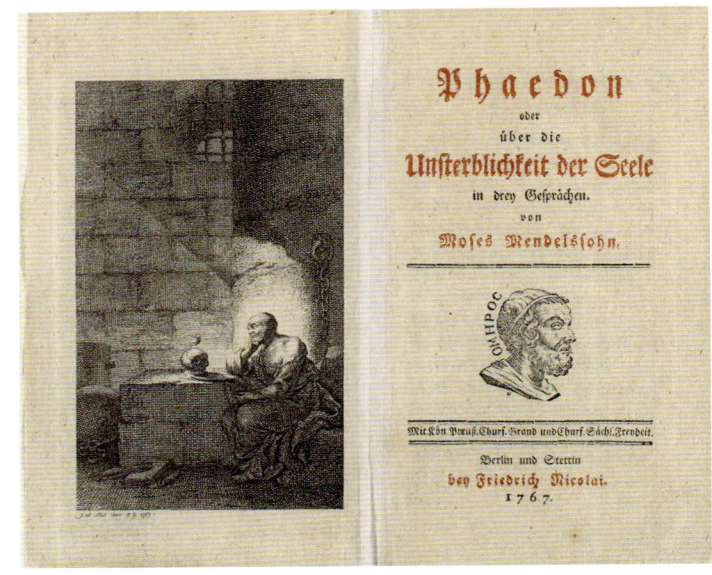

Nr. 191 Dritte Ansicht der Promenade vom Baad zu Pyrmont
Augsburg, ca. 1780
Kupferstich, koloriert
Museum im Schloss Bad Pyrmont

Nr. 192 Ansicht des Mineralischen Baades zu Pyrmont
Augsburg, ca. 1780
Kupferstich, koloriert
Museum im Schloss Bad Pyrmont

Nr. 193 Johann David Schleuen (1711–1771): Prospect des Gesundbrunnens bei Berlin. Ansicht der Kuranlagen
Berlin, ca. 1770
Kupferstich, koloriert
JMB (Foto: Roman März)

Nr. 195 Moses Mendelssohn (1729–1786): Gedicht (Abschrift)
undatiert
Papier, Tinte
Mendelsohn-Gesellschaft, Berlin, Leihgabe Sammlung Dopfer
Überwindet dieser Geist den zerbrechlichen Körper? Der Kontrast verstört und fasziniert seine Zeitgenossen. Mendelssohn ist schwächlich und schüchtern, ein Stotterer, jahrelang nervenkrank, braucht oft Ärzte und Kuraufenthalte. Er stirbt mit 56.
Can the mind overcome the frailties of the body? The contrast between the two disturbs and fascinates Mendelssohn's contemporaries. He stutters, is frail and shy, suffers from a nervous disease for years, and is in constant need of doctors' care and spa treatments. He dies at fifty-six.

Nr. 196: Moses Mendelssohn (1729–1786): Phaedon oder über die Unsterblichkeit der Seele in drey Gesprächen
Berlin und Stettin: Nicolai, 1767
Privatbesitz
Mendelssohns „Phädon" erscheint in zahlreichen Übersetzungen und Auflagen. Die von Platon aufgeschriebenen Dialoge des zum Tode verurteilten Sokrates bezieht er auf aktuelle Fragen nach dem Sinn des Lebens.
Mendelssohn's "Phaedon" is published in numerous translations and editions. Mendelssohn revisits the dialogues of the condemned Socrates, recorded by Plato, and applies them to present-day questions about the meaning of life.

Nr. 197 Moses Mendelssohn (1729–1786): Phédon, ou Entretiens sur la spiritualité et l'immortalité de l'âme
Paris: Saillant, 1772
JMB

Nr. 198 Moses Mendelssohn (1729–1786): Fedon. Hu sefer hascharat ha-nefesch
Berlin: Jüdische Freischule, 1787
JMB

Nr. 199 Moses Mendelssohn (1729–1786): Phedon of over de onsterflykheid der zeile, in drie t'zamenspraaken, Door Moses Mendelssohn
Graavenhaage: Pieter van Cleef, 1776
SBB PK, Musikabteilung mit Mendelssohn-Archiv

Nr. 200 Moses Mendelssohn (1729–1786) : Fedone, o dell' immortalitá dell'anima. In tre dialoghi
Coira, 1773
JMB

Nr. 201 Moses Mendelssohn (1729–1786): Fedon o niesmiertelnosci duszy: Przez slawnego filozofa M. Mendelssohna przekladu Jakóba Tugendholda
Warschau: Piotra Baryckiego, 1842
Staatsbibliothek zu Berlin –
Preußischer Kulturbesitz

Nr. 203 Moses Mendelssohn (1729–1786): Eintrag zur „Bestimmung des Menschen" im Stammbuch Hersleb, Band 2
23.12.1780
Papier, Tinte
Goethe-Museum Düsseldorf
Nr. 204 Stammbuchblatt von
Moses Mendelssohn
20.12.1785
Papier, Tinte
SBB PK, Musikabteilung mit
Mendelssohn-Archiv
„Warheit erkennen; Schönheit lieben;
Gutes wollen; das Beste thun."
„Gott nachahmen heißt So, wie Er, das
Gute lieben, weil es gut ist; Nicht, weil
es Gott befohlen."
*"To recognize truth, to love beauty,
to wish for good, to do what is best."
"To emulate God is to love all that is
good—not because it is commanded
by God, but because it is good."*

Nr. 202 Moses Mendelssohn (1729–1786): Abhandlung über das Kommerz zwischen Seele und Körper
Berlin, 1788
JMB
Auf dem gottbestimmten Weg zur
Vervollkommnung seiner sozialen
Tugenden überwindet der Mensch die
Begrenzungen der Seele und des
Körpers.
*By following the path ordained by
God for perfecting his social virtues,
man can overcome the limitations
of body and mind.*

Nr. 205 Johann Georg Zimmermann (1728–1795): Von der Diät der Seele
1764
Papier, Tinte
Gottfried Wilhelm Leibniz Bibliothek -
Niedersächsische Landesbibliothek
In Mendelsohns „elendestem und
unter uns Thoren verachtetsten Leib"
wohne, so formuliert es der Arzt,
„eine göttliche Seele", der „Schöpfung
zur Zierde".
*In Mendelssohn's "most miserable
and most despised body by us fools"
dwells, as the doctor puts it, "a divine
soul" that "adorns creation".*

Stegreifgedicht Mendelssohns im Gelehrten Kaffeehaus, um 1755

„Gros nennt Ihr den Demosthen den
stotternden Orator von Athen
Aesop der Höckrige galt Euch für weise
Triumph! ich werd in Eurem Kreise
Gedoppelt gros und weise seyn,
Der glücklich ich in mir verein
Was man getrennt im Demosthen,
und im Aesop gehöret und gesehen."

Impromptu poem by Mendelssohn at the Learned Coffee House, around 1755

*"Great you call Demosthenes,
Stuttering orator of Greece;
Hunchbacked Aesop you deem wise;—
In your circle I surmise
I am doubly wise and great.
What in each was separate
You in me united find—
Hump and heavy tongue combined."
(Translation as cited in Benson Bobrick:
Knotted Tongues: Stuttering in History
and the Quest for a Cure; New York:
Simon & Schuster 1995, p. 78.)*

Judenporzellan

Jewish Porcelain

Zu mancher Lieferkette gehört die Ausblendung von Menschenrechten. Preußen braucht Devisen, produziert Luxusgüter. Du als Jude willst heiraten, ein Haus kaufen, ein zweites Kind „ansetzen"? Die Sondersteuer dafür funktioniert so: Porzellan aus Königs Fabrik kaufen und im Ausland absetzen.

Bis 1945 verwahren Mendelssohn-Nachkommen aus so einem Zwangsdeal hässliche Keramik-Affen. Wie Trophäen überwundener Schikanen! Oder sollte man Diskriminierung von einst irgendwann vergessen?

Der Künstler Izhar Patkin montiert Zerbrechliches aus der guten Stube und Porträts aus der Mendelssohn-Familie zur Laubhütten-Tapete. Seine Kunst verbindet Motive arrivierter Bürgerlichkeit mit dem Provisorium des Migranten.

Supply chains often disregard human rights. Prussia needs foreign currency and produces luxury goods. You are Jewish and you want to get married, buy a house, or have a second child? If so, you are subject to a special tax: You have to buy porcelain from the royal factory, then sell it abroad.

The ugly ceramic monkeys from one such forced deal were kept by Mendelssohn's family until 1985—like trophies of injustices overcome. Or should past discrimination be forgotten after enough time has gone by?

Artist Izhar Patkin has created a wall hanging for a sukkah that combines delicate parlor pieces with portraits of the Mendelssohns, juxtaposing motifs of the Nouveau Riche with an immigrant's makeshift solutions.

zu Nr. 247

OBJEKTVERZEICHNIS

Nr. 242 Johann Joachim Kaendler (1706–1775): Affe mit Schnupftabakdose
Meißen, Modell: 1732, Ausformung: 1924/33
Porzellan
Meißen Porzellan-Stiftung

o. Nr. Porzellanaffe aus der Mendelssohn-Familie
Aufnahme von der 1929er Moses-Mendelssohn-Ausstellung
Fotografie
Mendelssohn-Gesellschaft, Berlin
Moses' Urenkel Sebastian Hensel berichtet 1879 über die Zwangsabnahme von Porzellan:
„So bekam Moses Mendelssohn zwanzig lebensgroße, massiv porzellanene Affen, von denen sich noch einige in der Familie erhalten haben." Sahen sie aus wie diese?

In 1878, Sebastian Hensel reports on the compulsory purchase of porcelain: "Thus, Moses Mendelssohn received twenty life-sized solid porcelain apes, a few of which still remain in the family." Did they look like this one?

Nr. 245 Verpflichtung der Juden zu Abnahme und Export von Porzellan aus der Königlichen Porzellan-Manufaktur gemäss Kabinettsordres 09.03. und 07.06.1769
Papier, Tinte, Wachs
Geheimes Staatsarchiv Preußischer Kulturbesitz, Berlin
Nr. 246 Abschrift der Verfügungen vom 28.01.1770 und 19.03.1772
Papier, Tinte
Geheimes Staatsarchiv Preußischer Kulturbesitz, Berlin

Für Hauskauf, Heirat und andere Genehmigungen müssen Juden seit 1769 der staatlichen Manufaktur Porzellan im Wert von 300 Talern abkaufen und ins Ausland exportieren. 300 Taler entsprechen einem auskömmlichen Jahresgehalt für eine Familie.

Starting in 1769, Jews seeking to buy a house, get married, or obtain other permits must first buy and export 300 talers worth of porcelain from the royal factory. This amount, 300 talers, comes up to a decent family income for a year.

Nr. 243 Bestätigung für Isaac Moses über den Ankauf und Export von Porzellan
Berlin, 11.06.1783
Papier, Tinte
JMB

Nr. 247 Izhar Patkin (geb. 1955): Sukka-Installation mit 23 Objekten aus der Serie „Judenporzellan"
1998–2002
JMB
Der in New York lebende israelische Künstler Izhar Patkin setzt sich mit Mendelssohn, dessen Vermächtnis und der Erfolgsgeschichte der Familie auseinander. In seinem Kunstwerk verbindet er die traditionelle Ausschmückung der Sukka mit der im 18. Jahrhundert beliebten Technik des Scherenschnitts.

The New York-based Israeli artist Izhar Patkin picks up the threads of Mendelssohn, his legacy, and his family's success story. In his artwork, he links traditional Sukkah decorations with the art of paper cutting, which was popular in the eighteenth century.

Was wird aus Moses Mendelssohn?

What is Moses Mendelssohn's Legacy?

Viele schwören auf Veränderungen. Andere auf Bewahrung. Manche werfen alles über Bord. Für den Weg in die Zukunft modelliert man sich Helden nach Bedarf.

Dem Trauerzug Mendelssohns folgt noch die ganze Jüdische Gemeinde, samt Mitgliedern des Hofes. Bald bilden sich Denkmalfraktionen. Für Haskala-Aktivisten ist er der Aufklärer. Für Neoorthodoxe der Gesetzestreue. Für Schtetl-Bewohner der Tora-Übersetzer. Für Patrioten der „Moses der deutschen Juden".

Die Gesellschaft polarisiert sich. Für Marx ist dieser Vermittler ein „Seichtbeutel". Zionisten sagen: Er sei schuld an der Assimilation. Schwächt Integration die kulturelle Identität? Für Nazis wird er zum Feindbild.

Many insist on the urgency of change. Others on the urgency of conservation. Some throw everything overboard. When building roads to the future, everyone designs the heroes they desire.

The whole Jewish community walks in Mendelssohn's funeral procession, including members of the royal court. Soon enough, various factions disagree about his legacy. For Haskalah activists, he is the Enlightenment thinker. For the Orthodox, he is the pious follower of the commandments. For shtetl residents, he is the Torah translator. For the patriotic, he is the "Moses of the German Jews."

Society polarizes. Marx dismisses him as wishy-washy. Zionists blame him for assimilation. Does social integration weaken cultural identity? Ultimately, the Nazis demonize him.

ZU NR. 255

o. Nr. Friedrich Albert Schwartz (1836–1906): Das Wohnhaus Mendelssohns in der Spandauer Strasse 68
Berlin, 1886
Fotografie
Privatbesitz
In diesem 1886 abgerissenen Haus, einem Treffpunkt der „Berliner Aufklärung" und der Haskala, hatten vor Mendelssohn mit Familie auch seine Mitstreiter Lessing, Nicolai und Ramler gewohnt.
Mendelssohn's comrades-in-arms Lessing, Nicolai and Ramler lived in this house, a meeting place of the "Berlin Enlightenment", before Mendelssohn and his family. The building was demolished in 1886.

Nr. 253 Gedenktafel für Moses Mendelssohn
Berlin, 1829
Marmor
Stiftung Neue Synagoge Berlin – Centrum Judaicum, Berlin
Die Gedenktafel befand sich am ehemaligen Wohnhaus Mendelssohns in der Spandauer Straße 68 – eine der frühesten Ehrungen für einen Bürgerlichen im öffentlichen Raum.
This memorial plaque was affixed to Mendelssohn's former home on Spandauer Straße 68—one of the earliest tributes to a commoner in public space.

Nr. 254 Micha Ullman (geb. 1939: Haus Mendelssohn, Projektion
Nr. 255 Micha Ullman (geb. 1939): Haus Mendelssohn, Fassade
2015
Bleistift, aquarelliert
JMB
Auf Initiative der Mendelssohn-Gesellschaft konzipiert Micha Ullman eine Bodenskulptur am Ort des Wohnhauses. Über dem Türsturz: die Gedenktafel.
On the initiative of the Mendelssohn Society, Micha Ullman designs a ground sculpture for the site of Mendelssohn's home. Above the lintel: the memorial plaque.

OBJEKTVERZEICHNIS

Nr. 248 Andres Stöttrup (1754–1812): Gedenkblatt Moses Mendelssohn (Moses Mendelssohn Grab)
ca. 1790
Radierung
Leo Baeck Institute, New York City
Pläne für ein Mendelssohn-Denkmal gibt es schon bald nach seinem Tod. Sie scheitern an der Finanzierung und leben in der Fantasie fort.
Plans for a Mendelssohn memorial emerge shortly after his death. They fail due to a lack of funding, yet endure in the imagination.

Nr. 251 Moses Mendelssohn im Kreise von Schriftstellern und Philosophen
ca. 1900
Lithografie
ÖNB
Zeitgenossen, liberal und traditionell, verehren Mendelssohn gleichermaßen.

Nr. 256 Moses Mendelssohn (1729–1786): Gesammelte Schriften. Jubiläumsausgabe
Herausgegeben von Alexander Altmann, Michael Brocke, Eva J. Engel und Daniel Krochmalnik. In Gemeinschaft mit Fritz Bamberger, H. Borodianski (Bar-Dayan), Simon Rawidowicz, Bruno Strauss, L. Strauss und Werner Weinberg. Begonnen von Ismar Elbogen, Julius Guttmann und Eugen Mittwoch
40 Bände
Stuttgart-Bad Cannstatt: frommann-holzboog Verlag e. K., 1972–2022
Die Jubiläumsausgabe der Gesammelten Schriften beginnt 1929 mit Unterstützung der Nachkommen zum 200. Geburtstag. 1938 vernichtet die Gestapo den gerade erschienenen

Band 14 bis auf wenige Exemplare. 2023 soll die seit 1972 fortgesetzte Jubiläumsausgabe fertiggestellt werden.
With support from Mendelssohn's descendants, the preparation of an anniversary edition of his collected writings is initiated in 1929 to commemorate his two-hundredth birthday. In 1938, the Gestapo destroys all but a few copies of the most recent volume. The project was resumed in 1972 and is scheduled to be completed in 2023.

NR. 257 MOSES MENDELSSOHN (1729–1786): GESAMMELTE SCHRIFTEN, BAND 14. HEBRÄISCHE SCHRIFTEN I
Breslau: Stefan Münz/Jüdischer Buchverlag, 1938
SBB PK

NR. 258 LUDWIG PASSINI (1832–1903): PORTRÄT ERNST VON MENDELSSOHN-BARTHOLDY (1846–1909) IN SEINEM ARBEITSZIMMER MIT MINIATURBÜSTE MOSES MENDELSSOHNS
1894
Tempera auf Velin, auf Faserplatte aufgezogen
Privatbesitz
(Foto Manfred Claudi)

NR. 259 OTTO ILLEMANN (1869–1929): MEDAILLE MOSES MENDELSSOHN
Berlin, 1929
Bronze, patiniert
JMB

NR. 260 FRIEDRICH WILHELM HÖRNLEIN (1873–1945): MEDAILLE MOSES MENDELSSOHN
1929
Silber
SMB PK, Münzkabinett

NR. 261 JACOB PLESSNER (1871–1936): BÜSTE MOSES MENDELSSOHN
1929, Guss nach dem Entwurf von 1909
Bronze, patiniert
JMB

NR. 262 KÖNIGLICHE PORZELLAN-MANUFAKTUR: BÜSTE MOSES MENDELSSOHN (NACH ANTOINE TASSAERT) (1727–1788)
Berlin, nach 1785
Porzellan
JMB

NR. 263 PORZELLANMANUFAKTUR FÜRSTENBERG: BÜSTE MOSES MENDELSSOHN (NACH ANTOINE TASSAERT)
2006, Abguss nach der Originalform von 1785–1790
Porzellan
JMB

NR. 264 POKAL MIT PORTRÄT MOSES MENDELSSOHN
Nordböhmen, ca. 1835 (Pokal), 1886 (Gravur, signiert K. B.)
Glas
JMB

NR. 265 LESSING-MENDELSSOHN-GEDENKBUCH. ZUR HUNDERTFÜNFZIGJÄHRIGEN GEBURTSFEIER VON GOTTHOLD EPHRAIM LESSING UND MOSES MENDELSSOHN SOWIE ZUR SÄKULARFEIER VON LESSINGS „NATHAN", HG. V. DEUTSCH-ISRAELITISCHEN GEMEINDEBUND
Leipzig: Baumgärtner, 1879
JMB

NR. 266 ANGELINA SCHÜLER UND MARIE-CHRISTIN BEHRENDT: HOMMAGE
2015
Inkjet auf Leinwand
Privatbesitz, Berlin
[Christoph Schulte]

NR. 269 FREUNDE IN PREUSSEN ODER: OB EIN EDLER JUDE ETWAS UNWAHRSCHEINLICHES SEI (AUSSCHNITTE)
Friends in Prussia, or Whether a Noble Jew is an Unlikely Thing (Excerpts)
Deutschland, 1981
Spielfilm, 95 Minuten, Farbe
Regie: Rolf Busch,
Drehbuch: Heiner Michel
Produktion: Allianz Film Produktion GmbH mit Unterstützung der DEFA im Auftrag des ZDF
ZDF

NR. 270 AUF DER SUCHE NACH HERRN MOSES (AUSSCHNITTE)
Searching for Mr Moses (Excerpts)
Deutschland, 1990
Dokumentarfilm, 60 Minuten, Farbe
Regie: Tamara Wyss
Produktion: Leon Janucek für ESON-Film im Auftrag des ZDF
Alice Wyss

o. Nr. Typex: Entwürfe für die Graphic Novel „Moische. Sechs Anekdoten aus dem Leben des Moses Mendelssohn" 2022

Anhang *Appendix*

ANHANG

Medienstationen

Media Stations

Hörtext: Brief von Christoph Friedrich Nicolai an Johann Peter Uz

„Berlin den 26. März 1759
Insbesonders Hochzuehrender Herr und Freund

Erlauben Sie mir immer daß ich mich des letztern Titels bediene, den ich noch nicht habe verdienen können, denn ich werde Ihrer Freundschaft nötig haben, um mich wegen des langen Ausbleibens meiner Antwort auf Dero angenehmes Schreiben zu entschuldigen – Einigermaßen entschuldigt mich das Gewühl von Geschäften in welchen ich lebe, ich komme kaum zu mir selber […]

Ich warf mich gleichsam in diese Bahn ohne zu bedenken wie viele Mühe mich erwartete. Herr Moses half mir hernach, und bloß seine Freundschaft gegen mich macht, daß er sich noch mit den schönen Wissenschaften beschäftigt, da sonst dieselben eigentlich nicht sein Werk sind.

Herr Moses hält sich zur Synagoge und warum sollte er dieses nicht thun? – Er ist eines der größten Genies die Deutschland je gehabt, die Geschichte seiner Zunahme in den Wißenschaften überzeugt mich recht sehr von der Unnützlichkeit unseres Universitätsstudierens. – Herr Moses hat keiner mündlichen Unterweisung etwas zu danken. Er ist aus Deßau gebürtig, und konnte bis in sein vierzehntes Jahr kei-

Listening text: Letter from Christoph Friedrich Nicolai to Johann Peter Uz

"Berlin, March 26, 1759
Most Honorable Sir and Friend

I hope you will allow me to refer to you by the latter title, which I have not yet had the chance to earn, as I will require your friendship to excuse myself for the long delay in my reply to your kind letter—to some degree, my excuse is the bustle of business dealings amongst which I live; I scarcely find time for myself. […]

I threw myself onto this track, as it were, without considering how much toil would await me. Herr Moses helped me afterwards, and being my friend is his sole reason for remaining occupied with the arts and letters, which are otherwise not his domain.

Mr. Moses keeps to the synagogue, and why should he not?—He is one of the greatest geniuses Germany has ever had; the story of his acquisition of knowledge persuades me very greatly of the uselessness of our university studies.— Herr Moses owes nothing to any oral instruction. He is a native of Dessau, and until age fourteen could read no language but Hebrew, not even proper German. By then the Jews considered him a great Talmudist, and he was already meant to marry a rabbi's daughter. Around that time, he succumbed to a kind of nervous condi-

ne Sprache als hebräisch, ja nicht einmal recht Deutsch lesen. Inzwischen war er unter den Juden für einen großen Talmudisten gehalten, und er sollte schon die Tochter eines Rabbinens heirathen. Er fiel um diese Zeit in eine Art von Nerven oder engischer Krankheit, wodurch er bucklicht wurde da er sonst grade gewachsen gewesen. Er ging zu Fuße nach Berlin, wo ihm ein Jude als einem armen Jungen einen Verschlag auf dem Boden einräumte, wo er im Talmud studieren könnte. Hier studierte er Tag und Nacht, und wußte von der übrigen Welt nichts. Er studierte auch aus hebräischen Schriften die Philosophie und Mathematik. [...] Er hatte für sich in kurzer Zeit Lateinisch Französisch und Engländisch gelernt. Von einem Juden Hern Gumpertz (einem guten Mathematico) lernte er Wolfen [den Philosophen] kennen, dessen sämtliche lateinische Schriften er mit großem Bedachte durchgelesen welches sich wenige werden anrühmen können.

Eben dieser Doctor Gumpertz brachte ihn zu einem jüdischen Kaufmann als Hofmeister für deßen Kinder; nachdem er den Sohn und Tochter sehr vernünfig erzogen, so dirigiret er seit einigen Jahren dieses Kaufmannes Isaac Bernhard Seidenfabrique. Er ist bis etwa Nachmittag um 4 Uhr im Contor und wendet die übrige Zeit bis Mitternacht zum studiren an. Hr Leßing brachte ihn zu erst darauf, sich um die schönen Wissenschaften zu bekümmern, und dieser war es auch der ihm die philosophischen Bücher so er herausgegeben gleichsam ablokte. [...] Seit ein paar Jahren lesen wir unter Anführung eines erfahrenen Griechen griechische Schriftsteller, wir sind izt beim Homer, dieser Dichter ist außerordentlich nach Herrn Moses Geschmake.

Er hat das beste Herz, wie glücklich wäre ich wenn ich immer um ihn sein könnte, ich habe nie einen innigern Freund gehabt. [...]"

tion or English ailment, which caused him to hunch although he had previously stood erect. He walked to Berlin on foot, where as an impoverished boy, a Jew offered him a garret where he could study Talmud. There, he studied day and night and knew nothing of the outside world. He also studied philosophy and mathematics from Hebrew texts. [...] Within a short time, he taught himself Latin, French, and English. From a Jew, Herr Gumpertz (a good mathematician), he became familiar with Wolff [the philosopher] and soon read all of Wolff's Latin writings very attentively, writings very few can boast of having read.

The same Dr. Gumpertz recommended him to a Jewish merchant as a tutor for the man's children; and after educating the son and daughter most judiciously, he has been entrusted with running the silk factory belonging to said merchant, Isaac Bernhard, for several years now. He works at the office until around 4 o'clock in the afternoon and spends his remaining hours, until midnight, studying. Herr Lessing first led him to concern himself with the arts and letters, and it was he who also coaxed his philosophical books out of him, so to speak, which he then published. [...] For a few years now, we have read Greek authors with the guidance of an experienced Hellenist; we have now moved on to Homer, a poet exceedingly to Herr Moses's taste.

He has the best heart. How happy I would be if I could always be around him. I have never had a dearer friend. [...]"

Papiertheater

Die Hörstationen an den Papiertheatern verbinden eine Moses-Figur des Zeichners Typex mit den Legenden und biografischen Episoden, von denen seine Graphic Novel „Moische" inspiriert wurde.

Hörtext: Das Stadttor
Der 14-jährige Moische, so sagt eine oft wiederholte Legende, soll am Ende seiner Wanderung von Dessau nach Berlin die Stadt noch einmal zwangsweise zu Fuß halb umrundet haben. Weil arme Juden nur im Norden, durchs Rosenthaler Tor, hätten einreisen dürfen. Hier gab es für sie eine Herberge. Lernen wolle er, habe der Junge als Reisegrund genannt. Der Torschreiber habe ihn daraufhin, neben sechs Ochsen und zwei Schweinen, als Einreisenden vermerkt.

    Tatsächlich folgt Moische seinem verehrten Lehrer Fränkel nach Berlin. Vielleicht nutzt er dabei auch die Postkutsche. Jedenfalls darf er das Hallesche Tor im Süden passieren, marschiert dann vorbei am Kollegienhaus, dem heutigen Jüdischen Museum, zur Stadtmitte. Neben der Nikolaikirche findet er in Chaim Bambergers Dachstube sein erstes Quartier.

Hörtext: Mendelssohn und Lavater
Ein populäres Gemälde fasst als legendäre Szene einen dramatischen Streit zusammen: Mendelssohn und sein Freund Lessing begegnen in Mendelssohns guter Stube dem Schweizer Theologen Lavater. Der fordert den jüdischen Gelehrten heraus: Dieser soll, da er so ein edler Mensch sei, entweder das Christentum widerlegen oder sich taufen lassen. Lessing schaut angewidert über den Theologen hinweg.

    In Wahrheit hat Lavater schon als junger Mann den weithin bekannten Gelehrten kon-

Paper Theater

The listening stations at the paper theaters connect a Moses character by the cartoonist Typex with the legends and biographical episodes from which his graphic novel "Moishe" was inspired.

Listening text: At the Gate
According to legend, fourteen-year-old Moishe, having just completed the long journey from Dessau to Berlin on foot, was nevertheless forced to walk halfway around the city before he could enter it. Supposedly poor Jews were only allowed through the city's northern gate, the Rosenthaler Tor, where an almshouse that would accommodate them was located. When asked his reason for traveling, the boy said he wanted to learn. As the story goes, the gatekeeper noted his arrival along with the entry of six oxen and two pigs.

    In fact, Moishe was following his distinguished teacher Fränkel to Berlin. Fränkel may have traveled by stagecoach. In any case, he was allowed to enter through the southern gate, the Hallesches Tor, and would have passed the Kollegienhaus, today's Jewish Museum, on his way to the city center. Moishe first stayed near the Nikolaikirche—the Church of St. Nicolas—as a lodger in Chaim Bamberger's attic.

Listening text: Mendelssohn and Lavater
A popular painting shows a dramatic dispute, boiled down to a single legendary scene. Mendelssohn and his friend Lessing meet the Swiss theologian Lavater in the parlor of Mendelssohn's home. Lavater challenges the Jewish scholar's honor: he must either refute Christianity or get baptized himself. Lessing looks away from the theologian in disgust.

taktiert. Der Bekehrungsversuch folgt später: durch ein Buch, das Mendelssohn zur öffentlichen Reaktion zwingt. Pro und Contra-Schriften erscheinen europaweit. Mendelssohn lehnt selbstverständlich ab, sich taufen zu lassen – und gilt als moralischer Sieger. Doch dieser Stress macht ihn, der mit dem Kaufmannsberuf seine Familie ernährt, schwerkrank und setzt ihn für einige Zeit außer Gefecht.

Hörtext: Mendelssohn und Friedrich II.

Wenn Friedrich II. den berühmtesten Juden seiner Zeit zu sich rufen lässt und ihm auf Philosophen-Ebene begegnet, muss die Gleichberechtigung endlich kommen. So denken und träumen wohl viele deutsche Juden. Das legendäre Treffen beider Männer wird weitererzählt und ausgeschmückt: wie unverblümt Mendelssohn dem größten Preußenkönig geantwortet hat!

Aber der echte Alte Fritz ist ein Judenfeind. Er fördert nur den nützlichen Textilkaufmann Mendelssohn, seine Aufnahme in die Akademie der Wissenschaften stoppt er, seiner Familie verweigert er Aufenthaltsgarantien. Nach Potsdam zitiert er ihn, weil sein Gast Baron Fritsche den berühmten Gelehrten sehen will. So fährt Mendelssohn mit einem Feiertagsdispens der Rabbiner am 30. September 1771 von Berlin nach Potsdam. Er spricht lange mit seinem Verehrer Fritsche. Majestät hingegen bleiben unter sich.

Hörtext: Mendelssohn und Abba Glosk

Die Geschichte von Mendelssohn und Abba Glosk ist wahr, nur kaum bekannt. Mit Persönlichkeiten, die von jüdischen Autoritäten gebannt oder verfolgt werden, hat Mendelssohn öfter zu tun. Doch keiner drängt sich ihm so ungestüm auf wie der obdachlose, hochgelehrte Alkoholiker Abba Glosk.

In fact, Lavater had once, years earlier as a young man, sought contact with the well-known scholar. His attempt to convert him only came later: through a book that forced Mendelssohn to react publicly. Arguments on both sides were published across Europe. Of course, Mendelssohn declined to convert to Christianity—and won the moral victory. But the stressful situation made him gravely ill, jeopardized his ability to support his family as a merchant, and forced him to withdraw from the public eye for several years.

Listening text: Mendelssohn and Frederick II

When Frederick II summoned the era's most famous Jew for a philosophical discussion, equal rights were in reach. Or at least, that was what many German Jews hoped and dreamed. The legend of the two men's meeting was told and retold with many embellishments: What blunt terms Mendelssohn used in his response to the great King of Prussia!

But the real Old Fritz was an enemy of the Jews. He only supported Mendelssohn as a useful fabric merchant. He blocked his membership in the Academy of Sciences and denied his family any guarantees of residency. The reason he called him to Potsdam was because his guest Baron Fritsche wanted to meet the famous scholar. And so, with rabbinical dispensation to travel on a holiday, Mendelssohn rode from Berlin to Potsdam on September 30, 1771. He had a long conversation with his admirer Fritsche. His Majesty, however, kept his distance.

Listening text: Mendelssohn and Abba Glosk

The story of Mendelssohn and Abba Glosk is true, but little known. Mendelssohn often dealt with people who had been excommunicated or persecuted by the Jewish authorities. But no one approached him as impetuously as the scholarly but homeless and alcoholic Abba Glosk.

Aufgrund seiner schroffen, prophetischen Kritik am Zustand der Synagogengemeinden gerät dieser polnische Dissident überall in Konflikt mit Glaubensgenossen: im heimatlichen Schtetl, in Holland, in England. Er wird gejagt, misshandelt, vertrieben. Im aufgeklärten Berlin hofft er auf Liberalität und schafft sich auch hier bald wieder Feinde. Aber durch Wissen, scharfsinnige Diskussion und Offenheit gewinnt er die Freundschaft Mendelssohns. Der versteckt den Störenfried ohne Aufenthaltserlaubnis am Stadtrand, im Villenpark des Gemeindeältesten Itzig.

Because of his harsh, prophetic criticism of the state of Jewish congregations, this dissident clashed with his fellow Jews wherever he went: in his native Polish shtetl, in the Netherlands, and in England. He had been hounded, abused, and banished. He hoped to find liberalism in Enlightened Berlin, but he quickly made enemies here too. And yet, thanks to his knowledge, his astute remarks, and his open mind, he gained the friendship of Mendelssohn, who hid the undocumented troublemaker at the city's outskirts—on the grounds of community leader Daniel Itzig's mansion.

Projektion: Freunde und Feinde

Am Ende der Ausstellung steht die Frage „Was wird aus Moses Mendelssohn?" Eine Collage der Zitate aus dem 19. und 20. Jahrhundert skizziert das weite und widersprüchliche Spektrum der Mendelssohn-Deutungen.

Projection: Friends and Foes

The exhibition ends with the question "What will become of Moses Mendelssohn?" A collage of quotations from the 19th and 20th centuries outlines the wide and contradictory spectrum of Mendelssohn interpretations.

London 1870 Karl Marx
Dieser Urtyp eines Seichtbeutels![1]
That prototype of a windbag!

Hamburg 1929 Ernst Cassirer
Verkünder einer geistigen Zukunft.[2]
The harbinger of an intellectual future.

New York 1951 Hannah Arendt
Der erste assimilierte Jude ist Moses Mendelssohn, und er ist auch der erste, der charakteristische Züge eines Intellektuellen trägt.[3]
It is important to bear in mind that assimilation as a group phenomenon really existed only among Jewish intellectuals. It is no accident that the first educated Jew, Moses Mendelssohn, was also the first who … was admitted to non-Jewish society.

Paris 1897 Max Nordau
Mendelssohn war ein so erfolgreicher Assimilator, daß alle seine Nachkommen heute gute Christen sind.[4]
Mendelssohn was such a successful assimilationist that today all his descendants are good Christians.

Breslau 1870 Heinrich Graetz
Er erweckte unwillkürlich die schlummernde Begabung des jüdischen Stammes.[5]
He aroused the slumbering genius of the Jewish race.

Leipzig 1865 Friedrich Friedrich
Vereint mit Lessing trat er auf die Bahn, / Der Kaufmann mit dem Dichter und Gelehrten, Der Jude mit dem Christen, beide schufen / Dem deutschen Volk die Freiheit des Gedankens.[6]
United, he and Lessing soon embarked / The merchant with the learned scholar-poet / On Germans, Jew and Christian would bestow / The liberty to ponder for oneself.

Bonn 1843 Bruno Bauer
Und womit hat Mendelssohn gewirkt? Mit den schalsten Resten einer Philosophie, die längst im Untergehen begriffen war.[7]
And what did Mendelssohn employ in his work? The stalest remnants of a philosophy that had long been in decline.

Padua 1862 Samuel David Luzzatto
Gott hätte ihm fünfzehn weitere Lebensjahre gönnen und sie meinem Leben abziehen sollen.[8]
God should have granted him fifteen more years of life and deducted them from mine.

Amsterdam 1936 Otto Zarek
Die Aufklärung triumphierte im

Zynismus; Mendelssohn führte sie zur Höhe neuer Religiosität.[9]
The Enlightenment triumphed in cynicism; Mendelssohn guided it to the heights of new religiosity.

Weimar 1786 Johann Gottfried Herder
Ein zu pfiffiger Hebräer, als daß ein ehrlicher Christ mit ihm auskäme.[10]
A Hebrew too shrewd for an honest Christian to stomach.

Karlsruhe 1811 Johann Peter Hebel
Man muss um des Bartes willen den Kopf nicht verachten, an dem er waechst.[11]
You mustn't judge a man's head by the length of the beard that grows from it.

Frankfurt am Main 1933 Margarete Susman
Und doch war die Gestalt, die Moses Mendelssohn erschuf: die des geistigen deutschen Juden, etwas Großes und Einziges.[12]
And yet the figure Moses Mendelssohn called into being—that of the intellectual German Jew—was something grand and unique.

Jena 1943 Walter Grundmann
Der Philosophenmantel, den sich Mendelssohn umhängt, dient der Tarnung des jüdischen Propagandisten.[13]
The philosopher's cloak in which Mendelssohn drapes himself has the function of disguising the Jewish propagandist.

Berlin 1938 Carl Schmitt
Mendelssohn hat vom Staat Gewissensfreiheit verlangt; mit dem unbeirrbaren Instinkt dafür, daß eine solche Aushöhlung der Macht zur Emanzipation des eigenen jüdischen Volkes am besten dient.[14]
Mendelssohn … demanded from the state freedom of thought; … he was endowed with the unerring instinct for the undermining of state power that served to emancipate his own Jewish folk.

London 1956 Leo Baeck
Ohne ihn ist das Judentum auch unserer Tage und von Tagen, die kommen werden, nicht zu denken.[15]
The Judaism of our own day, and of days to come, would be unimaginable without him.

Paris 1834 Heinrich Heine
Mendelssohn war der Reformator der deutschen Israeliten, er stürzte das Ansehen des Talmudismus, er begründete den reinen Mosaismus.[16]
Mendelssohn … was the reformer of the German Israelites, his co-religionists; he destroyed the reputation of talmudism and founded the pure Mosaic religion.

Marburg 1919 Hermann Cohen
Seine politische, seine kulturelle Wirksamkeit war messianisch.[17]
His political and cultural effect has been messianic.

München 1929 Ludwig Feuchtwanger
Mendelssohn war als deutscher Schriftsteller eine Modegröße, als Jude dagegen von überwältigender, sprengender Wirkung.[18]
As a German writer, Mendelssohn was a passing fancy. As a Jew, however, his impact was staggering, explosive.

Lemberg 1864 Rabbi Hillel Lichtenstein
Der Ketzer, der Zerrütter Israels, der Name der Frevler wird verwesen.[19]
A heretic, a destroyer of Israel. May the blasphemer's name be blotted out.

Liverpool 1825 Moses Samuels
Mose, der Sohn des Amran, befreite seine Brüder aus der körperlichen Sklaverei; die glorreiche Aufgabe, ihren Geist zu befreien, war Mose, dem Sohn des Mendel, vorbehalten.[20]
Moses, the son of Amran, delivered his brethren from bodily slavery: the glorious task of emancipating their minds was reserved for Moses, the son of Mendel.

Pressburg 1836 Rabbi Moses Sofer (Chatam Sofer)
Die Mendelssohn'schen Bibelbände / Lass nicht berühren Deine Hände.[21]
Your fingertips had better shun / The bible books from Mendelssohn

Altona 1840 Salomon Ludwig Steinheim
Mendelssohn hat den großen, heiligen Offenbarungsgedanken verkannt, verflacht, mißdeutet und dem seichten Rationalismus Tür und Tor geöffnet.[22]
Mendelssohn misunderstood, flattened, and misinterpreted the great, sacred idea of revelation and opened the floodgates to trivial rationalism.

Madison, Wisconsin 1999 David Sorkin
Die nachfolgenden Interpreten schufen ein Bild Mendelssohns, das den Konflikten entsprach, die die nächsten zwei Jahrhunderte bestimmten.[23]
Successive interpreters shaped an image of Mendelssohn according to the conflicts that filled the next two centuries.

Frankfurt / Main 1920 Franz Rosenzweig
Mendelssohn ist gar kein einheitlicher Mensch […] Er ist weder noch. […] Unbegreiflich für die Zeitgenossen. Wie sollten sie begreifen, daß hier nicht ein Mensch vor ihnen stand, sondern zwei. Beide dabei ohne Bewußtsein. Mendelssohns Treue war ebenso bewußtlos wie seine Abtrünnigkeit.[24]
Mendelssohn is not a uniform man at all […] He is neither. […] Incomprehensible for the contemporaries. How should they understand that here not one man stood before them, but two. Both of them without consciousness. Mendelssohn's loyalty was just as unconscious as his apostasy.

ANHANG

Quellenverzeichnis

[1] Brief v. Karl Marx an Ludwig Kugelmann, v. 27. Juni 1870, in: Marx-Engels-Werke, Bd. 32, Briefe: Januar 1868 bis Mitte Juli 1870, Hildegard Scheibler (Bearb.), Institut für Marxismus-Leninismus (Hg.), Berlin 1965, S. 686. – *English source: Marx, Karl. "Letter to Ludwig Kugelmann, June 27, 1870." Karl Marx, Frederick Engels: Collected Works, vol. 32. Various translators. New York: International Publishers, 1988, 529.*

[2] Die Idee der Religion bei Lessing und Mendelssohn, in: Gesammelte Werke. Hamburger Ausgabe, Bd. 17. Aufsätze und kleine Schriften 1927–1931, S. 11.

[3] Elemente und Ursprünge totaler Herrschaft, München: Piper, 1991, S. 157. – *Arendt, Hannah. The Origins of Totalitarianism. San Diego: Harcourt, Brace, & Company, [1951] 1979, 62.*

[4] Max Nordau: Ein Tempelstreit, in der Zeitschrift „Welt" vom 11. Juni 1897, Wien.

[5] Geschichte der Juden. Von den ältesten Zeiten bis auf die Gegenwart. Bd. 11: Vom Beginn der Mendelssohn'schen Zeit (1750) bis in die neueste Zeit (1848), Leipzig 1870, S. 3. –
Graetz, Heinrich. History of the Jews, vol. 5. Philadelphia: Jewish Publication Society of America, 1895, 929 f.

[6] Prolog zur Mendelssohn-Feier am 4. Januar 1865, S. 7 f. in: Reden und Gedichte vorgetragen bei der am Todestage Moses Mendelssohns 4. Januar 1865 vom „Verein zur Förderung geistiger Interessen im Judenthume" veranstalteten Gedächtnisfeier. Zweite Folge. Hrsg. zum Besten des Fonds für das angekaufte Geburtshaus Moses Mendelssohns in Dessau. Leipzig 1866.

[7] Die Judenfrage, Braunschweig 1843, S. 83.

[8] David Luzzatto an Meyer Kayserling, Juni 1862, in: Samuel David Luzzatto, Epistolario italiano, francese, latono, Padua 1890, S. 1004. Zitiert nach: Dominique Bourel: Moses Mendelssohn. Begründer des modernen Judentums, Zürich 2007, S. 45.

[9] Moses Mendelssohn. Ein jüdisches Schicksal in Deutschland, Amsterdam, Querido [1936], S. 379.

[10] Toot Hoffmann, Herders Briefe an Joh. Georg Hamann, Berlin 1889, S. 223, Brief vom 02.01.1786.

[11] Schatzkästlein des rheinischen Hausfreundes, Stuttgart und Tübingen: Cotta, 1833, S. 176.

[12] Das Nah- und Fernsein des Fremden. Essays und Briefe, Frankfurt am Main: Jüdischer Verlag im Suhrkamp Verlag, 1992, S. 216.

[13] Mendelssohn und Hamann, in: Germanentum, Christentum und Judentum, Bd. 3, Leipzig 1943, S. 12.

[14] Der Leviathan in der Staatslehre des Thomas Hobbes, 1938, Neuausg. 1982, S. 92 f. – *Schmitt, Carl. The Leviathan in the State Theory of Thomas Hobbes: Meaning and Failure of a Political Symbol. Translated by George Schwab and Erna Hilfstein. Westport, CT: Greenwoof Press, 1996, 60.*

[15] Von Moses Mendelssohn zu Franz Rosenzweig. Typen jüdischen Selbstverständnisses in den letzten beiden Jahrhunderten. Franz Delitzsch-Vorlesungen 1955, Stuttgart, Kohlhammer (1958).

[16] Düsseldorfer Heine-Ausgabe, Bd. 8, Teil 1: Text, 1979, Teil 2: Apparat, 1981, Hamburg: Hoffmann und Campe. – *Heine, Heinrich. On the History of Religion and Philosophy in Germany and Other Writings. Translated by Howard Pollack-Milgate. Cambridge, UK: Cambridge University Press, 2007, 69.*

[17] Religion der Vernunft, 2. Aufl. 1928, 415, EA 1919 Hermann Cohen: Religion der Vernunft aus den Quellen des Judentums: Nach dem Manuskript des Verfassers neu durchgearbeitet und mit einem Nachwort versehen von Bruno Strauss, 2. Aufl., J. Kauffmann, Frankfurt, 1929, S. 415. – *Cohen, Hermann. Religion of Reason: Out of the Sources of Judaism. Translated by Simon Kaplan. Atlanta: Scholars Press, 1995, 357.*

[18] Das Bild Mendelssohns bei seinen Gegnern bis zum Tode Hegels, in: Zeitschrift für die Geschichte der Juden in Deutschland, Jg. 1 (1929/30) Heft 3 (Oktober 1929), S. 213–232, hier: S. 221.

[19] Lev ha-Ivri (1864), 52a, Zitiert nach: Meir Hildesheimer: The Attitude of the Hatam Sofer toward Moses Mendelssohn, in: Proceedings of the American Academy for Jewish Research Vol. 60 (1994), S. 141–187, hier: S. 155 f.

[20] Memoirs of Moses Mendelssohn, the Jewish Philosopher; including the Celebrated Correspondence, On the Christian Religion with J.C. Lavater, Minister of Zurich, London 1825. Zit nach: Gesammelte Schriften. Jubiläumsausgabe, Ismar Elbogen u. a. (Hg.), Berlin 1929-1938; neu hrsg. v. Alexander Altmann, Eva Engel, Daniel Krochmalnik u. a. (Hg.), Bd. 23, Dokumente II: Die frühen Mendelssohn-Biografie, Michael Albrecht (Bearb.), Stuttgart 1998, S. 430.

[21] Zitiert nach Immanuel Heinrich Ritter: David Friedländer. Sein Leben und sein Wirken im Zusammenhange mit den gleichzeitigen Culturverhältnissen und Reformbestrebungen im Judenthum, Berlin 1861, S. 59.

[22] Vom Bleibenden und Vergänglichen im Judentum (Vom Bleibenden und Vergänglichen im Judentum, in: Deutschjüdischer Weg. Eine Schriftenreihe, No. 3, S. 11–30). Vorwort von H. J. Schoeps. Erste Ausgabe, Vortrupp-Verlag, Berlin, 1935.

[23] Moses Mendelssohn und die theologische Aufklärung, Jüdische Denker, Bd. 4, Wien: Werner Eichbauer 1999, S. 186. – *Sorkin, David. „Conclusion." In: Moses Mendelssohn and the Religious Enlightenment. Berkeley, University of California Press, 1996, S. 148–149.*

[24] Aus einer Vortragsreihe (1920) für das Freie Jüdische Lehrhaus in Frankfurt: Franz Rosenzweig: (1920/84): Der jüdische Mensch, in: F. R.: Der Mensch und sein Werk, Gesammelte Schriften, Bd. 3: Zweistromland. S. 566.

Moses Mendelssohn (1729 – 1786) Biografische Daten und Zeitgeschichte

Moses Mendelssohn (1729 – 1786)
Biographical Data and Contemporary History

1729
Mosche Dessau (Moses Mendelssohn) wird am 6. September in Dessau geboren.
Mosche Dessau (Moses Mendelssohn) is born on September 6th in Dessau.

1735
Besuch der Talmud-Schule. Autodidaktische Lektüre der Tora, der Fünf Bücher Mose. Übungen in hebräischer Grammatik und Poesie.
Mendelssohn attends Talmudic school, with studies in the Torah as well as Hebrew grammar and poetry.

1737
Fromet Gugenheim, Mendelssohns spätere Ehefrau, wird in Altona geboren.
Birth of Fromet Gugenheim, Mendelssohn's future wife, in Altona.

1739
Rabbiner David Fränkel wird Mendelssohns Lehrer in Dessau.
Mendelssohn takes lessons with Rabbi David Fränkel in Dessau.

1740
Friedrich II. wird König von Preußen.
Frederick II becomes King of Prussia.

1743
Mendelssohn folgt David Fränkel nach Berlin, um weiter bei ihm zu lernen. Selbststudium der deutschen, lateinischen, französischen, englischen Sprache, der Philosophie und der Mathematik.
Mendelssohn follows David Fränkel to Berlin, studies German, Latin, French, and English, philosophy, and mathematics.

1750
Mendelssohn wird Hauslehrer bei dem Seidenhändler Bernhard Isaak. Der preußische König Friedrich II. erlässt das „revidierte General-Privilegium und Reglement für die Judenschaft im Königreich Preußen", das die Ansiedlung und Arbeitsmöglichkeiten der Juden stark einschränkt.
Mendelssohn tutors the children of silk merchant Isaak Bernhard. The Prussian king Frederic II decrees new, restrictive regulations regarding Jews.

1753
Beginn der Freundschaft zwischen Mendelssohn und dem Dichter Gotthold Ephraim Lessing.
Mendelssohn befriends poet Gotthold Ephraim Lessing.

1754
Mendelssohn wird Buchhalter in der Seidenmanufaktur von Bernhard Isaak. Beginn der Freundschaft mit dem Schriftsteller Friedrich Nicolai.
Mendelssohn becomes the bookkeeper for Bernhard Isaak's silk manufactory. Befriends the publicist Friedrich Nicolai.

1755
Mendelssohn wird Mitglied im aufgeklärten Gelehrten Kaffeehaus (100 Mitglieder) und ist zu Gast im Montagsclub (24 Mitglieder).
Mendelssohn joins the Scholarly Coffeehouse, an Enlightenment gathering place (100 members) and visits the Monday Society (24 members).

ANHANG

1756
Mendelssohn lernt Klavierspielen. Seine Mutter stirbt. Die briefliche Diskussion zwischen Mendelssohn, Lessing und Nicolai gipfelt im „Briefwechsel über das Trauerspiel".
Mendelssohn learns to play the piano. His mother dies. A mail discussion with Lessing and Nicolai leads to their "Correspondence on the Tragedy".

1757
Mendelssohn und Nicolai geben die „Bibliothek der Schönen Wissenschaften und der freyen Künste" heraus.
Mendelssohn and Nicolai publish the "Library of the Belles Lettres and Liberal Arts".

1760
Lessing verlässt Berlin.
Lessing leaves Berlin.

1761
Mendelssohn reist nach Hamburg und verlobt sich mit Fromet Gugenheim. Er wechselt Briefe mit Fromet, die „Brautbriefe". Seine „Philosophischen Schriften" erscheinen.
Mendelssohn becomes engaged to Fromet Gugenheim in Altona. He exchanges letters with her. Publishes "Philosophical Writings".

1762
Mendelssohn heiratet Fromet Gugenheim, nachdem er in Berlin das Niederlassungsrecht erhalten hat. Sie wohnen in der Spandauer Straße 68.
Mendelssohn marries Fromet Gugenheim after being granted residency rights in Berlin. They settle at Spandauer Straße 68.

1763
Mendelssohn erhält das Privileg eines außerordentlichen Schutzjuden. Erhält den ersten Preis der Akademie der Wissenschaften. Die Berliner Jüdische Gemeinde befreit ihn in Anerkennung seiner Verdienste von den ihr zustehenden Abgaben.
Mendelssohn receives status of an "Extraordinary Protected Jew." Receives first prize from the Academy of Sciences. The Jewish Community exempts him from dues.

1765
Mitarbeit Mendelssohns an Nicolais „Allgemeiner deutscher Bibliothek".
Mendelssohn collaborates on Friedrich Nicolai's "General German Library".

1766
Fünf Wochen nach seiner Geburt stirbt Mendelssohns erster Sohn Chaim.
Birth of his first son Chaim, who dies after only five weeks.

1767
Die Tochter Recha wird geboren. Mendelssohns erfolgreichstes Buch „Phaedon oder über die Unsterblichkeit der Seele" erscheint bei Nicolai. Es wird in zehn Sprachen übersetzt.
Birth of his daughter Recha. Mendelssohn publishes "Phaedon or On the Immortality of Souls", which will be his most successful book.

1768
Bernhard Isaak stirbt. Mendelssohn wird Teilhaber der Seidenfabrik. Der Sohn Mendel Abraham wird geboren.
Bernhard Isaak dies. Mendelssohn becomes co-owner of the silk factory. His son Mendel Abraham is born.

1769
Der Theologe Johann Caspar Lavater fordert Mendelssohn öffentlich auf, sich zum Christentum zu bekennen.
Mendelssohn has a public dispute with Christian theologian Johann Caspar Lavater, who challenges him to convert.

1770
Der Sohn Joseph wird geboren. Beginn der Arbeit an der Übersetzung der Psalmen.
Birth of his son Joseph. Mendelssohn begins translating the Psalms.

1771
König Friedrich II. verhindert Mendelssohns Aufnahme in die Akademie der Wissenschaften. Mendelssohn erkrankt schwer. Die Berliner Jüdische Gemeinde ehrt Mendelssohn
King Frederic II blocks Mendelssohn's admission to the Academy of Sciences. Mendelssohn becomes gravely ill. The Berlin Jewish Community honors Mendelssohn.

1772
Mendelssohn nimmt gegen die traditionell übliche sofortige Beerdigung der Juden Stellung.
Takes a stance against the traditional Jewish practice of early burial.

1773
Kur in Bad Pyrmont.
Stays at the Bad Pyrmont spa town.

1774
Beginn der Arbeit an der Tora-Übersetzung.
Mendelssohn begins work on Torah translation.

1775
Mendelssohns Tochter Jente (Henriette) wird geboren, sein Sohn Mendel Abraham stirbt.
Birth of his daughter Yente (Henriette), death of his son Mendel Abraham.

1776
Der Sohn Abraham, der spätere Vater von Fanny und Felix Mendelssohn Bartholdy, wird geboren.
Birth of his son Abraham, the future father of Fanny and Felix Mendelssohn Bartholdy.

1777
In Königsberg Gespräche mit Immanuel Kant. Letzter Besuch bei Lessing in Wolfenbüttel.
Mendelssohn converses with Immanuel Kant in Königsberg. Visits Lessing in Wolfenbüttel for the last time.

1778
David Friedländer und Isaac Daniel Itzig gründen, angeregt durch Mendelssohn, eine moderne jüdische Schule, die Jüdische Freischule in Berlin. Lessing sendet das Manuskript seines Schauspiels „Nathan der Weise" an Mendelssohn zur Durchsicht und Kritik.
David Friedländer and Isaac Daniel Itzig found the Jewish Free School at Mendelssohn's suggestion. Lessing sends the draft of his drama "Nathan the Wise" to Mendelssohn for revision.

1779
Friedrich II. lehnt Mendelssohns Antrag ab, seinen Schutzbrief auf seine Frau und seine Kinder auszudehnen.
King Frederic II denies Mendelssohn's request to have his letter of protection extended to his wife and children.

1780
Erscheinen des ersten Bandes von Mendelssohns Übersetzung der Tora ins Deutsche, gedruckt in hebräischen Lettern. Beratung Christian Dohms bei dessen Arbeit an dem bahnbrechenden Buch „Über die bürgerliche Verbesserung der Juden".
The first volume of Mendelssohn's Torah translation into German appears, printed in Hebrew letters. Consulted for Christian Dohm's treatise on Jewish emancipation.

1781
Mendelssohns Freund Lessing stirbt.
Mendelssohn's friend Lessing dies.

1782
Der Sohn Nathan wird geboren. Beginn der gutachterlichen Mitarbeit an dem von Friedrich II. auf den Weg gebrachten modernen Allgemeinen Preußischen Landrecht.
Birth of his son Nathan. Mendelssohn consults the work on Prussia's main legal code, the General State Laws.

1783
Mendelssohn wird Ehrenmitglied der Gesellschaft von Freunden der Aufklärung („Mittwochsgesellschaft"). Die Berliner Jüdische Gemeinde bestätigt ihn im Amt eines Vorstehers. „Die Psalmen. Übersetzung von Moses Mendelssohn" und Mendelssohns philosophisches Hauptwerk „Jerusalem oder über religiöse Macht und Judenthum" erscheinen.
Mendelssohn appointed honorary member of the Society of Friends of the Enlightenment ("Wednesday Society") and dignitary of the Jewish Community. Mendelssohn's translation of the Psalms and his philosophical magnum opus "Jerusalem" are published.

1784
Immanuel Kants Definition der Aufklärung und Johann Georg Hamanns Schrift gegen „Jerusalem" erscheinen.
Immanuel Kant's definition of Enlightenment and Johann Georg Hamann's book opposing "Jerusalem" are published.

1786
Im Beisein des Arztes Marcus Herz, seines langjährigen Schülers und Freundes, stirbt Moses Mendelssohn am 4. Januar.
Moses Mendelssohn dies on January 4th in the presence of the physician Marcus Herz, his long-time student and friend.

1812
Fromet Mendelssohn stirbt am 16. März in Altona.
Fromet Mendelssohn dies on March 16th in Altona.

ANHANG

Räume & Themen *Rooms & Topics*

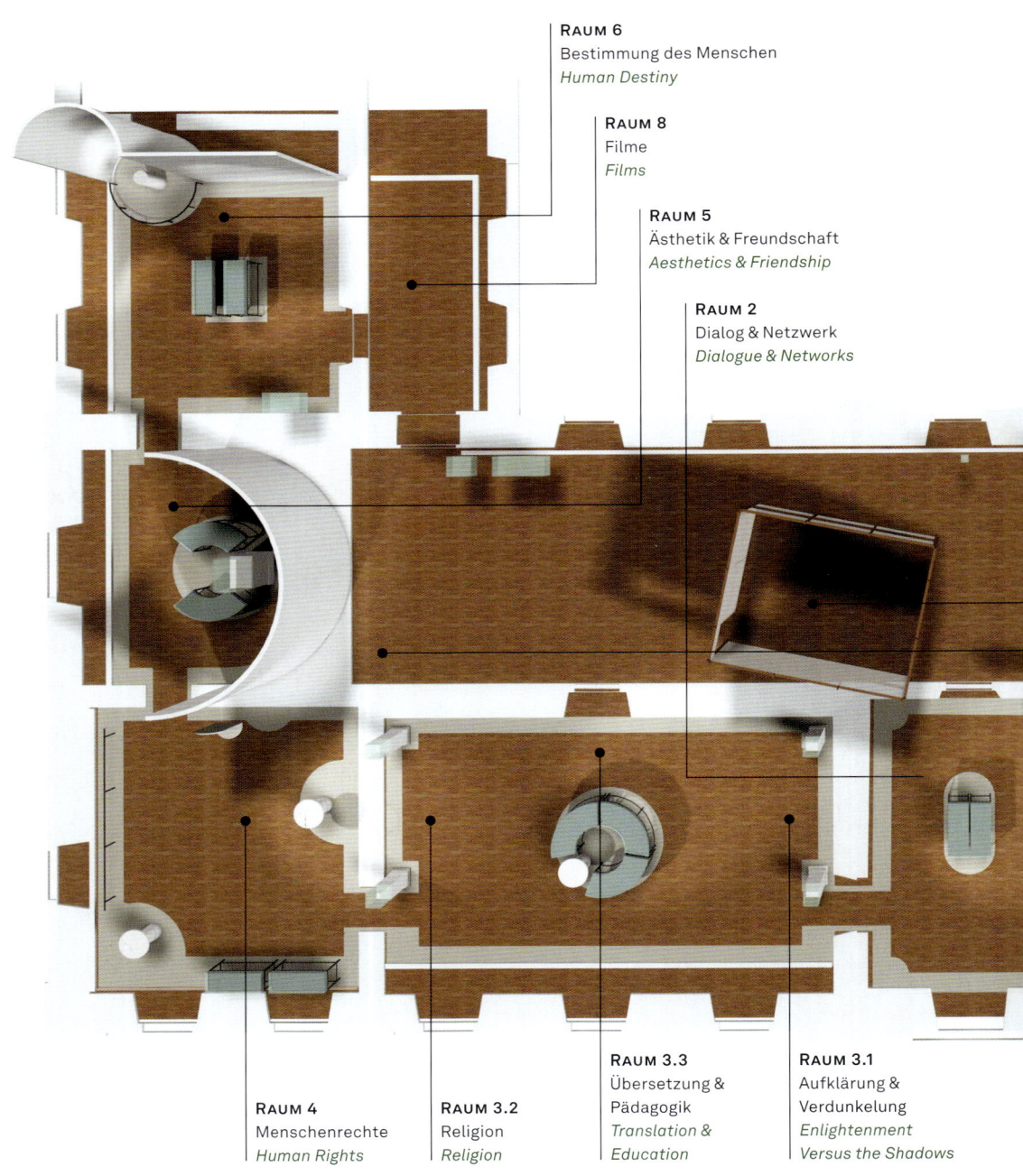

Raum 6
Bestimmung des Menschen
Human Destiny

Raum 8
Filme
Films

Raum 5
Ästhetik & Freundschaft
Aesthetics & Friendship

Raum 2
Dialog & Netzwerk
Dialogue & Networks

Raum 4
Menschenrechte
Human Rights

Raum 3.2
Religion
Religion

Raum 3.3
Übersetzung &
Pädagogik
*Translation &
Education*

Raum 3.1
Aufklärung &
Verdunkelung
*Enlightenment
Versus the Shadows*

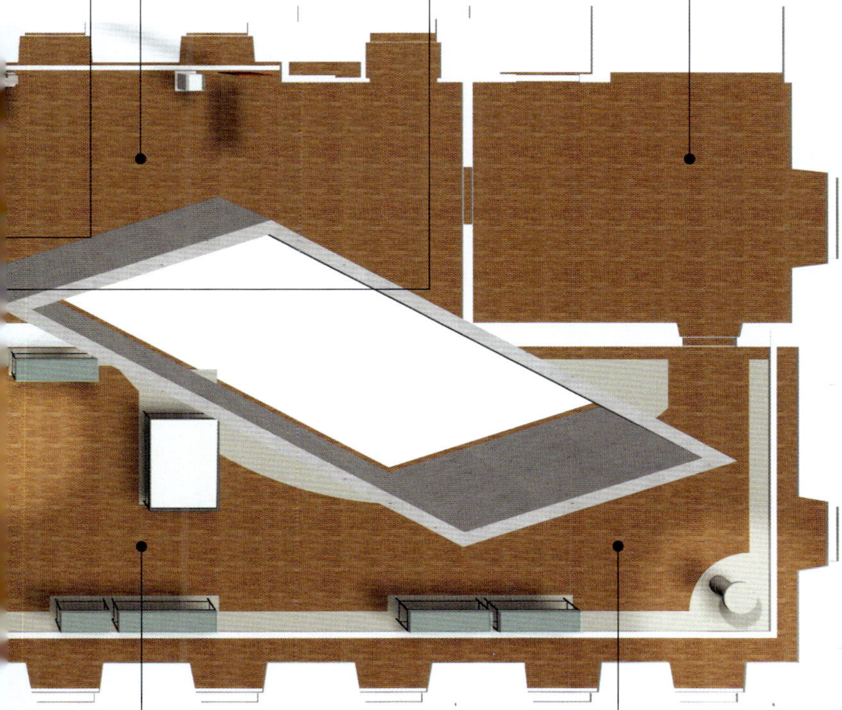

Raum 7.2
Judenporzellan
Jewish Porcelain

Raum 7.3
Was wird aus Moses Mendelssohn?
What is Moses Mendelssohn's Legacy?

Raum 7.1
Bilderfabrik
Image Factory

Introfragen & Biografie
Intro Questions & Biography

Raum 1.2
Der „Jude von Berlin"
The "Jew from Berlin"

Raum 1.1
Von Dessau nach Berlin
From Dessau to Berlin

Literaturhinweise (Auswahl)

Literature (Selection)

Werkausgaben, Editionen und Einzelschriften

Gesammelte Schriften. Jubiläumsausgabe, Ismar Elbogen u. a. (Hg.), Berlin 1929–1938; neu hrsg. v. Alexander Altmann, Eva Engel, Daniel Krochmalnik u. a. (Hg.), Stuttgart 1972 bis 2023.

Ausgewählte Werke. Studienausgabe, 2 Bde., Christoph Schulte, Andreas Kennecke, Grazyna Jurewicz (Hg.), Darmstadt 2009.

Ästhetische Schriften, Anne Pollock (Hg.), Hamburg 2013 (Philosophische Bibliothek, Bd. 571).

Brautbriefe, Ismar Elbogen (Hg.), Berlin 1936 (Nachdr. Königstein 1985).

Frühschriften zur Metaphysik, Michael Albrecht (Hg.), Tübingen 1969.

Geschäftspapiere. Kommentierte Edition, Eva Engel (Hg.), Wiesbaden 2009.

Jerusalem oder über religiöse Macht und Judentum. Mit dem Vorwort zu Manasse ben Israels Rettung der Juden und dem Entwurf zu Jerusalem, Michael Albrecht (Hg.), Hamburg 2013 (Philosophische Bibliothek, Bd. 565).

Metaphysische Schriften, Wolfgang Vogt (Hg.), Hamburg 2013 (Philosophische Bibliothek, Bd. 594).

Phädon oder über die Unsterblichkeit der Seele. Anne Pollock (Hg.), Hamburg 2013 (Philosophische Bibliothek, Bd. 595).

Schriften über Religion und Aufklärung, Martina Thom (Hg.), Darmstadt 1989.

Bibliographien, Forschungsberichte, Zeitschriften

Meyer, Herrmann M. Z.: Moses Mendelssohn Bibliographie, Berlin 1965.

Mendelssohn-Studien. Beiträge zur neueren deutschen Kulturgeschichte, Cécile Lowenthal-Hensel, Rudolf Elvers, Hans-Günter Klein, Roland Schmidt-Hensel, Christoph Schulte (Hg.), Bd. 1–22, Berlin, seit 1967.

Albrecht, Michael: Moses Mendelssohn. Ein Forschungsbericht 1965–1980, in: Deutsche Vierteljahresschrift für Literaturwissenschaft und Geistesgeschichte 57 (1983), S. 64–159.

Biografien und Gesamtdarstellungen

Albrecht, Michael (Bearb.): Die frühen Mendelssohn-Biografien, als: Gesammelte Schriften.Jubiläumsausgabe, Band 23: Dokumente II, Stuttgart 1998.

Albrecht, Michael: Moses Mendelssohn. Das Lebenswerk eines jüdischen Denkers der deutschen Aufklärung, Weinheim 1986 (Ausstellungskatalog Herzog August Bibliothek Wolfenbüttel, Nr. 51).

Altmann, Alexander: Moses Mendelssohn. A biographical study, London 1973.

Bourel, Dominque: Moses Mendelssohn. Begründer des modernen Judentums. Zürich 2007 (franz. 2004).

Feiner, Shumuel: Moses Mendelssohn. Ein jüdischer Denker in der Zeit der Aufklärung, Göttingen 2009 (hebr. 2005).

Knobloch, Heinz: Herr Moses in Berlin. Auf den Spuren eines Menschenfreundes, Berlin 1979.

Simon, Hermann: Moses Mendelssohn. Gesetzestreuer Jude und deutscher Aufklärer, Berlin 2012 (Jüdische Miniaturen, Bd. 1).

Sorkin, David: Moses Mendelssohn und die theologische Aufklärung, Wien 1999 (engl. 1996).

Tree, Stephen: Moses Mendelssohn, Reinbek 2007.

Forschungsliteratur, Sammelbände, Einzelaspekte

Albrecht, Michael / Engel, Eva J. / Hinske, Norbert (Hg.): Moses Mendelssohn und die Kreise seiner Wirksamkeit, Tübingen 1994 (Wolfenbütteler Studien zur Aufklärung, Bd. 19).

Altmann, Alexander: Moses Mendelssohns Kindheit in Dessau. Bulletin des Leo Baeck Instituts, Nr. 10 (1967), S. 237–275.

Altmann, Alexander: Die trostvolle Aufklärung. Studien zur Metaphysik und politischen Theorie Moses Mendelssohns, Stuttgart 1982.

Arnold, Heinz Ludwig, Berghahn, Cord-Friedrich (Hg.): Text + Kritik Sonderband Moses Mendelssohn, München 2011.

Behm, Britta: Moses Mendelsohn und die Transformation der jüdischen Erziehung in Berlin. Münster 2002.

Berghahn, Cord-Friedrich: Moses Mendelssohns „Jerusalem". Ein Beitrag zur Geschichte der Menschenrechte und der pluralistischen Gesellschaft in der deutschen Aufklärung, Tübingen 2001.

Freudenthal, Gideon: No Religion without Idolatry. Mendelssohn's Jewish Enlightenment, Notre Dame IN 2015.

Freudenthal, Max: Aus der Heimat Moses Mendelssohns. Moses Benjamin Wulff und seine Familie, die Nachkommen des Moses Isserles. Berlin 1900 / Reprint Dessau 2006.

Goldenbaum, Ursula / Meder, Stephan / Armgardt, Mattias: Moses Mendelssohns Rechtsphilosophie im Kontext, Hannover 2021.

Gottlieb, Micha / Manekin, Charles H.: Moses Mendelssohn. Enlightenment, Religion, Politics, Nationalism. Bethseda MD 2015.

Jurewicz, Grażyna: Moses Mendelssohn über die Bestimmung des Menschen. Eine deutsch-jüdische Begriffsgeschichte, Hannover 2018.

Meier, Brigitte: Jüdische Seidenunternehmer und die soziale Ordnung zur Zeit Friedrichs II. Moses Mendelssohn und Isaak Bernhard – Interaktion und Kommunikation als Basis einer erfolgreichen Unternehmensentwicklung, Berlin 2007.

Meyer, Herrmann M. Z.: Die Vorfahren von Moses und Fromet Mendelssohn. Familiengeschichtliche Notizen. Jerusalem 1967.

Pecina, Björn: Mendelssohns diskrete Religion, Tübingen 2016.

Pollok, Anne: Facetten des Menschen. Zur Anthropologie Moses Mendelssohns. Hamburg 2010.

Sacks, Elias: Moses Mendelssohn's Living Script. Philosophy, Practice, History, Judaism, Bloomington IN 2017.

Schulte, Christoph: Von Moses bis Moses … Der jüdische Mendelssohn. Hannover 2020.

Schwarz, Hans-Joachim / Schwarz, Renate: Moses Mendelssohn und die Krankheit der Gelehrten. Hannover 2013.

Steer, Martina: Moses Mendelssohn und seine Nachwelt. Eine Kulturgeschichte der jüdischen Erinnerung. Göttingen 2019.

Jüdische Aufklärung

Feiner, Shmuel: Haskala – jüdische Aufklärung. Geschichte einer kulturellen Revolution, Hildesheim 2007 (hebr. 2002).

Meyer, Michael A.: Von Moses Mendelssohn zu Leopold Zunz. Jüdische Identität in Deutschland 1749 – 1824, München 1994 (engl. 1967, 1992).

Pelli, Moshe: The Age of Haskalah. Studies in Hebrew Literature of the Enlightenment in Germany, Leiden 1979.

Schulte, Christoph: Die jüdische Aufklärung. Philosophie Religion Geschichte, München 2002.

Sorkin, David: The Berlin Haskalah and German Religious thought. Orphans of Knowledge, London 2000.

Wilde Mischung

In diesem Kapitel des Anhangs präsentiert die Katalogredaktion besonders interessante, nie publizierte oder ausgefallene Motive: Sehenswerte und in einigen Fällen auch kuriose Bilder, die aus organisatorischen, technischen oder Layout-Gründen nicht in anderen Kapiteln gezeigt werden konnten.

Wild Mixture

In this chapter of the appendix, the catalog editors present particularly interesting, never published or unusual motifs: pictures that are worth seeing and in some cases pictures that, for organizational, technical or layout reasons, could not be shown in other chapters.

Nr. 33 Porträt Joseph Mendelssohn (1770–1848)
undatiert
Grisaille, Öl auf Karton
Nachlass Angelika von Mendelssohn-Siebeck

Familienbilder
Family Portraits

Von Moses Mendelssohn wird häufig behauptet, alle seine Kinder hätten das Judentum verlassen. Die Porträts von **Joseph**, dem ältesten Sohn, und **Recha Meyer**, der zweitältesten Tochter, zeigen zwei Geschwister, die bei der Synagoge verblieben sind. Rechas Ehemann **Mendel Meyer** – diese Heirat hatte Moses selbst noch arrangiert – ließ sich nach seiner Scheidung taufen.

*It is often said of Moses Mendelssohn that all his children had left Judaism. The portraits of **Joseph**, the eldest son, and **Recha Meyer**, the second oldest daughter, show two siblings who remained with the synagogue. Recha's husband **Mendel Meyer**—this marriage had been arranged by Moses himself—was baptized after his divorce.*

ANHANG

Nr. 35 Porträt Recha Meyer, geb. Mendelssohn (1767–1831)
undatiert
Öl auf Leinwand
Privatbesitz, Köln

Nr. 36 Porträt Mendel Meyer (gest. 1831), Kaufmann
undatiert
Öl auf Leinwand
Privatbesitz, Köln

Nr. 88 Moses Mendelssohn (1729–1786): Abhandlung über die Evidenz in Metaphysischen Wissenschaften
Berlin: Haude & Spener, 1764
SBB PK, Abteilung Handschriften und Historische Drucke

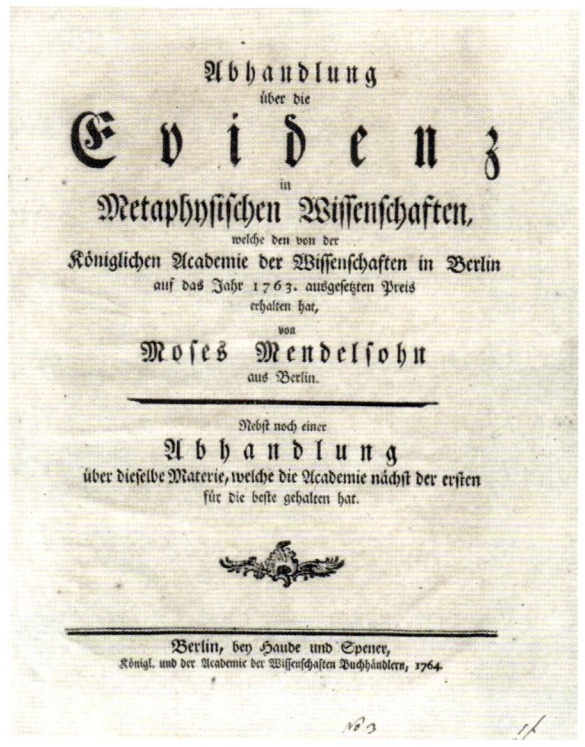

Der intellektuelle Star
The Intellectual Star

Ein **Essay Mendelssohns** beantwortete die Preisfrage der Königlichen Akademie der Wissenschaften: ob existenzielle Grundaussagen so beweisbar sind wie mathematische Gewissheiten. Der 34-Jährige erhält dafür den ersten Preis, sein damals noch wenig bekannter Kollege Kant den zweiten. Die Illustration der gedruckten Preisschrift, in der beide Texte veröffentlicht wurden, zeigt Natur, Künste und Wissenschaft als Elemente einer feudalen Gartenanlage – eine allegorische Erkenntnislandschaft.

*An **essay by Mendelssohn** answered the prize question of the Royal Academy of Sciences: Whether basic existential statements are as provable as mathematical certainties. The 34-year-old received the first prize, while his then little-known colleague Kant the second. The illustration of the brochure in which both texts were published shows nature, the arts and science as elements of a feudal garden—an allegorical landscape of knowledge.*

Einleitung.

Man macht der Weltweisheit gemeiniglich den Vorwurf, daß in ihren Lehren niemals eine sonderliche Ueberzeugung zu hoffen wäre, weil in jedem Jahrhunderte neue Lehrgebäude empor kommen, schimmern und wieder vergehen. Die Gedichte, die Reden, die historischen und kritischen Schriften, die Bildsäulen und übrigen Kunststücke der Alten, werden noch in unsern Tagen als Meisterstücke bewundert, und zum Theil noch mit grösserm Nutzen studiret, als die Natur selbst. Allein die philosophischen Schriften der vorigen Zeiten, sind in unsern Tagen fast unbrauchbar geworden.

Nr. 88 Moses Mendelssohn (1729–1786): Abhandlung über die Evidenz in Metaphysischen Wissenschaften
Berlin: Haude & Spener, 1764
SBB PK, Abteilung Handschriften und Historische Drucke

NR. 189 ADER-
LASSKASTEN MIT
SCHRÖPFKÖPFEN
UND ADERLASS-
DARSTELLUNG
1746/55
Holz, Glas, Metall,
textiles Gewebe
Deutsches
Hygiene-Museum,
Dresden

Zerbrechlichkeit und Herkunft des Homo sapiens
Fragility and Origin of Homo Sapiens

Der **Aderlasskasten** aus dem 18. Jahrhundert steht für eine Behandlung, durch die der kränkelnde Mendelssohn oft kuriert werden sollte. Die Skizzenevolution zwischen **Amphibie und „Dichter-Apoll"** (S. 228) gehört zur grafischen Sammlung des Physiognomik-Experten Lavater, der über den Zusammenhang von Erscheinung und Charakter spekulierte. Beide Objekte kommentieren in der Ausstellung das Thema „Bestimmung des Menschen". Bei Marcus Elieser Bloch, dem Naturforscher, Freund und Hausarzt Mendelssohns (Porträt Nr. 72), kommen Aderlasspraxis, Zoologie und Haskala-Ideale zusammen. In seinen „Medicinischen Bemerkungen" (1774) stellt er fest, dass das Seelenleben der Mutter und das des Embryos miteinander verbunden seien. Seine „Allgemeine Naturgeschichte der Fische" (1782–1795) wird zum Standardwerk.

*The **bloodletting box** from the 18th century stands for a treatment by which the ailing Mendelssohn was often to be cured. The sketch evolution between **amphibian and "poet-apoll"** (p. 228) belongs to the graphic collection of the physiognomic expert Lavater, who speculated on the connection between appearance and character. Both objects comment in the exhibition on the theme of the "determination of man". In Marcus Elieser Bloch, the naturalist, friend and Mendelssohn's family doctor (portrait no. 72), bloodletting practice, zoology and Haskalah ideals come together. In his "Medicinische Bemerkungen" (1774), he states that the inner life of the mother and that of the embryo are connected. His "General Natural History of the Fishes" (1782-1795) becomes a standard work.*

ANHANG

NR. 185 CHRISTIAN VON MECHEL (1737–1817): STUFENFOLGE VON DEM FROSCHE BIS ZUM APOLLO-PROFILE

Basel, 1797
Radierung, koloriert
Österreichische Nationalbibliothek Wien

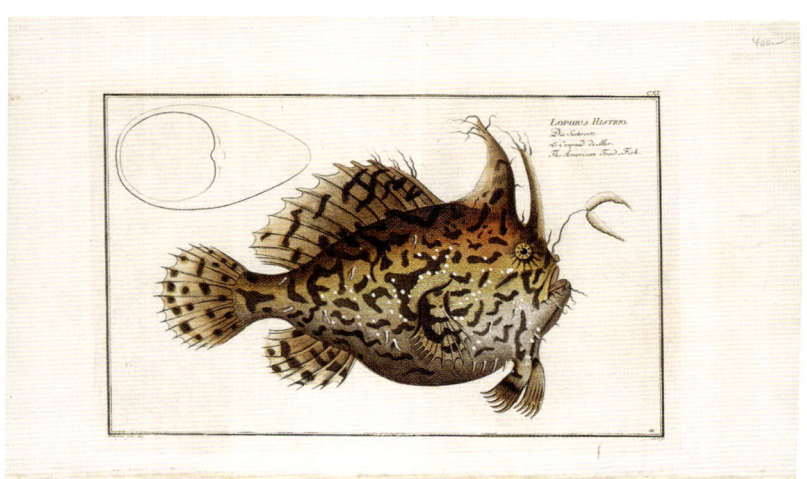

O. NR. LOPHIUS HISTRIO. DIE SEEKRÖTE

Aus Marcus Elieser Bloch's Naturgeschichte der ausländischen Fische. 1787
Kupferstich
JMB
Der Lieblingsfisch des Ausstellungsteams
The favorite fish of the exhibition team

O. NR. ZWEI MÄNNER AM FLUSS
Illustration aus der moralischen Wochenschrift „Der Chamäleon" (1756), herausgegeben von Johann Georg Philipp Müchler und Moses Mendelssohn
Bayerische Staatsbibliothek

Der Team-Player
The Team Player

Mit dem Verleger **Nicolai**, der hier als Bekämpfer der Gegenaufklärung gewürdigt wird (S. 230), realisiert Mendelssohn über drei Jahrzehnte Zeitschriftenprojekte. Für seine philosophischen Aufbrüche ist ihm der Dichter **Lessing** die wichtigste Instanz. Das Bild von Tischbein zeigt den jungen Lessing in den ersten Jahren des Freundschaftstrios. Das Gemälde war im Besitz der Freunde Mendelssohns, kam von Marcus Herz an die Familie Friedländer, die es der Nationalgalerie schenkte. Auf der Zeichnung des 19. Jahrhunderts begegnen sich dann, in Wolfenbüttel, Mendelssohn und Lessing als gesetzte Gelehrte. Ein weiterer wichtiger Partner für Moses' emanzipatorische, politische Projekte war der Jurist **Dohm**: auf diesem späten Porträt eher ein erschöpfter Kämpfer. **Mendelssohn** selbst ist hier in einer Version der Graff-Porträts zu sehen, die sich durch die Gelehrtenpose mit Buch und Lesezeichen von den bekannten Varianten unterscheidet. Ein verschollenes Gemälde oder eine Bearbeitung für das Magazin-Cover?

*With the publisher **Nicolai**, who is acknowledged here as a fighter against the Counter-Enlightenment (p. 230), Mendelssohn realizes magazine projects over three decades. For his philosophical awakenings, the poet **Lessing** is the most important authority. The picture by Tischbein shows the young Lessing in the first years of the friendship trio. The picture was in the possession of Mendelssohn's friends, came from Marcus Herz to the Friedländer family, who donated it to the National Gallery. On the drawing of the 19th century, then, in Wolfenbüttel, Mendelssohn and Lessing meet as seated scholars. Another important partner for Moses' emancipatory, political projects was the jurist **Dohm**: in this late portrait rather an exhausted fighter. **Mendelssohn** himself is shown here in a version of the Graff portraits, which differs from the known variants by the scholar's pose with book and bookmark. A lost painting or an adaptation for the magazine cover?*

ANHANG

NR. 55 JOHANN HEINRICH
TISCHBEIN D. Ä. (1722–1789):
JUGENDBILDNIS GOTTHOLD
EPHRAIM LESSING (1729–1781)
ca. 1755
Öl auf Leinwand
SMB PK, Alte Nationalgalerie

O. NR. FRITZ WERNER
(1827–1908): LESSING UND
MENDELSSOHN VOR LESSINGS
WOHNHAUS IN WOLFENBÜTTEL
um 1870
Zeichnung
Herzog August Bibliothek,
Wolfenbüttel

o. Nr. Porträt
Moses Mendelssohn
(1751–1820)
Umschlag des Jüdischen
Magazins September/
Oktober 1929
„Nach dem Gemälde von
A. Graff. Mit Genehmigung
der Familie v. Mendelssohn"
Verlag B. Pollak, Berlin
Staatsbibliothek zu Berlin

Nr. 76 Moses Samuel
Löwe (1756–1831):
Porträt Friedrich
Nicolai (1733–1811)
mit Vignette
Berlin, ca. 1806
Öl auf Leinwand
Stiftung Stadtmuseum
Berlin

Nr. 134 Georg Adolf
Schöner (1774–1841):
Porträt Christian
Wilhelm von Dohm
(1751–1820)
1801
Öl auf Leinwand
Museen der Stadt
Regensburg

O. NR. DER PROPHET MOSES, DIE GELEHRTEN MOSES MAIMONIDES UND MOSES MENDELSSOHN MIT MOSES MONTEFIORE (FÖRDERER DER AUSWANDERUNG NACH PALÄSTINA) UND BARON MAURICE DE HIRSCH (FÖRDERER JÜDISCHER KOLONISTEN IN ARGENTINIEN)
Karte aus dem Palästina-Album der Hebrew Publishing Company
New York, um 1900
Kedem Auction House, Jerusalem

Von Moses bis Moses war keiner wie Moses
From Moses to Moses, no one was like Moses

Die Postkarte versammelt den Moses des Exodus, Moses Maimonides und Moses Mendelssohn mit zwei Pionieren jüdischer Auswanderung. Der Buchtitel zeigt die Begegnung des Moses mit einem seiner schärfsten Kritiker, dem Prager Oberrabbiner Ezechiel Landau: ihre Umarmung im Paradies. Die Legitimation des Berliner Juden am Himmelstor beschreibt das Gedicht eines anonymen Lesers, notiert in einem Exemplar der „Morgenstunden oder Vorlesungen vom Daseyn Gottes" (1785).

The postcard gathers the Moses of the Exodus, Moses Maimonides and Mendelssohn with two pioneers of Jewish emigration. The book title shows Moses' encounter with one of his harshest critics, the Chief Rabbi of Prague, Ezekiel Landau: their embrace in paradise. The legitimation of the Berlin Jew at the Gate of Heaven describes the poem of an anonymous reader, noted in a copy of the "Morgenstunden oder Vorlesungen vom Daseyn Gottes" (1785).

Gedicht eines anonymen Lesers, eingetragen in die Ausgabe von Moses Mendelssohns „Morgenstunden" (1786)

Als *Mendelssohn* jüngst vor den Scheidewegen
Zum Himmel und zur Höll ankam
Und steil auf zum Visier den Sonnendohm sich nam
Um keinen Zerberus verlegen;

Sprang ihm von Kommandanten wegen
Sct. Peter, Luther und Calvin
Aus iren Schilderhäusergens entgegen
Und recta vor den Schlagbaum hin.

Tutti: Wohin? – Wohin? – Wohin? –
Mend. Zum Dohm!
Tutti: Den Pas! Den Pas! Den Pas!
Sct. Peter: Woher der Pas du kleiner Höckerschimmel?

Calvin: Von Genf? *Luther:* Von Wittenberg?
Sct. Peter: Von Rom?
Mend. Wi so?
Tutti: Wo ist dein Pas datirt zum Himmel?

Calvin: Zu Genf? *Luther:* Zu Wittenberg?
Sct. Peter: Zu Rom?
Sonst scher dich nur zum Teufel alter Schimmel! /
Mend.: Mein Pas ist alt; datirt in aller Früh
Im Hauptquartier zu Sinai!

Der Schlagbaum knarrte auf und Moses ging gen Himmel.

Poem by an Anonymous Reader recorded in Moses Mendelssohn's "Morning Hours, or Lectures on the Existence of God" (1786)

*When Mendelssohn, not so long ago,
To the fork twixt Hell and Heaven came,
And set his sights straight up to the sun's cupola,
Not shy of any hell-hound Cerberus,*

*There sprang from out their sentry boxes,
To confront him at the barrier gate,
Saint Peter, Luther, and Calvin, too,
On behalf of their Commander.*

*Tutti: Whereto? Whereto? Whereto?
Mend. To the Heavenly House!
Tutti: Let's see your pass! Your pass! Your pass!
St. Peter: Whence comes your pass, you little humpbacked nag?*

*Calvin: From Geneva? Luther: From Wittenberg?
St. Peter: From Rome?
Mend. Why ask you this?
Tutti: Where was your pass to Heaven dated?*

*Calvin: In Geneva? Luther: In Wittenberg?
St. Peter: In Rome?
If not, then devil take you, you old nag!
Mend.: My pass is ancient, dated in the earliest time,
In Sinai, at the High Command itself!*

Open creaked the barrier gate and up to heaven Moses flew.

O. NR. JOSEF HA-EFRATI:
ALON BACHUT
Wien, 1793
National Library of Israel,
Jerusalem

Personenregister

Index of Names

Abbt, Thomas
1738–1766, Philosoph, Mathematiker
13, 33, 69, 164
Abraham, Jakob
1723–1800, Medailleur 40, 77, 102
Abramson, Abraham
1752/54 -- 1811, Medailleur,
Münzmeister 40, 67, 71, 77, 102
Addison, Joseph
1672–1719, Dichter 23
Aesop
ca. 619 – ca. 561 v. Chr., Dichter 22
Albo, Josef
ca. 1380 – ca. 1444, Religionsphilosoph 54
Albrecht, Michael
1940–2021, Philosoph,
JubA-Mitarbeiter 214
Altmann, Alexander
1906–1987, Rabbiner, JubA-Hg. 28,
77, 204, 214
Andreae, Johann
1586–1654, Theologe 195
Arendt, Hannah
1906–1975, Philosophin 212, 214
Arndt, Wilhelm
1750–1813, Kupferstecher 71
Arnstein, Fanny, geb. Vögele Itzig
1768–1818, Philantropin 186

Bach, Maximilian
Germanist 77
Badt-Strauss, Bertha
1885–1970, Publizistin 77
Baeck, Leo
1873–1956, Rabbiner, Religionsphilosoph 213
Balzer, Johann
1738–1799, Kupferstecher 180
Bamberger, Chaim
gest. 1764, Hauswirt Mendelssohns
210

Bamberger, Fritz
1902–1984, Philosoph, JubA-Hg. 204
Bardou, Emanuel
1744–1818, Bildhauer 168
Basedow, Johann Bernhard
1724–1790, Pädagoge 40, 100
Bauer, Bruno
1809–1882, Theologe 212
Bause, Johann Friedrich
1738–1814, Kupferstecher 39, 40,
88, 93 f.
Becker, August
1878–1942, Maler, Holzschneider 44
Becker, Johann Gottlieb
1753–1813, Maler 76
Beer, Aaron
1739–1821, Kantor 69
Behrendt, Marie-Christin
Judaistin, Historikerin 12, 205
Bendavid, Lazarus
1762–1832, Mathematiker, Pädagoge
71, 181
Berckenhagen, Ekhart
* 1923, Kunsthistoriker 76
Berger, Gottfried Daniel
1744–1825, Kupferstecher 33, 41, 55,
71, 113, 181
Bernhard Isaak
gest. 1768, Seidenfabrikant 65, 157 f.,
209, 215 f.
Biester, Johann Erich
1749–1816, Jurist, Publizist 165
Bloch, Marcus Elieser
1723–1799, Arzt, Naturforscher 66, 70,
116, 168, 169, 231 f.
Bock, Tuvia (Tobias)
gest. 1755, Buchdrucker, Verleger 165
Boerhave, Herman
1668–1738, Mediziner 23
Bollinger, Friedrich Wilhelm
1777–1825, Kupferstecher 44

Borodianski, Chaim (Bar-Dayan)
1899–1978, Schriftsteller, JubA-Hg.
204
Bourel, Dominique, * 1952
Philosoph, Religionshistoriker 76, 78
Brann, Markus
1849–1920, Rabbiner, Geschichtsforscher 76
Brocke, Michael
* 1940, Judaist 204
Brockmann, Johann Franz
1745–1812, Schauspieler 190
Buchhorn, Ludwig
1770–1856, Maler 158
Busch, Rolf
1933–2014, Regisseur 205

Calvin, Johannes
1509–1564, Theologe, Reformator 237
Cassirer, Ernst
1874–1945, Philosoph 212
Charpentier, Françoise-Philippe
1734–1817, Kupferstecher 170
Chodowiecki, Daniel
1726–1801, Grafiker, Kupferstecher,
40 ff., 55, 58, 61, 66, 67, 69, 71, 79, 86,
96–103, 163, 168 ff., 190, 192, 195,
Cleef, Pieter van
1781–1851, Maler 196
Cohen, Hermann
1842–1918, Philosoph 213, 214
Cohen, Raphael
1722–1803, Rabbiner 180
Cohen, Richard I.
* 1946, Historiker 36, 76, 78
Curländer, David Joseph
1761–1852, Autor, Illustrator 34
Czok, Claudia
* 1964, Kunsthistorikerin 77

Darbes, Joseph Friedrich August
1747–1810, Maler 58 f., 68, 70 f., 125, 158, 163
David, König
um 1000 v.Chr. 60
Degen, Dismar
ca. 1690–1753, Maler 25, 158
Demosthenes
384–322 v. Chr., Politiker 22
Diner, Dan
* 1946, Historiker, 35
Dohm, Christian
1751–1820, Jurist, politischer Schriftsteller 185 ff., 217, 233, 235
Dr. P. S. (vermutlich Elimelech Pilta ben Schimschon Rofe)
Maler 48–51, 50, 53, 78, 83 ff.
Dubno, Solomon ben Joel
1738–1813, Biurist, Dichter 181

Eybeschütz, Jonathan
1690–1764, Talmudist, Kabbalist 49–52, 54, 78, 180
Einstein Albert
1879–1955, Physiker 82
Elbogen, Ismar
1874–1943, Rabbiner, JubA-Hg., 204, 214
Engel, Eva J.
1919–2013, Germanistin, JubA-Hg., 204, 214
Engel, Johann Jakob
1741–1802, Theaterdirektor, Philosoph 180
Ephraim, Marcus Samuel
1777–1854, Kaufmann 73
Ephraim, Veitel Heine
1703–1775, Hofjuwelier, Münzunternehmer 73
Euchel, Isaak Abraham
1756–1804, Maskil 55, 113, 165

Fechhelm, Carl Traugott
1748–1819, Maler 14, 157
Feiner, Shmuel
* 1955, Historiker 78
Feuchtwanger, Ludwig
1885–1947, Jurist, Autor, 213, 214
Fischer, Johann
um 1760, Maler 41
Formey, Jean Henri Samuel
1711–1797, Theologe 33
Franciscus, Samson
1780–1810, Maler 181
Fränkel, David Hirschel
1707–1762, Talmudist 20, 150, 152 f., 210, 215
Freimark, Peter
1934–2008, Judaist 78
Friedländer, David
1750–1834, Aufklärer, Seidenfabrikant 44, 61, 66, 70, 181, 214, 217
Friedländer, Familie
70
Friedrich II.
1712–1786, König von Preußen 141, 145, 157, 124, 186, 211, 215 f.
Friedrich Wilhelm II.
1744–1794, König von Preußen 62
Friedrich, Friedrich
1828–1890, Schriftsteller 212
Frisch, Johann Christoph
1738–1815, Maler 6, 19, 43 ff., 53, 55, 60 f., 66 f., 69 f., 110–113, 116–121, 168, 175, 186
Fritsch, Karl Wilhelm von
1769–1850, sächsischer Minister 39
Fritsch, Thomas Freiherr von
1700–1775, kursächsischer Minister 211
Fritzsch, Christian Friedrich
ca. 1719–1774, Kupferstecher 50, 56 f.
Fritzsch, Claudius Ditlev
1765–1841, Maler 78

Fürst, Jacob Paul Livius
1840–1907, Schriftsteller, Kinderarzt 33

Garve, Anna Katharina
1717–1792, Mutter Christian Garves 39
Garve, Christian
1742–1798, Philosoph 39
Gassner, Joseph
1727–1779, Ordensmann, Exorzist 170
Gedike, Friedrich
1754–1803, Theologe, Pädagoge 165
Geiger, Ludwig
1848–1919, Kulturhistoriker 35
Gleim, Johann Wilhelm Ludwig
1719–1803, Dichter, Sammler 36, 38, 76, 87, 164, 170, 181
Glosk, Abba
gest. nach 1772, Aufklärer, Talmudgelehrter 26, 211
Goethe, Johann Wolfgang von
1749–1832, Dichter 35
Graetz, Heinrich
1817–1891, Historiker 212, 214
Graetz, Michael
1933–2018, Rabbiner, Autor 79
Graff, Anton
1736–1813, Maler 6, 38 ff., 55, 57, 61, 66, 69 ff., 76 f., 79, 88, f., 90–93, 94 f., 107, 110, 169, 181, 164
Grassi, Joseph Matthias
1757–1838, Maler 163
Grote, Ludwig
1893–1974, Kunsthistoriker 76
Grundmann, Walter
1906–1976, Theologe 213
Grunwald, Max
1871–1953, Rabbiner, Autor 78
Gumpertz, Aaron
1723–1769, Arzt, Gelehrter 158, 209
Guttmann, Julius
1880–1950, Religionsphilosoph 204

Haass, Peter
1754–1804, Kupferstecher 40, 100
Halevi, Jehuda
1074–1141, Philosoph, Dichter 54
Hamann, Johann Georg
1730–1788, Philosoph 37, 76, 185 ff., 214, 217
Hayyum, Elias
1709–1766, kurfürstlicher Hoffaktor 48
Hebel, Johann Peter
1760–1826, Dichter 213
Heine, Heinrich
1797–1856, Dichter 213, 214
Heinemann, Jeremias
1778–1855, Übersetzer, Orientalist 115
Held, Julius
1905–2002, Kunsthistoriker 58
Henkel, Arthur
1915–2005, Germanist 76
Henne, Eberhard Siegfried
1759–1828, Kupferstecher 57, 113, 185
Hennings, August Adolph von
1746–1726, Aufklärer, Politiker 33, 41 f., 77
Hensel, Fanny, geb. Mendelssohn
1805–1847, Komponistin 217
Hensel, Sebastian
1830–1898, Manager, Autor 200
Hensler, Erwin
1882–1935, Kunsthistoriker 77
Herder, Johann Gottfried
1744–1803, Theologe, Kulturphilosoph 37, 76, 213 f.
Herz, Henriette, geb. de Lemos
1764–1847, Saloniere 46, 66, 70
Herz, Marcus
1747–1803, Arzt, Philosoph 66, 71, 116, 164, 168, 217
Heymann Jente
1723–1769, Schwester Mendelssohns 153

Hildesheimer, Meir
1864–1934, Rabbiner 214
Hirsch, Maurice de
1831–1896, Philanthrop 236
Hirsch, Michel
1719–1777, Rabbiner 65
Hirsch, Samson Raphael
1808–1888, Rabbiner 54, 78
Hirschenberg, Samuel
1865–1908, Maler, 26
Hobbes, Thomas
1588–1679, Philosoph 214
Hochman, Leah
Judaistin 36, 76
Hoffmann, Tassilo
1887–1951, Numismatiker 77
Hogarth, William
1697–1764, Maler, Grafiker 190
Hohenzollern-Hechingen, Friedrich von
1776–1838, Fürst 59
Hohenzollern-Hechingen, Konstantin von
1801–1869, Fürst 59
Holzalb, Johann Rudolph
1723–1806, Radierer 170
Holzboog, Günther
1927–2006, Verleger 28
Homberg, Herz
1749–1841, Erzieher 180
Horaz
65–8 v. Chr., Dichter 18
Hörnlein, Friedrich Wilhelm
1873–1945, Medailleur 205
Houdon, Jean-Antoine
1741–1828, Bildhauer 196

Illemann, Otto
1869–1929, Medailleur 205
Isaak ben Scheschet
1326–1408, Gelehrter 152

Issachar Bär Cohen (Berend Cohen)
1635–1728, Gründer der ältesten Hamburger Klaus 48
Itzig, Daniel
1723–1799, Münzunternehmer, Gemeindeältester 70 f., 212
Isaak Daniel
1750–1806, Bankier, Hofbaurat 66, 69, 71, 116, 181, 217
Itzig, Miriam, geb. Wulff
1727–1788, 68, 71, 78

Jacob-Friesen, Holger
* 1967, Kunsthistoriker 36, 76
Jacobi, Friedrich Heinrich
1743–1819, Philosoph 171
Jacobsson, Johann Karl Gottfried
1725–1789, technologischer Schriftsteller 157
Jantzen, Friedrich
1815–1901, Lithograf 94
Jenisch, Daniel
1762–1804, Theologe, Schriftsteller 33
Jordan, Carl
1826–1907, Maler, 38, 164

Kaendler, Johann Joachim
1706–1775, Porzellan-Modelleur 200
Kant, Immanuel
1724–1804, Philosoph 37 f., 76, 168, 217, 229
Kanter, Johann Jacob
1731–1786, Buchhändler 37, 54, 165
Karl Wilhelm Ferdinand von Braunschweig-Wolfenbüttel
1735–1806, Herzog 176
Karo, Isaak
1458–1535, Prediger, Arzt 54

Karsch, Anna Louisa
1722–1791, Dichterin 33
Kaselowsky, August Theodor
1810–1891, Maler 76 f.
Katz, Dietmar
Fotograf 158
Katzenstein, Louis
1824–1907, Maler 144
Kauder, Samuel Loeb
1768–1838, Rabbiner 54, 78
Kaufmann, David
1852–1899, Talmudgelehrter 35, 76
Kaulla, Challe (Karolina)
1739–1809, Hoffaktorin 78
Kayserling, Meyer
1829–1905, Rabbiner, Historiker 57, 77 f., 214
Keith, James von
1696–1758, schottisch-preußischer Feldmarschall 124
Kempner, Margarethe, geb. von Mendelssohn
1894–1961, 77
Kempner, Paul
1889–1956, Bankier, Unternehmer 77
Kisch, Abraham
1725–1803, jüdischer Gemeindearzt in Prag 158
Klauber, Markus
Kupferstecher 180
Klauber, Martin Gottlieb
1742–1801, Bildhauer 177
Klein, Hans-Günter
1939–2016, Musikwissenschaftler 4
Kleinhardt, Wilhelm
1695–1773, Miniaturma.er 180
Klopstock, Friedrich Gottlieb
1724–1803, Dichter 195
Knoblauch, Karl
1756–1794, Publizist, Jurist, 170
Knobloch, Heinz
1926–2003, Feuilletonist 28

Kober, Bertram
* 1961, Fotograf 163
Kölbele, Johann Balthasar
1722–1778, Jurist, Theologe 41
Köves, Izso (Isidor)
1853–1917, Maler 145
Krochmalnik, Daniel
* 1956, Judaist, JubA-Hg. 204, 214
Krüger, Johann Conrad
1733–1791, Kupferstecher 37, 55, 76, 87, 169, 180, 192
Kuczynski, Thomas
* 1944, Wirtschaftshistoriker 33
Künzl, Hannelore
1940–2000, Kunsthistorikerin 78
Kugelmann, Ludwig
1828–1902, Mediziner 33, 214
Kuh, Ephraim, Moses
1731–1790, Dichter 18
Kurland, Dorothea von, geb. von Medem
1761–1821, Herzogin 58 f., 70, 125, 163
Lacher, Reimar
* 1969, Kunsthistoriker 77
Landau, Ezechiel
1713–1793, Oberrabbiner von Prag und Böhmen 180, 236
Landsofer, Yonah ben Eliyahu
1678–1712, Talmudist, Euklid-Kommentator, 157
Lange, Friedrich Albert
1828–1875, Philosoph 33
Lavater, Johann Caspar
1741–1801, Theologe 6, 22, 38, 41, 67 f., 89, 96, 104, 141 f., 175, 177, 210, 216, 231 f.
Lehmstedt, Mark
* 1961, Germanist 76
Leibniz
1646–1716, Philosoph, 23, 195
Lemercier, Joseph
1803–1887, Lithograph 142

Lessing, Eva Katharina, geb. Hahn, verw. König
1736–1778, 180
Lessing, Gotthold Ephraim
1729–1781, Dramatiker 27, 33, 35, 40 f., 69, 79, 107, 141 f., 164, 170, 175, 180, 186 f., 192, 205, Lessing 209, 210, 215 ff., 233 f.
Levin, Marcus Theodor (Mordechai)
1772–1826, Bruder von Rahel Levin 67 ff.
Levin, Marcus
1723–1790, Juwelenhändler, Vater von Rahel Levin 68 f.
Levin, Rahel, verh. Varnhagen von Ense
1771–1833, Salonière, Schriftstellerin 67 ff.
Levy, Samuel Salomon
1760–1806, Bankier 70
Levy, Sara, geb. Itzig
1761–1854, Saloniere 70 f.
Lichtenstein, Hillel
1814–1891, Rabbi 2013
Liebmann, Jost
1639–1702, Hoffaktor 65
Liepmann, Jakob
1803–1865, Maler 146
Lilti, Antoine
* 1972, Historiker 79
Lindner, Johann
1839–1906, Kupferstecher 95
Loebel, Hirschel, auch Hirschel Levin
1721–1800, Oberlandesrabbiner 54, 180
Loewen, Johann Friedrich
1727–1771, Dichter, Theatertheoretiker 33
Lonsing, François
1739–1799, Maler 185

Lorenz, Ina Susanne
* 1940, Historikerin 78
Löwe (auch Lowe), Moses Samuel, später Johann Michael Siegfried
1756–1831, Maler, Kupferstecher 32, 57, 71, 103, 114 f., 169, 181
Lowenstein, Steven M.
1945–2020, Historiker 79
Lowenthal-Hensel, Cécile
1923–2012, Historikerin 44
Luther, Martin
1483–1546
Theologe, Reformator 237
Luzzatto, Samuel David
1800–1865, Dichter, Aufklärer 212, 214

Maimon, Salomon
1753–1800, Philosoph, Maskil, 71
Maimonides, Moses (Mosche ben Maimon)
1135/38–1204, Philosoph, Rechtsgelehrter, Arzt 25, 33, 54, 150, 153, 236
Mann, Vivian B.
1943–2019, Kunsthistorikerin 78
Marcuse, Rudolf
1878–1940, Bildhauer 63 f.
Marpurg, Friedrich Wilhelm
1718–1795, Musiktheoretiker 191
Marquis d'Argens, d. i. Marc René de Voyer de Paulmy
1652–1721, Staatsmann 110
Marx, Karl
1818–1883, Philosoph 17, 33, 201, 212, 214
Mechel, Christian von
1737–1817, Kupferstecher 195
Mendel Dessau (Heymann)
1683–1766, Tora-Schreiber, Vater Mendelssohns 15, 150

Mendelssohn, Brendel/Dorothea, gesch. Veit, verh. (von) Schlegel
1764–1839, Übersetzerin, Schriftstellerin 21, 43, 70, 116, 158, 160
Mendelssohn, Chaim
1766–1766, 216
Mendelssohn, Fromet, geb. Gugenheim
1737–1812, S. 15, 29, 36, 46 f., 50, 52, 56 f., 78, 80, 83, 141, 154, 156–160, 215 f.
Mendelssohn, Jente (Henriette Maria)
1775–1831, Erzieherin 217
Mendelssohn, Joseph
1770–1848, Bankier 35, 43 f., 110, 159, 216, 227
Mendelssohn, Mendel Abraham
1769–1775, 216 f.
Mendelssohn, Nathan
1782–1852, Mechanikus 158, 217
Mendelssohn, Susgen
1778–1778, 159
Mendelssohn, Abraham Moses, nach der Taufe Abraham Ernst Mendelssohn Bartholdy
1776–1835, Bankier 16, 217
Mendelssohn Bartholdy, Albrecht
1874–1936, Völkerrechtler 44
Mendelssohn Bartholdy, Felix
1809–1847, Komponist 16, 33, 217
Mendelssohn-Bartholdy, Ernst von
1846–1909, Bankier 205
Mendelssohn-Siebeck, Angelika von
1939–2021, Lehrerin, 100
Meyer, Herrmann M. Z.
1901–1972, Buchhändler, Verleger 36, 43, 76 f.

Meyer, Mendel, später Johann Martin Meyer
gest. 1832, Schwiegersohn Mendelssohns 33, 159, 227 f.
Meyer, Recha (Reikel), geb. Mendelssohn
1767–1831, Erzieherin 159, 160, 216, 227 f.
Michaelis, David
1717–1791, Theologe, Orientalist, 185 ff.
Michel, Heiner
Drehbuchautor 205
Mirabeau, Honoré Gabriel Victor de Riqueti, Comte de
1749–1791, Politiker 185 f.
Mittwoch Eugen
1876–1942, Orientalist, JubA-Hg. 204
Moehsen, Johann Carl Wilhelm
1722–1795, Leibarzt, Aufklärer 165
Montefiore, Moses
1784–1885, Philantrop, Vordenker des Zionismus 236
Montgolfier, Joseph
1740–1810, und **Jacques**
1745–1799, Erfinder des Heißluftballons 170
Moses
Prophet 236 f.
Mosse, George L.
1918–1999, Historiker 64
Müchler, Johann Georg
1724–1819, Publizist 165, 233
Müller, Johann Friedrich Wilhelm
1782–1816, Kupferstecher 44, 121
Müller, Johann Gotthard von
1747–1830, Kupferstecher 61, 121
Münz, Stefan
Verleger in Breslau, 205
Murr, Christoph Gottlieb von
1733–1811, Jurist, Bibliograf, 192

NACHAMA, ANDREAS
* 1951, Historiker 78
NACHMANIDES (MOSES BEN NACHMAN)
1194–1270, Arzt, Philosoph, Dichter 54
NICOLAI, FRIEDRICH
1733–1811, Buchhändler, Verleger, Schriftsteller 19, 27, 32, 43, 45, 56, 73, 78 f., 86, 109, 164 f., 169, 170, 187, 191 f., 196, 208, 215, 216, 233, 235
NIEWÖHNER, FRIEDRICH
1941–2005, Philosophiehistoriker 33
NOACK, HERMANN
1895–1977, Bronzegießer 46
NORDAU, MAX
1849–1923, Mitgründer der Zionistischen Weltorganisation 212, 214

OPPENHEIM, MORITZ DANIEL
1800–1882, Maler 141 f.
OPPENHEIMER, SAMUEL
1630–1703, kaiserlicher Hoffaktor 48

PASCHELES, WOLF
1814–1857, Verleger 53 f., 139
PASSINI, LUDWIG
1832–1903, Maler 205
PATKIN, IZHAR
* 1955, Maler, Bildhauer, 30, 75, 198
PAULINE VON BIRON, VERH. FÜRSTIN VON HOHENZOLLERN-HECHINGEN
1782–1845, 59
PETHER, WILLIAM
ca. 1738–1821, Maler 195
PETRUS, SIMON
gest. 65/67, Apostel 236
PFENNINGER, JOHANNES
1765–1825, Maler 107
PLATON
428/427–348/347, Philosoph 23
PLESSNER, JAKOB
1871–1936, Bildhauer 62 f., 205

POLLEM, HEINRICH
1804–1844, Lithograf 136
PONHEIMER, KILIAN
1757–1828, Kupferstecher 180
POPE, ALEXANDER
1688–1744, Dichter, 23
PORSTMANN, GISBERT
* 1963, Kunsthistoriker 36, 43, 76 f., 79
PSILLE, ARNE
Fotograf 91

RABE, JOHANN JACOB
1710–1798, Hebraist 33
RAMLER, KARL WILHELM
1725–1798, Dichter 33, 37–40, 76
RÄNTZ, CHRISTIAN
1751–1794, Grafiker 132 f.
RASCHKE, GEORG FRIEDRICH
1772–1849, Maler 158
RAWIDOWICZ, SIMON
1897–1957, Philosoph 204
RECKE, ELISA VON DER
1754–1833, Schriftstellerin 58 f., 158, 163
REICH, PHILIPP ERASMUS
1717–1787, Buchhändler 38 f., 54, 76, 89
REICHARDT, JOHANN FRIEDRICH
1752–1814, Komponist 191
REIMARUS, ELISE
1735–1805, Schriftstellerin 41 f., 45, 77
REIMARUS, JOHANN ALBERT
1729–1814, Nationalökonom 33
REINBECK, JOHANN GUSTAV
1682–1741, Theologe 158
REMBRANDT VAN RIJN
1606–1669, Maler 66
RITTER, IMMANUEL HEINRICH
1825–1890, Rabbiner, Historiker 214
RODE, CHRISTIAN BERNHARD
1725–1797, Maler 6, 37 f., 55, 66 f., 71, 86 f., 96, 110

ROSE, JOSEPH & SONS
1765–1784, Uhrmacher 171
ROSENBERG, DAVID
* 1793, Lithograf, Kabbalist 131
ROSENBERG, JOHANN GEORG
1739–1808, Maler, Kupferstecher 71
ROSENTHAL, FERDINAND
1839–1921, Rabbiner 76
ROSENZWEIG, FRANZ
1886–1929, Historiker, Philosoph 213, 214
ROUSSEAU, JEAN-JACQUES
1712–1778, Philosoph 17, 35, 186
RUBENS, ALFRED
1903–1998, Sammler, Historiker 78

SAHLER, OTTO CHRISTIAN
1720–1811, Porträtmaler, Zeichner 41, 106
SALFELD, SIEGMUND
1843–1926, Rabbiner, Pädagoge 35, 76
SAMOSZ, ISRAEL
1700–1772, Gelehrter 158
SAMUEL, MOSES
1795–1860, Uhrmacher, Gelehrter 213 f.
SCHADOW, JOHANN GOTTFRIED
1764–1850, Zeichner, Bildhauer 41, 60, 72 f., 77, 123, 128, 186
SCHELLENBERG, JOHANN ULRICH
1709–1795, Maler, Radierer 41, 136
SCHLEUEN, JOHANN DAVID
1711–1771, Kupferstecher 21, 164, 196
SCHLÜTER, ANDREAS
1634/59–1714, Architekt, Bildhauer 73
SCHMIDT, FRIEDRICH WILHELM
1756–1798, Kupferstecher 169
SCHMIDT, GEORG FRIEDRICH
1712–1775, Radierer 65
SCHMITT, CARL
1888–1985, Staatsrechtler 213, 214
SCHMITZ, ANDRÉ
* 1957, Jurist, Politiker 10

SCHOEPS, HANS-JOACHIM
1909–1980, Historiker 214
SCHÖNER, GEORG ADOLPH
1774–1841, Porträtmaler 185
SCHOONJANS, ANTON
1655–1726, Maler 65
SCHULE, CHRISTIAN
1764–1816, Kupferstecher 107
SCHÜLER, ANGELINA
Illustratorin 12, 205
SCHULTE, CHRISTOPH
* 1958, Judaist, Philosophiehistoriker 73, 79
SCHÜTZ, FRIEDRICH WILHELM VON
1758–1834, Publizist 56
SCHWARZ, AGNES SOPHIE, GEB. BECKER
1754–1789, Schriftstellerin 163
SCHWARZ, KARL
1885–1962, Kunsthistoriker 76
SEYDLITZ-KURZBACH, FRIEDRICH WILHELM FREIHERR VON
1721–1773, Generalleutnant 124
SHAFTESBURY, ANTHONY ASHLEY COOPER, EARL
1671–1713, Philosoph 171
SIMON, HERMANN
* 1949, Historiker 36, 77
SOFER, MOSES (CHATAM SOFER) 213
SOKRATES
469–399 v. Chr., Philosoph, 23, 33, 55, 77, 123 f., 127
SOLMS-LAUBACH, CHRISTIANE VON
1754–1815, Gräfin, Malerin 58, 67, 79
SORKIN, DAVID
* 1958, Historiker, Judaist 76, 213
SPALDING, JOHANN JOACHIM
1714–1804, Theologe, Popularphilosoph 38 ff., 76

SPIESS, JOHANN JAKOB
1730–1814, Numismatiker, Bibliothekar 77
SPINOZA, BARUCH DE
1632–1677, Philosoph 26, 33
STARKE, GEORG FRIEDRICH
Verleger 182
STEER, MARTINA
Historikerin 76
STEINHEIM, SALOMON LUDWIG
1789–1866, Religionsphilosoph 213 f.
STEINLA, MORITZ (FRANZ ANTON ERICH MORITZ MÜLLER)
1791–1858, Kupferstecher 44, 63, 121
STERN, MORITZ
1864–1939, Gemeindebibliothekar 35, 41, 76 f.
STERN, SÜSSKIND
gest. 1686, Kaufmann 48
STÖTTHUP, ANDREAS
1754–1812, Radierer 203
STRAUSS, BRUNO
1889–1969, Philosophiehistoriker 204, 2014
SULZER, JOHANN GEORG
1720–1779, Theologe, Philosoph 19, 38 ff., 76, 192,
SUSMAN, MARGARETE, VERH. VON BENDEMANN
1872–1966, Religionsphilosophin 213

TASSAERT, JEAN JOSEPH FRANÇOIS
1765–1825, Graveur 60, 129
TASSAERT, ANTOINE
1727–1788, Bildhauer 6, 33, 45, 47, 57, 59, 64, 67, 124 ff., 129, 205
THERBUSCH, ANNA DOROTHEA, GEB. LISIEWSKA
1721–1782, Malerin 66
TIKTIN, ABRAHAM
1764–1820, Talmudist, Oberrabbiner 54, 78

TISCHBEIN, JOHANN HEINRICH, DER ÄLTERE
1722–1789, Maler 66, 164
TRUBLET, NICOLAS-CHARLES-JOSEPH
1697–1770, Mitglied der Académie française, 33
TUGENDHOLD, JAKUB
1794–1871, Maskil 197
TYPEX
* 1962, Illustrator, Comic-Zeichner, Maler 15, 29, 210

ULBRICH, BERND G.
* 1954, Historiker 36, 76
ULLMAN, MICHA
* 1939, Bildhauer 203
UZ, JOHANN PETER
1720–1796, Dichter 208

VEIT, JOHANNES
1790–1854, Nazarener-Maler, Enkel Mendelssohns 158
VEIT, SALOMON
1751–1827, Bankier 72 f.
VEIT, SIMON
1754–1819, Bankier 43, 158
VELTEN, JOHANN
1807–1883, Maler 142
VOLTAIRE, D. I. FRANÇOIS-MARIE AROUET
1694–1778, Schriftsteller 35
VOSS, CHRISTIAN FRIEDRICH
Verleger 172, 175, 186 f., 191 f.

WAHL, PAUL
1892–1954, Bibliothekar 76
WEIDEMANN, MORITZ GEORG
1658–1693, Buchhändler 38
WEINBERG, WERNER
1915–1997, Hebraist, JubA-Hg. 204
WEISS/WEISZ, VIKTOR
1913–1966, Zeichner, Karikaturist 153

Weitsch, Friedrich Georg
1758–1828, Maler 70, 71, 170, 181
Werner, Anna Maria, geb. Haid
1688–1753 Kupferstecherin 180
Wertheimer, Samson
1658–1724, kaiserlicher Hoffaktor 48
Wessely, Moses
(oder Mausche Wesel)
1737–1792, Kaufmann 66, 68, 157
Wessely, Hartwig, auch
Naphtali Herz Weisel
1725–1805, Schriftsteller 71, 181
Wilhelm Aarland
1822–1906, Holzstecher 142
Wolf, Albert
Sammler 35, 57, 76, 78, 79
Wolff, Christian Freiherr von
1679–1754, Aufklärer 157, 209
Wright of Derby, Joseph
1734–1797, Maler 195
Wyss, Tamara
1950–2016, Filmemacherin 205

Zadikow, Arnold
1884–1943, Bildhauer 46
Zarek, Otto
1898–1958, Schriftsteller 212
Ziegenhagen, Franz Heinrich
1753–1806, Kaufmann,
Sozialutopist 195
Ziesemer, Walther
1882–1951, Germanist 76
Zimmermann, Johann Georg
1723–1795, Arzt, Schriftsteller
5, 23, 169, 171, 195, 197
Zingg, Adrian
1734–1816, Maler 6, 41 f., 77, 107, 109
Zoffoli, Giacomo
1731–1785, Bronzegießer 190
Zöllner, Johann Friedrich
1753–1804, Pfarrer 55

ANHANG

Leihgeber der Ausstellung

Lenders of the Exhibition

- Akademie der Künste, Berlin
- Deutsches Historisches Museum, Berlin
- Deutsches Hygiene-Museum, Dresden
- Evangelischer Friedhofsverband Berlin Stadtmitte
- frommann-holzboog Verlag e. K., Stuttgart
- Geheimes Staatsarchiv PK, Berlin
- Germanisches Nationalmuseum, Nürnberg
- Gleimhaus – Museum der deutschen Aufklärung, Halberstadt
- Goethe-Museum, Düsseldorf
- Gottfried Wilhelm Leibniz Bibliothek, Hannover
- Herzog Anton Ulrich-Museum, Braunschweig
- Herzog August Bibliothek, Wolfenbüttel
- The Israel Museum, Jerusalem
- Jewish Historical Institute Emanuel Ringelblum, Warschau
- Jüdische Gemeinde zu Berlin
- Jüdisches Museum, Prag
- Leo Baeck Institute, New York
- Lessing-Museum, Kamenz
- Lindenau-Museum, Altenburg
- Meißen Porzellan-Stiftung
- Mendelssohn Gesellschaft e. V., Berlin
- Musée des Beaux-Arts de Bordeaux
- Museen der Stadt Regensburg
- Museum für Naturkunde, Berlin
- Museum für Stadtgeschichte, Dessau
- Museum im Schloss Bad Pyrmont
- Niedersächsisches Landesarchiv, Abteilung Bückeburg
- Österreichische Nationalbibliothek, Wien
- Privatbesitz
  Cornelie von Bismarck, Berlin
  Thomas Lackmann, Berlin
  Christian Siebeck, Lastreille
  und weitere private Leihgeber
- The Royal Collections, Stockholm
- Staatliche Kunstsammlungen Dresden, Kupferstichkabinett
- Staatliche Museen zu Berlin, Preußischer Kulturbesitz
  Gemäldegalerie
  Gipsformerei
  Kupferstichkabinett
  Münzkabinett
  Museum Europäischer Kulturen
- Staatsbibliothek zu Berlin, Preußischer Kulturbesitz
  Abteilung Handschriften und Historische Drucke
  Musikabteilung mit Mendelssohn-Archiv
- Stadtbibliothek Lübeck
- Stadtmuseum Düsseldorf
- Stiftung Preußische Schlösser und Gärten, Potsdam
- Stiftung Stadtmuseum Berlin
- Stiftung Neue Synagoge – Centrum Judaicum, Berlin
- Universität der Künste, Universitätsbibliothek, Berlin
- Universität Leipzig, Kustodie
- Universität Leipzig, Universitätsbibliothek
- Universität Rostock, Universitätsbibliothek
- University of California, Berkeley, Magnes Collection of Jewish Art and Life
- Württembergische Landesbibliothek, Stuttgart
- Zentralbibliothek Zürich
- Zilkens Fine Art, Köln

Abbildungsverzeichnis

Table of Figures

- Bayerische Staatsbibliothek, München: S. 95, 136 oben, 187 (Standort Bamberg), 229
- Carlsen Verlag, Hamburg: S. 29
- Deutsches Historisches Museum, Berlin: S. 91 (Nr. 214b), 102 (Nr. 223)
- Deutsches Hygiene-Museum, Dresden, Sammlung Schwarzkopf: S. 213, 227
- Germanisches Nationalmuseum, Nürnberg: S. 196 (Nr. 188 – Leihgabe der Friedrich von Praun'schen Familienstiftung)
- Gleimhaus Halberstadt – Museum der deutschen Aufklärung: S. 38 (Nr. 52), 87 (Nr. 49/50)
- Haus Hohenzollern, SKH Georg Friedrich Prinz von Preußen, SPSG: S. 14 (DLn Hz II 1987 GK I 9246)
- Herzog Anton Ulrich-Museum, Kunstmuseum des Landes Niedersachsen, Braunschweig: S. 189 (Nr. 151), 191 (Nr. 156)
- Herzog August Bibliothek, Wolfenbüttel: S. 93 (Nr. 215), 120 (Nr. 209), 137 (Nr. 241), 169 (Nr. 71), 230 unten
- Historical Society on Pennsylvania, Philadelphia: S. 182 (Nr. 127)
- Israel Museum, Jerusalem: S. 70 (Nr. 117), 109 (Nr. 226), 147 (Nr. 110 – Bequest of Mrs. S. B. Dimson, London), 168 (Nr. 72), 169 (Nr. 70)
- Jewish Museum, London/United Synagogue: S. 54 (Nr. 108)
- The Jewish Museum, New York, gift of Mr. and Mrs. J. Snyderman: S. 37
- Jüdische Gemeinde zu Berlin: S. 126/27 (Nr. 180)
- Jüdisches Historisches Institut „Emanuel Ringelblum", Warschau: S. 139 (Nr. 252), 145 (Nr. 131), 180 (Nr. 104), 186 (Nr. 135), 247 (Nr. 221)
- JMB: S. 21 (Nr. 193), 34, 45, 47 (Nr. 262), 53 (Nr. 29), 62, 65, 68, 69, 72, 75 (Nr. 247), 84 (Nr. 207), 85 (Nr. 208), 87 (Nr. 211), 94 (Nr. 216), 98 (Nr. 219), 111 (Nr. 236), 113 (Nr. 237), 116 (Nr. 227), 121 (Nr. 231), 128 (Nr. 235), 129 (Nr. 234), 131 (Nr. 249), 133 (Nr. 178), 138, 155 (Nr. 43), 163 (Nr. 48), 165 (Nr. 56), 181 (Nr. 97), 192 (Nr. 175), 195 (Nr. 181), 199 (Nr. 247), 202 (Nr. 255), 228 unten
- Jüdisches Museum, Prag: S. 151 (Nr. 16)
- Kedem Auctions, Jerusalem: S. 232
- Kulturstiftung Dessau-Wörlitz: S. 41
- Kursker Staatliche Gemäldegalerie „A. A. Dejneka", Russische Föderation: S. 26
- LBI, New York: S. 8/9 (Nr. 233), S. 125 (Nr. 233), S. 158 (Nr. 37)
- Lessing-Museum, Kamenz: S. 175 (Nr. 136)
- Lindau-Museum, Altenburg: S. 162 (Nr. 47)
- Mairie de Bordeaux, musée des Beaux-Arts: S. 184 (Nr. 133)
- Mendelssohn-Gesellschaft, Berlin: S. 83 (Nr. 206), 91 (Nr. 214), 94 (Nr. 217 – Leihgabe Sammlung Dopfer), 142, 143, 158 (Nr. 34 und 30), 160 (Nr. 32a), 167 (Nr. 90), 200 (MA Depos. MG, Fot. 5)
- Museen der Stadt Regensburg, Inv.-Nr. K 1961/50: S. 321 (Nr. 134)
- Museum für Naturkunde, Berlin: S. 168 (Nr. 73 – Inv.-Nr. ZMB/8567)
- Museumslandschaft Hessen Kassel, Neue Galerie, Städtischer Kunstbesitz: S. 144
- Nachlass Angelika von Mendelssohn-Siebeck: S. 100 (Nr. 222), 223 (Nr. 33)
- National Library of Israel, Jerusalem: S. 233 (Sign. SR 59 A 3774)
- Niedersächsisches Landesarchiv, Abteilung Bückeburg: S. 165 (Nr. 57)
- Österreichische Nationalbibliothek, Wien: S. 106 (Nr. 225), 106/07 (Nr. 173), 195 (Nr. 185), 228 (Nr. 185)
- Privatbesitz: S. 12 (Nr. 266), 22, 42 (Nr. 250), 83 (Nr. 28), 97 (Nr. 218), 105, 107, 112 (Nr. 250), 113 unten, 115, 153 (Nr. 4), 172 (Nr. 92), 196 (Nr. 196), 203 oben, 204 (Nr. 258), 224 (Nr. 35 und 36)
- Rijksmuseum, Amsterdam: U2, S. 56
- Royal Collections, Stockholm: S. 190 (Nr. 150)
- SPSG: S. 25, 59 (Nr. 180), 90 (Nr. 212 – Leihgabe des Berliner Senats), 157 (Nr. 23 – Neues Palais)
- SMB PK, Alte Nationalgalerie: S. 66, 230 (Nr. 55)
- SMB PK: Gipsformerei: S. 185 (Nr. 138)
- SMB PK, Kunstbibliothek: S. 156 (Nr. 12)
- SMB PK, Kupferstichkabinett: S. 99 (Nr. 220), 123 (Nr. 177), 174 (Nr. 109), 194 (183)

ANHANG

- SMB PK, Münzkabinett: S. 205 (Nr. 260)
- SMB PK, Museum Europäischer Kulturen: S. 170 (Nr. 81)
- SBB PK, Abteilung Handschriften und Historische Drucke: S. 67 (Sammlung Varnhagen, gzgr 8365/SBB K 17), 87 (Nr. 49 – Portr.-Slg/Philos.gr/Mendelssohn, Moses, Nr. 12), 119 (Nr. 230 – Autogr. I/600), 132, 225 und 226 (beide: Nr. 88 – Nm 2698:R)
- SBB PK, Musikabteilung mit Mendelssohn-Archiv: S. 90 (Nr. 213), 95, 101, 103 (Nr. 130 – MA BA 151), 105 unten, 112 (Nr. 239 – MA BA 188,28), 114 (Nr. 238 – MA BA 325), 117 (Nr. 228 – MA BA 137), 118 (Nr. 229 – MA Nachl. 22/C,5), 121 unten, 134 (Nr. 210 – MA BA 29), 135, 136 unten, 160 (Nr. 40 – MA Nachl. 4,77), 231 oben (Zsn 22574)
- Stiftung Neue Synagoge – Centrum Judaicum, Berlin: S. 120 (Nr. 232)
- Stiftung Stadtmuseum Berlin: S. 32, 92, 163 (Nr. 46), 231 (unten rechts)
- Studio OTW, Amsterdam: S. 218/19
- Typex, Amsterdam: S. 15, 206/07
- ULB Sachsen-Anhalt, Halle (Saale): S. 17
- Universität Hamburg, Universitätsbibliothek: S. 51
- Universität Leipzig, Kunstsammlung, Kustodie: S. 89, 164 (Nr. 54)
- Universität Rostock, Universitätsbibliothek: S. 179 (Nr. 126)
- University of California, Berkeley, Magnes Collection of Jewish Art and Life – Gift of Vernon Stroud, Eva Linker, Gerda Mathan, Ilse Feiger and Irwin Straus in memory of Frederick and Edith Straus: S. 80/81 (Nr. 95), 140 (Nr. 95)
- Zentralbibliothek Zürich: S. 177 (Nr. 96)

Abkürzungsverzeichnis

List of Abbreviations

DEFA	Deutsche Film Aktiengesellschaft
JMB	Jüdisches Museum Berlin
JubA	Moses Mendelssohn: Gesammelte Schriften. Jubiläumsausgabe
LBI	Leo Baeck Institute, New York City
PK	Stiftung Preußischer Kulturbesitz
SBB PK	Staatsbibliothek zu Berlin – Preußischer Kulturbesitz
SKH	Seine Königliche Hoheit
SMB PK	Staatliche Museen zu Berlin – Preußischer Kulturbesitz
SPSG	Stiftung Preußische Schlösser und Gärten
ULB	Universitäts- und Landesbibliothek
ZDF	Zweites Deutsches Fernsehen

Danksagung *Acknowledgments*

Herausgeber und Mendelssohn-Gesellschaft danken allen Institutionen, Förderern, Kollegen, Freunden und vielen Nachfahren Moses Mendelssohns für die Unterstützung der Ausstellung und dieses Katalogprojektes. Auf die Ankündigung der Ausstellung und der Publikation des Kataloges sowie der Graphic Novel „Moische. Sechs Anekdoten aus dem Leben Moses Mendelssohns" haben sie mit Begeisterung und Ermutigung reagiert. Ohne Ratschläge, Kritik und Bestätigung von vielen Begleitern wäre die Entdeckungsfahrt dieser Ausstellung und ihre Dokumentation nicht möglich geworden. Wir danken allen institutionellen und den privaten Leihgebern, auch jenen, die namentlich nicht genannt werden wollen.

Der LOTTO-Stiftung Berlin danken wir für ihre großzügige Förderung der Ausstellung. Der Hermann Reemtsma Stiftung, der Moses Mendelssohn Stiftung, der Axel Springer Stiftung, der Historischen Gesellschaft der Deutschen Bank und der Stiftung Irène Bollag-Herzheimer verdanken wir die großzügige finanzielle Förderung des Kataloges. Die Stiftung Preußische Seehandlung war bereit, Begleitveranstaltungen der Mendelssohn-Gesellschaft mit wissenschaftlichen Recherchen für Ausstellung und Katalog zu finanzieren. Ebenso danken wir Mitgliedern der Mendelssohn-Gesellschaft für Spenden und Teammitgliedern der Mendelssohn-Remise für Mitarbeit an der Katalog-Produktion, dem Grafikteam Alexandra und Gerald Geffert, Carmen von Schöning und den Samson-Übersetzungen, dem Katalogredakteur und Mendelssohnforscher Sebastian Panwitz, den

The editors and the Mendelssohn-Gesellschaft wish to thank all the institutions, sponsors, colleagues, and friends, as well as the many descendants of Moses Mendelssohn who supported the exhibition and our catalogue project. Their enthusiasm and encouragement were inspiring when the plans to mount the exhibition and publish an accompanying catalogue plus the graphic novel "Moische: Six Anecdotes from the Life of Moses Mendelssohn" were announced. Without the suggestions, constructive criticism, and affirmation provided by the many people involved, we could never have embarked upon the journey of discovery that this exhibition and its documentation ultimately became. Our sincere thanks also go out to each of the institutional and private lenders, including those who prefer not to be mentioned by name.

We are grateful to LOTTO-Stiftung Berlin for its generous financial support of the exhibition. Our thanks also go to Hermann Reemtsma Stiftung, Moses Mendelssohn Stiftung, Axel Springer Stiftung, the Historical Association of Deutsche Bank, and the Stiftung Irène Bollag-Herzheimer for their generous support of the catalogue's production. Stiftung Preussische Seehandlung very kindly was willing to fund the research-centered events the Mendelssohn-Gesellschaft organized in conjunction with the exhibition and catalogue. We also thank the members of the Mendelssohn-Gesellschaft for their donations; the staff of the Mendelssohn Remise museum for their help in producing the catalogue; Alexandra and Gerald Geffert for their graphics work; Carmen v. Schöning and her team

Mitarbeitern des Wienand Verlages, dem Ausstellungsteam und hilfreichen Kolleginnen und Kollegen des Jüdischen Museums Berlin.

Wir danken weiteren Mendelssohnforschern und Fachkollegen, deren Rat uns wichtige Orientierungen und Impulse gegeben hat: besonders Dominique Bourel, Christoph Schulte, Daniel Krochmalnik, Chana Schütz und Hermann Simon. Museen und Archive haben unsere vielen Nachfragen geduldig beantwortet. Viele Fotoarchive und Digitalisierungszentren haben uns schneller beliefert, als wir erhoffen konnten. Besonderer Dank für gute Zusammenarbeit geht an die Musikabteilung mit Mendelssohn-Archiv sowie an die Abteilung Handschriften und Historische Drucke der Staatsbibliothek zu Berlin, an das Bildarchiv Preußischer Kulturbesitz, an den Steinrestaurator Andreas Hoferik, Anna Fischer von der Stiftung Neue Synagoge Berlin – Centrum Judaicum und Ute Winkelmann von der Kulturstiftung Dessau Wörlitz. Großer Dank an all jene, die hier nicht speziell erwähnt werden können: Ausstellung und Katalog sind das Ergebnis von zahlreichen Dialogen und intensiver Zusammenarbeit im schönsten Sinne Moses Mendelssohns. Danke!

at Samson-Übersetzungen for the translations; Sebastian Panwitz, for editing the catalogue in his capacity as a Mendelssohn scholar; the associates of the Wienand Verlag publishing house; the entire exhibition team; and the helpful staffers of the Jewish Museum Berlin.

Our particular thanks go to the many Mendelssohn scholars and specialists who provided us with useful guidance and ideas, particularly Dominique Bourel, Christoph Schulte, Daniel Krochmalnik, Chana Schütz, and Hermann Simon. Various museums and the Mendelssohn Archive fielded our many enquiries with great patience. We appreciate the unexpected rapidity with which many of the photo archives and digitalization centers delivered the requested material. We are especially grateful for the excellent cooperation we obtained from the Berlin State Library's Music Department with its Mendelssohn Archive and the Departments of Manuscripts and Early Printed Books; the Image Archive of the Stiftung Preussischer Kulturbesitz; Mr. Andreas Hoferik, a specialist in stonework restoration; Ms. Anna Fischer at the Stiftung Neue Synagoge Berlin—Centrum Judaicum; as well as Ute Winkelmann at the Kulturstiftung Dessau Wörlitz. Heartfelt thanks also go out to all those who could not be specifically mentioned here: The exhibition and its catalogue are the result of uncounted dialogues and intensive collaboration, entirely in keeping with the spirit of Moses Mendelssohn himself. Thank you all!

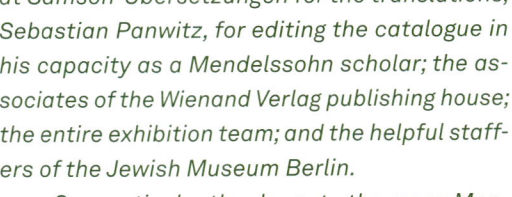

**Nr. 221 Daniel Nikolaus Chodowiecki (1726–1801)
Porträt Moses Mendelssohn**
undatiert
Handzeichnung, Aquarell, Rötel, schwarze Kreide
45,5 × 32 cm (Trägerkarton)
Jüdisches Historisches Institut „Emanuel Ringelblum", Warschau

Die Zeichnung wurde 1903 von dem Dresdener Sammler Albert Wolf erworben, der sie 1907 der Jüdischen Gemeinde zu Berlin hinterließ. Als Teil der Grafik- und Fotosammlung des ehemaligen Jüdischen Museums wurde sie 1938 von deutschen Behörden geraubt. Nach dem Krieg in Polen aufgefunden, wird sie heute im Jüdischen Historischen Institut in Warschau bewahrt.

The drawing was acquired in 1903 by the Dresden collector Albert Wolf, who left it to the Jewish Community of Berlin in 1907. Part of the graphic and photographic collection of the former Jewish Museum, it was looted by German authorities in 1938. Found in Poland after the war, it is now preserved in the Jewish Historical Institute in Warsaw.

ANHANG

Impressum

Credits

Dieser Katalog erscheint anlässlich der Ausstellung „'Wir träumten von nichts als Aufklärung.' Moses Mendelssohn", 14. April – 11. September 2022. Eine Ausstellung des Jüdischen Museums Berlin in Zusammenarbeit mit der Mendelssohn-Gesellschaft, Berlin.
This catalogue is published on the occasion of the exhibition "'We dreamed of nothing but enlightenment.' Moses Mendelssohn", April 14 – September 11, 2022. An exhibition of the Jewish Museum Berlin in cooperation with Mendelssohn Society, Berlin.

Kuratoren der Ausstellung *Curators of the exhibition*: Inka Bertz (Jüdisches Museum Berlin), Thomas Lackmann (Mendelssohn-Gesellschaft)

Kuratorische Assistenz *Curatorial assistant*: Barbara Heinrich

Ausstellungsarchitektur *Exhibition design*: Jelena Stefanović, Studio OTW, Amsterdam

Textredaktion und -management *Text editing and coordination*: Maren Krüger, Martina Lüdicke

Übersetzung *English translations*: Jake Schneider, Adam Blauhut

Fotoakquise, -produktion und Rechteklärung *Photograph acquisitions, production and rights clearance*: Christina Hecht

Herausgeber des Katalogs *Editors*: Inka Bertz und Thomas Lackmann im Auftrag der Mendelssohn-Gesellschaft e.V.

Redaktion *Editing*: Sebastian Panwitz

Lektorat *Copy Editing*: Hauptstadtstudio Freier Lektoren, Frank Elminowski, Berlin; Lektorat Irmer, Stephanie Irmer, Berlin

Übersetzung *Translation*: Samson-Übersetzungen GmbH, Berlin

Gestaltung *Graphic design*: Gerald Geffert, Berlin

Projektmanagement Verlag *Project management publisher*: Freia Schleyerbach

Gesamtherstellung *Production*: Wienand Verlag
Gedruckt in Europa *Printed in Europe*
Erschienen im *Published by*:
Wienand Verlag
www.wienand-verlag.de
Weyertal 59, 50937 Köln

© 2022 Wienand Verlag, Köln, und die Autoren *and the authors*

ISBN 978-3-86832-690-1

Die Deutsche Nationalbibliothek verzeichnet diese Publikation in der Deutschen Nationalbibliografie; detaillierte bibliografische Daten sind im Internet über http://dnb.d-nb.de abrufbar.
The Deutsche Nationalbibliothek lists this publication in the Deutsche Nationalbibliografie; detailed bibliographic data are available on the Internet at http://dnb.d-nb.de.

Umschlagabbildungen *Cover illustrations*
1 Johann Christoph Frisch: Porträt Moses Mendelssohn, 1783 (Jüdisches Museum Berlin)
2 Daniel Chodowiecki: Toleranz. Aus „Sechs große Begebenheiten des vorletzten Decenniums", 1791 (Jüdisches Museum Berlin)
3 Daniel Chodowiecki: Aufklärung. Aus „Sechs große Begebenheiten des vorletzten Decenniums", 1791 (Herzog August Bibliothek, Wolfenbüttel)
4 Izhar Patkin: Moses Mendelssohn. Aus der Installation „Judenporzellan", 1998 (Jüdisches Museum Berlin)

Eine weitere Begleitpublikation zur Ausstellung ist die Graphic Novel „Moische. Sechs Anekdoten aus dem Leben des Moses Mendelssohn" von Typex. Sie erscheint auf deutsch, niederländisch und englisch bei Scratch Books, Amsterdam (ISBN 978-94-93166-58-5).
The exhibition is also accompanied by the graphic novel "Moishe. Six anecdotes from the life of Moses Mendelssohn" by Typex. It will be published in German, Durch and Englisch at Scratch Books, Amsterdam (ISBN 978-94-93166-59-2).